start here

start here

**OPEN THE BIBLE
ENTER ITS STORY
WALK ITS PATH**

Stephen Cheyney

© 2025 Stephen Roberts Cheyney

All rights reserved. No part of this book may be reproduced or transmitted in any form or by any means, electronic or mechanical, including photocopying, recording, or by any information storage and retrieval system, without permission in writing from the publisher.

Scripture Acknowledgments

Scripture quotations marked (NIV) are taken from the Holy Bible, New International Version® (NIV®). Copyright © 1973, 1978, 1984, 2011 by Biblica, Inc.™ Used by permission. All rights reserved worldwide. www.Zondervan.com

Scripture quotations marked (ESV) are from The Holy Bible, English Standard Version® (ESV®), copyright © 2001 by Crossway, a publishing ministry of Good News Publishers. Used by permission. All rights reserved. www.crossway.org

Scripture quotations marked (CEB) are from the Common English Bible (CEB), © 2011 by Common English Bible. Used by permission. All rights reserved. www.CommonEnglishBible.com

Scripture quotations marked (NRSVUE) are from the New Revised Standard Version Updated Edition (NRSVUE), copyright © 2021 National Council of Churches of Christ in the United States of America. Used by permission. All rights reserved worldwide.

Scripture quotations marked (VOICE) are taken from The Voice™ Bible, copyright © 2012 by Ecclesia Bible Society. Used by permission. All rights reserved.

Scripture quotations that are unmarked are the author's own translation.

All rights reserved. Used by permission.

ISBN 978-0-9889559-3-6 — Paperback edition, printed on lightweight white offset paper
ISBN 978-0-9889559-7-4 — Paperback edition, printed on cream trade book paper
ISBN 978-0-9889559-8-1 — Hardcover edition with matte printed case
ISBN 978-0-9889559-6-7 — Hardcover edition with dust jacket

Part 1: Open the Bible
Discover Its Purpose and Power

Chapter 1 - Why Read the Bible? 5

Chapter 2 - What Is the Bible's Past? 15

Chapter 3 - Why Translate? 35

Chapter 4 - Where Do I Begin? 61

Part 2: Enter Its Story
Explore the Heart of Scripture

Chapter 5 - What Is God's Story? 77

Chapter 6 - What Matters Most? 111

Chapter 7 - What Also Matters? 163

Chapter 8 - Who is God? 263

Chapter 9 - Who is Jesus Christ? 271

Part 3: Walk Its Path
Transform Your Journey

Chapter 10 - What Is Faith in Action? 291

Chapter 11 - Where Can I Find Hope? 305

Chapter 12 - How Do I Grow? 313

Chapter 13 - What Is God's Plan? 323

Chapter 14 - What Verses We Love? 329

Chapter 15 - What Is Discipleship? 339

Your word
is a lamp
to my feet
& a light
to my path.

PSALM 119:105

part 1

Open the Bible
Discover Its Purpose and Power

chapter 1

Why Read the Bible?

My dad's father grew up in Philadelphia, and, unsurprisingly, he was a Quaker. My dad's mother was from North Carolina and grew up Methodist. My mom's parents, originally Baptist in Virginia, eventually became Episcopalian. My parents were active in church when I was very young, and I was baptized United Methodist.

Despite the legacy, I didn't grow up in a particularly religious family. As the youngest of four boys, I came along at a time when my parents had stopped attending church altogether. Though I was told we were United Methodist, I couldn't have told you where our church was. We didn't go to church, not even on Christmas Eve or Easter.

My first real memory of church came through a neighbor's invitation to Vacation Bible School at the local Baptist church. They were great at bringing friends along, and my oldest brother, Bill, became especially active there. As a little kid, I was struck by the towering architecture of the church. It felt impressive and almost larger than life. But more than that, it was a happy place. My neighbors were happy there, my brother was happy there, and I felt happy there, too.

Growing up, I felt very loved and surrounded by people I admired. But Bill was exceptional. He wasn't just my older brother; he was my hero. Bill seemed good at everything. The kind of person who could pick up anything and just excel. He was a phenomenal athlete, the one everyone wanted on their team, and an academic standout, especially in astronomy. My parents gave him this incredible telescope that made the stars feel like they were just within reach. He'd spend hours peering through it, mapping constellations, and tossing around big philosophical ideas as if 19-year-olds were supposed to carry the weight of the universe.

And then there was his art, a gifted hand that could turn a pencil into magic. I still remember one drawing, every detail so vivid it felt like it could breathe. But it didn't stop there. Music was his other universe. His vinyl collection? Legendary. The Beatles. Led Zeppelin. Even autographed albums and letters from Cat Stevens. It wasn't just a collection, it was a masterpiece, a window into his soul, curated with the care of someone who truly understood the art of sound. He was the kind of person you couldn't help but look up to.

When I was two or three, we visited my Aunt Anne in rural North Carolina. Like any curious toddler, I wandered off. In the backyard, I opened the door to a little wooden playhouse and started to play with a ball. Except I wasn't old enough to realize it was a chicken coup and the ball was actually a hornet's nest. So, as you can imagine, the moment I pulled it down, chaos erupted. Swarms of hornets attacked, and I was left screaming.

I don't remember the day with the hornets. I remember hearing the story countless times, though, especially when Bill came to my rescue. Without a second thought, he sprinted toward me, wrapped his arms around my tiny body, and shielded me from the angry swarm. He carried me to safety, and while I escaped with only a few stings, Bill bore the brunt of their fury. By the time it was over, he had been stung more than 200 times and ended up in the hospital. Bill didn't have to save my life (he was just a kid himself), but he did without hesitation.

There was another time. An event I don't remember but have heard so many times it's etched into my soul. My mom was driving the four of us kids across a mountain in Virginia when, on one of the dangerous curves, she became deathly ill. Somehow, she managed to pull the car to the side of the road.

Bill was thirteen, which means I must have been one. He pulled her out of the driver's seat, took the wheel, and drove us down the mountain to the nearest hospital in a town he didn't know. He found a hospital, the University of Virginia. Not a small, rural clinic but a major medical center. A miracle in itself.

That's when we learned my mom had suffered a massive stroke. The kind of stroke that could have taken her life if it weren't for Bill's quick thinking and courage. I believe in miracles, like how God worked through my brother that day to save my mom, my brothers, and me. It wasn't just bravery. It was divine. And Bill? He was the hands and feet of it.

So, I'm not exaggerating when I say Bill was my hero growing up. He wasn't just my hero; he was also a hero to my two other older brothers, David and Bryan. I didn't fully realize at the time, though, that Bill was simply following in the footsteps of his hero, our dad. In many ways, Bill's bravery and selflessness reflected the example our dad set for all of us.

Tragically, though, when I was twelve years old, my hero, Bill, died. His loss left a hole in my heart that I carry with me to this day.

Fast forward, I'm nineteen and home from college one Christmas break, and as I meander through the bookshelf in our den, I find Bill's Bible. It was a Good News Bible with a bright golden hardcover. If you've seen this brand of Bibles, what pops out are the basic stick figure drawings throughout. Bill's Bible, though, was even more intriguing. It had been thoroughly read, and you could see that he had written extensive notes scrawled all over its margins.

I can see it now. My eyebrows raised, I checked my shoulders, and seeing no one, I quietly slipped this Bible into my book bag. I thought if I were to take this Bible back with me to college, I could study his personal notes and reconnect with my brother, who had died seven years earlier.

No one ever taught me how to read the Bible. I knew it was a different kind of book, but I didn't think it could be read differently. So, one snowy week in January, at the start of my spring semester, I began my journey through Bill's Good News Bible, starting with page one. By spring break, I had finished.

At first, I was captivated by my brother's notes. The words were written in blue felt-tip ink on the first page: "Every inch of creation pulses with God's purpose." His notes continued page after page. As I read them, I could sometimes picture what he wore or how he looked when writing a particular thought. Those notes gave me a glimpse into my brother's mind and heart, insights I might never have known otherwise.

I didn't realize that something even more profound was happening as I read his notes and the Bible passages alongside them. Slowly, I began to encounter the Bible's central figure, the creator of the universe.

This is where I met God.

The Biblical Predicament

I didn't realize it at the time, but the religious world I was born into, like so many in America, wasn't an outlier. It reflected something deeper, a symptom of a broader struggle within the church. My parents called themselves Christians, but not in a way the early church would have recognized. We didn't go to church. We didn't talk about Jesus. Still, they held on to some of his ethical teachings, like being kind, helping others, and telling the truth, which was enough to pass the label on to me. They handed me the word "Christian" like a family trait, something inherited, like green eyes or a last name.

This kind of nominal Christianity is more common than we like to admit. In fact, in many places, it may be the norm. But it often leaves people wandering, spiritually curious, yet disconnected. My parents would have said they were "too busy" for church, a phrase I now recognize as a cover for something more complex: disappointment, disillusionment, or maybe just the slow drift of a comfortably secular life. Maybe they were hurt by the church. Maybe they were simply bored. Either way, we were unchurched. And I grew up without something I now know is vital: the shared, formative rhythm of reading Scripture in community.

I believe this is one of the great pastoral challenges of our time, what I've come to call the Biblical Predicament. We're serving generations who know the words of Christianity but not its language. Some grew up in churches focused solely on conversion: "Just accept Jesus, and you're good." Others were shaped by churches centered on activism, community, or contemplation, spaces that assumed people already knew the stories of Scripture. One group never learned the depth of the Bible. The other missed its simplicity. Both are left hungry, though in different ways.

If you're a pastor in a local church, you might not always see this gap. But in campus ministry, it's unmistakable. I meet students from every spiritual background imaginable. Many have never opened a Bible. Some have, but only alone, confused, uncertain, without a guide. I understand their frustration. I lived it. My family didn't have the tools to teach me the faith they claimed.

That's what led me to write this book. Not to argue that the Bible is true. If you've read this far, I trust you already suspect it might be. What struck me, though, is that Christianity is different. I was driving through a rural area recently when I passed a fire station, a clinic, an elementary school, and a handful of churches. I had no doubt that the firefighters were professionally trained, that the physicians were board-certified, and that the teachers were licensed by the state. But the churches? That's harder to know. When you walk into a church, there's often no clear way to tell how well-trained the pastor is. Each denomination has its own standards, and for someone searching for a spiritual home, that can make things confusing.

So let me offer this: I work with four major Christian denominations. I hold two graduate degrees in theology. What I share in these pages has been shaped by serious theological voices, tested in the fires of both ministry and scholarship. It may not be groundbreaking, unless you've never encountered the Bible for yourself. And yet, for all of that, this book isn't like the others.

That's why I wrote this book. Not because I had something completely new to say, but because I couldn't find the kind of book my students needed. If there had been one, I would have handed it to them. But there wasn't. So I wrote this, hoping it meets you right where you are, no matter how you got here. And here's the good news: you don't need to have everything figured out before you start. You don't have to believe perfectly to begin. Grace comes first. It always has. The gospel doesn't wait for you to be ready. I've discovered, time and again, that the gospel doesn't wait at the end of the road. It meets you in the middle of your story.

How to Read the Bible Without Giving Up

My best advice about reading the Bible is to start with a purpose. Reading the Bible just to read or finish it can quickly become overwhelming. That's why many people start with good intentions but eventually give up. Forcing yourself to slog through the tedious sections of Leviticus just to get through it isn't a strong enough reason to stick with it. It's like trying to power through a boring episode on Netflix; you're distracted and disengaged. And if a show has too many boring episodes, you'll stop watching entirely. Sadly, I've seen too many people walk away from the Bible before they even finish season one.

When you approach the Bible with a purpose, even a deeply personal one, it changes everything. A purpose gives your reading meaning and direction, keeping you connected and engaged. For me, that purpose was to reconnect with my brother. I didn't realize how much that simple, unspiritual goal mattered then, but I've learned this: having a purpose gives God something to work with.

I believe God was perfectly okay with my desire to reconnect with Bill. In fact, I'm convinced the specific purpose matters less than not having one at all. If the Bible were an ocean, diving in without a purpose is like trying to swim across. It's overwhelming and you'll quickly drown. Think of it this way: your purpose is your boat. It carries you through the tough parts, helps you stay afloat during the repetitive sections, and provides shelter when the journey feels exhausting. A boat keeps you moving forward.

For me, that boat was rattled and worn, a traumatized vessel beaten and bruised by grief. But it was still a boat, still a purpose. And as I read, God began to reshape it. He built on it, refined it, and made it stronger. My boat looks much different today. It's sturdier, steadier, and far better equipped. But it all started with the simple, imperfect purpose of reconnecting with my brother.

That's the beauty of having a reason to read the Bible. Your purpose doesn't have to be perfect or profound. It just has to be something. Without a purpose, you risk reading without intention, and it becomes harder to sense how God might want to move in your life. But when you bring even a seemingly obscure purpose to the table, you open the door for God to take it, transform it, and make it His.

Discover Your Purpose

I invite you to approach the Bible with a sense of purpose. Perhaps you're troubled by the violence and division in the world; your purpose could be to uncover wisdom about peacemaking and reconciliation.

Maybe you're surrounded by shallow relationships and long for deeper, more meaningful connections, your purpose might be to explore what true love, forgiveness, and integrity look like. Or perhaps you've been hurt by the church and carry wounds from that experience; your purpose could be to separate the flawed actions of people from the heart of God, seeking healing and clarity.

Whatever it is, let your purpose guide you. The Bible is vast and complex, but a clear purpose will help you navigate its stories, teachings, and challenges with meaning and direction.

Take time to reflect and think it through; why do you want to read the Bible? Be honest with yourself, and don't be afraid to dig deep. You may find more than one reason. You may uncover ten or even twenty. Use this book to explore your motivations and let your purpose take shape. The more precise your purpose, the richer your journey.

chapter 2

What Is the Bible's Past?

Many picture the Bible as a single, pristine volume that descended from heaven, bound in leather and untouched by time. But the truth is far more profound and, dare we say, human. The Bible is actually a sprawling collection of writings, narratives, songs, letters, and visions crafted, edited, and cherished over centuries. Thus, it is deeply human in its origins yet divinely inspired in its purpose.

The Bible is a Library, not a Single Book

The Bible is not a single book but a library, filled with history, poetry, prophecy, and letters. Each has its own voice, its own story, and its own moment in time. The word Bible originates from the Greek word *biblia*, meaning books or scrolls. Over time, the Bible has symbolized ultimate authority in many aspects of life. Consider how we refer to a definitive guide as the Cooking Bible, implying it's the only recipe book you'll ever need. We swear oaths on the Bible and pass down cherished family Bibles through generations. In some traditions, the Bible isn't just held; it's gripped, almost like it's part of the preacher's body. Picture that leather-bound book, flapping wildly with every gesture, nearly alive, a visible reminder that this isn't just a book; it's the heartbeat of their faith, the rhythm of every word they speak.

The Bible is Inspired, but not Imposed

We must take the Bible seriously, but not always literally. To take the Bible seriously is not to shrink it down to rigid literalism but to step into its depths. To wrestle, to question, and to discover a truth that is living, layered, and alive. The Bible didn't simply drop from the heavens, fully formed. When people say, "the Bible says," it can sometimes feel as though the Bible is being personified, as if it has a voice or mind of its own. But the truth is, the Bible doesn't speak. Instead, the Bible reveals. It reveals wisdom and truths, guidance and praise, sorrow and hope, and, most importantly, stories about God and what it means to be part of God's story.

If we want to really see the Bible's beauty, depth, and rawness, we have to take it on its own terms. Be honest with it. Struggle with it. Let it breathe. In 2 Timothy 3:16, we read that "all Scripture is inspired by God." But that word inspired, in the original Greek, *theopneustos*, means more than we might think. It means "God-breathed." It carries the image of divine breath, of the Spirit of God moving, speaking, stirring.

The book you're reading right now is a collection of words on a page. I hope you enjoy it and that it speaks to you in some way. But the Bible is something more. It's not just words on a page; it's the Spirit at work. In prayer, Scripture shapes us. In worship, it lifts us. In everyday life, it calls us to act justly, love deeply, and live faithfully.

So when Paul says, "All Scripture is God-breathed," he is not just telling us where it came from. He is showing us what it does. The Spirit who breathed it out is the same Spirit who breathes it in, into hearts, into communities, and into the Church. Thus, the Bible is inspired not simply because of how it was written but because of how it continues to work. It is alive. It transforms. It bears witness.

> 2 Timothy 3:16
> All scripture is inspired by God and is useful for teaching, for reproof, for correction, and for training in righteousness.
> NRSVue

The Bible is Sacred, but not Literal

People often ask, "should we take the Bible literally?" And that's a fair question. But let's pause for a moment and ask a deeper one: What do we even mean by "literal"? Because as soon as we say the Bible is literal, we run into a problem. It's not that simple. And it's not consistent.

Look at how Jesus taught. He used parables, stories filled with imagery, exaggeration, and metaphor. No one walked away from the parable of the Prodigal Son thinking it was a news report. But they did walk away changed. The point wasn't whether the story happened. The point was what it revealed.

Now, here's where it gets tricky. A lot of people who claim to read the Bible "literally" don't actually do that across the board. They take some parts literally and others figuratively, depending on what fits their theology, their politics, or their comfort zone. For example, someone might insist the six days of creation in Genesis were literal

24-hour days, but then say Jesus calling himself "the door" is obviously a metaphor. They might quote verses from Leviticus to condemn certain behaviors, while ignoring other verses in the same book that talk about not eating shellfish or wearing mixed fabrics. Or they'll take the book of Revelation as a coded map of future world events, but treat Jesus' command to "love your enemies" as more of a nice idea than a literal directive. That's not a flaw in the Bible. That's human nature.

But when we approach the Bible this way, insisting everything be literal, we risk turning something mysterious, beautiful, and transformative into something rigid and shallow. Worse, we risk using it like a weapon. History has shown us how literalism has been used to exclude, to judge, and to justify things the heart of God never would.

Now think about this. If we demand that everything in the Bible must be literally or historically true in order for our faith to be valid... why? What kind of faith needs proof to survive? That's not faith. That's evidence. And faith, by definition, is what we hold on to when evidence runs out.

Maybe the deeper question is this. Isn't it a greater act of faith to trust in something even when you can't verify every detail? Isn't that the point?

The Bible is History, but not Historical

Some folks are out there on mountain slopes, searching for Noah's Ark like it's a holy treasure map. Others dig with just as much intensity, hoping to disprove the resurrection. These are two extremes, but both have something in common. They think proof is the point.

It's understandable to want clarity, certainty, and evidence. But let's be honest. When it comes to the big, sweeping events of Scripture, like Noah's flood, the parting of the Red Sea, or Jesus' empty tomb, no definitive archaeological proof has ever settled the case. Not for the believers. Not for the skeptics.

And that's okay. Faith isn't a fossil you can find. It's not a bone you can carbon-date. It's a relationship. It's a story you're invited into. People in the ancient world didn't write history the way we do today. They weren't filming documentaries. They were telling the story of how they encountered the Divine in their chaos. In floods. In deserts. In wilderness wanderings. In exile. These stories weren't just facts. They were meaning. They were theology wrapped in narrative.

What's truly fascinating is that many of these stories echo the same themes over and over. Water as a path to salvation. Wilderness as a place of testing. Resurrection as the final word. You don't need to "prove" these things happened to see their truth. These are truths that transcend history.

I've thought about baptism a lot. I don't believe in the power of those waters because scientists measured the Jordan River. I believe because I've been in the water and I know what it's like to come up from the depths.

I still wrestle with the tension of the Bible's historic accuracy. Some things are historical, some are metaphorical, and many live somewhere in between. But in the wrestling, I've found the power of Scripture isn't in proving it happened, but in discovering it still happens.

The Bible is Authoritative, but not Inerrant

The authority of the Bible was not originally based on the concepts of inerrancy or infallibility. Inerrancy refers to the belief that the Bible is completely free from error or contradiction in all matters it addresses, including history, science, and morality. Infallibility, on the other hand, is the belief that the Bible is entirely trustworthy and authoritative in matters of faith and practice, though it may contain minor errors in less significant details.

These ideas emerged later, primarily advocated by some evangelicals in the late 1800s. Early church fathers, such as Origen, interpreted difficult or strange passages allegorically rather than viewing them as errors. Augustine acknowledged the reality of copyist mistakes and cautioned against overly rigid, literal interpretations that could potentially harm faith. In fact, the notions of inerrancy and infallibility assume a fixed, closed, and perfectly preserved collection that simply did not exist during the formative centuries of Christian theology.

Today, thousands of churches adhere to this belief, revealing a deep and tragic problem. This belief often confuses science with theology and combines "what we know" with "what we believe." If our belief in Jesus' resurrection is based solely on accuracy and proof, we encounter a significant issue. The Bible does not argue for belief based on empirical evidence. Instead, it invites us to believe in Jesus' resurrection because we have encountered the risen Christ.

I wish churches would stop making these claims. A more faithful and biblically accurate approach would be to assert that the Bible's authority lies in its capacity to narrate God's ongoing covenant with creation, culminating in Jesus, the crucified and risen Messiah. This approach does not rely on a modern obsession with proving to nonbelievers that the Bible is not fiction.

To demand scientific certainty or historical airtightness is to examine the Bible under the wrong lens. Scripture is not intended to satisfy the modern hunger for provable data; rather, it aims to form a people who bear witness to the resurrection through lives transformed by grace. The purpose of the Bible is not to provide accurate information to believe in, but to immerse us in a narrative through which we come to live faithfully.

The Bible is the Word of God, but not God

The Bible is called the word of God because it is a divinely inspired testimony of God's work in the world. It is not just a historical text but a living witness to His character and purpose. Through scripture we see how God has acted in history and continues to be at work today. It reveals His laws, prophecies, and teachings and shapes our understanding of who He is and how He relates to us.

However, it is important to distinguish between the word of God as Scripture and the Word of God as Jesus Christ. In John 1:1–14 Jesus is called the eternal *Logos*. It's a complex word. In ancient Greek philosophy, *Logos* referred to the divine principle of order and reason that governed the universe.

John's use of *Logos* connects Jewish and Greek thought. In Jewish tradition, God's word was His creative power, as seen in Genesis when He spoke the world into existence. By calling Jesus the *Logos*, John was showing that Jesus is not just a messenger of God's truth but the very expression of God Himself.

The Bible is a Story, but not a Simple One

At its heart, the Bible is a story. It is not a lifeless document or a static decree but a grand, untamed, deeply human narrative of a God who loves relentlessly. It is not a monologue but a centuries-old conversation that is still unfolding and still inviting us in. At places, the Bible is wild, messy, beautiful, and divine. It was written by people who were trying to make sense of existence, why we are here, why we are broken, and why, despite everything, God continues to choose us.

Within its pages are historical accounts nestled beside poetic verses. Prophetic warnings share space with apocalyptic dreams. Letters of advice mingle with ancient wisdom. Each piece invites us to read differently to adapt our engagement based on its nature.

The Bible's story is as much about its formation as it is about the stories it tells. It's a testament to how people, throughout time, have wrestled with God, life, and meaning. It's alive and dynamic, both ancient and immediate. And that's the invitation: to enter not a monologue but a conversation centuries in the making.

Historical Development
How did the Bible take shape?

The Old Testament is a book unlike any other. It is the heartbeat of a people, pulsing with stories of struggle, faith, and identity. First, its truths were carried on the tongues of elders. Then, as Israel became a nation, they were written on scrolls, preserved through generations, and woven into a sacred narrative that still speaks today.

From Word Spoken to Word Written

There's something sacred about the way family stories unfold. The way your grandmother's voice lowers just a little when she gets to the serious part, or how your uncle always jumps in to correct a detail, like, "no, it wasn't a Tuesday, it was Sunday after church, don't you remember?" There's a rhythm to it, a choreography where everyone knows their part, their line, their moment to lean in or nod knowingly. It's more than a story; it's THE story.

This is why churches have always leaned on preaching, the spoken word. We've always been storytellers. It's how we pass on who we are. And this, too, is how the Old Testament came to be: stories spoken aloud by mothers, fathers, and elders, told around fires and tables and gathering places, passed hand to hand like something precious. These stories didn't begin as words etched in stone; they began as breath spoken into the air.

From Scrolls to Books

Over time, the stories of the people of Israel were first shared through word of mouth, told around campfires and passed from parents to children. As the community grew and changed, moving from scattered tribes to a more organized society with shared laws, leaders, and worship practices, these important stories began to be written down. What started as oral tradition became sacred written records, helping preserve the faith and history of a growing nation.

Scholars believe that the Old Testament began to take shape during the reigns of King David and King Solomon, around 1000 to 930 BCE. Their rule brought political stability, centralized resources, and an increasing need for documentation. This period also marked the rise of Jerusalem as a cultural and religious center, making it an ideal time to preserve the traditions and history of Israel.

In 1979, amid the dust and ruins of Jerusalem's infamous Hinnom Valley, a place long shadowed by judgment and suffering, archaeologists unearthed something astonishing. Two tiny silver scrolls were found inscribed with the priestly blessing from the book of Numbers. Even in a valley of despair, the word of God endured.

Known in Hebrew as *Ge-Hinnom*. The valley is referenced by Jesus in the New Testament, the name was transliterated into Greek as *Gehenna*. *Gehenna*, was notorious because it was Jerusalem's landfill. Over 2,000 years ago, cities lacked modern conveniences such as running water, waste management, and refrigeration. Landfills like *Gehenna* were chaotic, pungent, and unsanitary. Unlike the regulated dumpsites of today, the landfills of the past became the last refuge for the destitute and forgotten. In their shadowed depths, the unhoused and impoverished carved out a grim existence, scavenging for scraps to survive. They were the unseen keepers, tending fires that burned through the night and not just for warmth, but for survival itself. Actually landfill communities persist today. In the hidden corners of the world, there are those who, driven by crushing poverty, find themselves living on the edges of landfills, or within them.

As language evolves, so do the meanings of words. And sometimes, those meanings carry the weight of centuries. The Hinnom Valley, with its perpetual fires, suffocating stench, and pervasive misery, became the symbol of unending torment. In 2 Kings 23:10 and Jeremiah 7:31, the valley is named as a site of unspeakable child sacrifices to the god Molech.

By the time of Jesus, the valley was still being used as a landfill. Everyone who lived in or visited Jerusalem during and before the days of Jesus knew the valley well. They recognized its smell before they ever saw its smoke. Children were still warned: Behave, or you may end up there. Jesus referenced the valley too. In nearly every English translation of the Bible, when Jesus referenced the place *Gehenna*, the translators wrote the word hell.

> Mark 9:43-44
> If your hand causes you to sin, cut it off;
> it is better for you to enter life maimed
> than to have two hands and to go to hell,
> to the unquenchable fire.
> NRSVue

To be clear, Jesus wasn't describing some otherworldly place of torment. He was pointing to this world. He was talking about that valley, the landfill that reeked of judgment and despair. And in his mind, no one should ever want to go there.

But in 1979 these archaeologists did. Literally digging in hell, they found two tiny silver scrolls hidden in a burial cave. Painstakingly etched in paleo-Hebrew, the inscriptions were so minuscule they needed a literal microscope to read. They contained the priestly blessing from he book of Numbers:

> Numbers 6:24-26
> The LORD bless you and keep you;
> the LORD make his face shine on you and be gracious to you;
> the LORD turn his face toward you and give you peace.
> NIV

During the Babylonian Exile, when the Temple was destroyed and important symbols like the ark of the covenant and the tablets of the Law were lost, the people of Israel turned to their stories. In this time of crisis, they began to collect, organize, and write down what would later become the Hebrew Bible. This included the *Torah* (the Law), the *Nevi'im* (the Prophets), and the *Ketuvim* (the Writings). These sacred texts gave the people a sense of identity and hope during a difficult time. Written on scrolls, the stories could be copied, shared, and carried with them, helping their faith survive and continue to inspire others for generations..

Their preservation worked. These ancient scrolls are the oldest known written fragments of the Bible, a discovery that invites us to pause and reflect. What strikes me most is where they were discarded and found. *Gehenna*, a place long associated with destruction, judgment, and even hell itself. Yet, something sacred emerged from the very depths of this symbol of despair and condemnation: the priestly blessing, one of the most significant passages in Scripture.

Think about that. God's Word still rose from a place that represented the worst of human failure and ruin. This blessing survived the ravages of time, enduring through the hell of empires, wars, and attempts to destroy it. It stands as a profound testament to the enduring nature of God's word, a word that cannot be silenced no matter how dark or hopeless the circumstances. What was cast into a place of destruction became a symbol of divine hope, proving that nothing, not even hell, can extinguish the light of God's truth.

This discovery reminds us of Scripture's resilience. It refuses to be forgotten and continually resurfaces to inspire and guide each generation. It also highlights the importance of curiosity and diligent research as historians and archaeologists uncover profound truths in the most unexpected places. Just as importantly, it honors the faithfulness of those who preserved God's Word, stewards who carefully transitioned sacred stories from oral tradition to written texts so that future generations, like us, could encounter its beauty and truth.

From Hebrew to Greek

By the 3rd century BCE, a few centuries after the Babylonian Exile much had changed for the Jewish people. The Exile had scattered communities far and wide. Under the influence of Hellenistic culture, Greek had become the common language of the Mediterranean world. Jewish scholars translated their sacred Scriptures into Greek. This monumental work became known as the *Septuagint*.

The name *Septuagint* comes from the Latin word for seventy, referencing the tradition that seventy (or seventy-two) Jewish elders worked on the translation. This version of the Scriptures made Jewish sacred texts accessible to Greek-speaking Jews outside Judea, many of whom no longer spoke Hebrew as their daily language. By bridging the linguistic divide, the *Septuagint* preserved the connection between dispersed Jewish communities and their shared heritage while also opening the Scriptures to the broader Greco-Roman world.

Hebrew texts continued to be used alongside the *Septuagint* (the Greek texts), especially in synagogues and communities still connected to their linguistic and cultural roots. However, for early Christians, the *Septuagint* became their Bible. It shaped how they understood Jesus as the fulfillment of Jewish prophecies and promises. Over time, as these texts were shared and circulated, they began to resemble something closer to a written book, bound together for ease of use rather than individual scrolls. This shift made Scripture portable and accessible, solidifying its role as both an anchor for Jewish identity and a foundation for the Christian story.

From Words to Life

Jesus was a Jewish rabbi steeped in the Hebrew Scriptures, likely having memorized large portions of the Hebrew Bible, if not all. In the Jewish tradition, Scripture was recited, absorbed, and lived. This was the air Jesus breathed, shaping his teachings, parables, and understanding of God's kingdom. Likewise, the Gospel writers and Paul were deeply rooted in these sacred texts. They knew Scripture intimately; they were formed by it.

Yet, when they began to tell the story of Jesus, they weren't setting out to write Scripture in the way we understand it today. Like the earliest Israelites who passed down their sacred stories orally, the New Testament writers were driven by something urgent: the need to tell what they had seen, heard, and experienced. They weren't striving for theological permanence but rather responding to a moment, bearing witness to what they believed God had done in Jesus. Their words weren't intended to be biblical; they were testimony.

Stories shared in the community and letters written to struggling churches all were anchored in the conviction that this Jesus fulfilled the very Scriptures they had known and loved. These were urgent communications, pastoral responses to real crises, and passionate attempts to make sense of an extraordinary life. The writers were addressing immediate needs in their communities while simultaneously wrestling with how this Jesus fit into the grand narrative they had inherited from their ancestors.

The Canonization of the Bible

The history of the Bible's formation and preservation offers a profound testament to the faithfulness of God's people. What we refer to today as the Bible is known among pastors and scholars as the canon of Scripture. The term canon comes from the Greek word *kanon*, meaning "measuring rod" or "standard," and it describes the collection of writings recognized as the "standard" for faith and practice. These books are distinct from other ancient religious texts that may appear biblical but are not considered part of the canon.

The final push to establish the biblical canon came during the 4th century CE. This process unfolded against the Roman Empire's shifting politics, especially under Constantine's rule. After the Edict of Milan in 313 CE, which legalized Christianity, the Church gained the stability it needed to tackle big questions about doctrine and scripture.

The effort to separate canonical texts from non-canonical ones gained momentum during this period. The Council of Nicaea in 325 CE, though focused mainly on theological issues, set an important example of bringing the Church together to resolve disputes. This spirit of unity paved the way for broader agreements about scripture.

By the late 300s, the 27 books of the New Testament were widely recognized by Christian communities. Leaders like Athanasius of Alexandria helped promote this list of books. Local church councils, or meetings of church leaders, in cities such as Hippo (in North Africa, in what is now Algeria) in 393 CE and Carthage (also in North Africa, near modern-day Tunisia) in 397 CE officially approved this group of writings. They based their decisions on several key factors: how the books were used in churches, whether their teachings matched core Christian beliefs, and whether they were connected to the apostles. This important time helped shape the New Testament as we know it today and built a strong foundation for the Christian faith.

The Handwritten Bible

In the early centuries of the Christian church, access to the Bible was a privilege reserved for a select few. Hand-copying manuscripts made Bibles extraordinarily expensive, which meant only the clergy and the wealthiest could afford them. This exclusivity was compounded by widespread illiteracy, meaning that even when people encountered Scripture, they often relied on religious authorities to interpret it. Furthermore, the Bible was primarily available in Latin, Greek, or Hebrew, languages that weren't commonly practiced by the uneducated.

In some cases, these barriers were merely practical limitations of the time, reflecting the technological and educational constraints of the era. However, there were also instances where restricted access was a tool for maintaining church authority. Church leaders could control theological interpretation and preserve their influence over religious teachings by keeping the Bible in a language unfamiliar to ordinary people and limiting its availability. This dynamic persisted for centuries until the advent of the printing press and the push for translations in common languages, which played a crucial role in the Reformation and the eventual spread of biblical knowledge to all people.

While access to the Bible was often limited for social or political reasons, the physical form of the Bible also played a role in how it was shared and preserved. Understanding how the Bible was written and copied helps us see how both its message and its materials shaped its reach.

The earliest biblical texts were written on papyrus, an ancient form of paper made from reeds, and assembled into scrolls or early codices (books). Over time, as the need for durability grew, scribes transitioned to vellum, a type of parchment made from carefully prepared animal skins. Vellum lasted longer and allowed writing on both sides, making it ideal for preserving extensive manuscripts. Two of the oldest and most significant complete Bible manuscripts, the *Codex Sinaiticus* and *Codex Vaticanus*, date to the 4th century. Written on vellum, these manuscripts include both the Old and New Testaments and reflect the shift to a more formalized and accessible Bible.

As Christianity spread, the task of copying Scripture fell to monks and scribes, who worked in dedicated rooms called scriptoriums. These scribes used meticulous methods to ensure accuracy, counting letters and words to verify that their copies matched the originals. While minor variations, like spelling differences, occasionally appeared, the core message of Scripture remained remarkably consistent.

As the Christian faith spread to new regions, it became more and more important to translate the Bible into different languages so people everywhere could understand it. Some of the earliest translations were into Coptic (used in Egypt), Ethiopian, and Latin. These helped people in different parts of the world connect with the message of Scripture.

One major milestone came in 405 CE, when a priest named Jerome, who was born in the Balkans, completed the first full translation of the Bible into Latin. This version was called the *Vulgate*. The name comes from the Latin word *vulgata*, which means "common" or "for the people." (It's where we get the modern word vulgar, which originally just meant something used by ordinary people.) For over 1,000 years, the *Vulgate* was the official Bible used by the Western Church and became the basis for many later versions.

For people who speak English, one of the most important steps in making the Bible easier to read came in the early 1200s. A church leader named Stephen Langton, the Archbishop of Canterbury (England), introduced the chapter divisions we still use today. These divisions made it much easier to find and study specific passages.

Then, in the 1300s, an English scholar named John Wycliffe helped make the Bible available to more people by translating the entire Bible into English for the first time. His work, known as the *Wycliffe Bible*, was completed in 1382 and gave everyday readers in England access to Scripture in their own language, something that had never been done before.

The Printing Press

The invention of the printing press by Johannes Gutenberg in the 1400s changed everything. For the first time, the Bible could be copied quickly and accurately, without the mistakes that came from writing by hand. This breakthrough made the Bible easier to get than ever before, setting the stage for people everywhere to read and study it.

The Reformation brought new energy to translating the Bible into everyday languages. In 1516, Erasmus published a Greek New

Testament with his own Latin translation, inspiring others to do the same. Martin Luther's German translation, finished in 1534, gave ordinary people direct access to the Bible and influenced many other translations across Europe.

Around the same time, another important change happened. In 1551, Robert Estienne published a Greek New Testament that was the first Bible to include verse numbers. A few years later, in 1555, he released his Latin edition, the first complete Bible with verse divisions. This numbering system became the standard that we still use today.

chapter 3

Why Translate?

This chapter gets technical, really technical. If you'd rather skip the nuts and bolts of translation, no hard feelings. Turn the page and move on. But if you're the kind of person who loves peeling back the layers, digging into the details, and seeing how the magic happens, then strap in. We are about to take a deep dive into the mechanics of meaning.

The Bible was written in three different ancient languages. Most of the Hebrew Bible (Old Testament) was written in biblical Hebrew, while the New Testament was composed in Koine Greek. Aramaic appears in parts of both testaments, specifically in sections of Daniel and Ezra in the Hebrew Bible and in a few preserved phrases in the Greek New Testament.

To explore the languages of the Bible effectively, we first need to understand two key terms you will encounter in Bible study: transliteration and translation.

- **Transliteration** is the process of representing the letters or characters of one writing system using those of another, allowing readers to approximate the original pronunciation.

    - The Hebrew word מָשִׁיחַ is transliterated to Messiah.

    - The Greek word Χριστός is transliterated as Christos.

- **Translation** is the process of conveying the meaning of text from one language into another language.

    - The Hebrew word מָשִׁיחַ is translated as "anointed one."

    - The Greek word Χριστός, is translated as "anointed one."

Understanding the difference between transliteration and translation helps readers appreciate how biblical words are brought into English, and what might be gained or lost in the process. A transliteration like *Christos* preserves the sound of the original but not its meaning, while a translation like "Anointed One" conveys the meaning but loses the linguistic and cultural resonance of the original term. Without this distinction, readers might assume "Christ" is simply Jesus's last name, rather than a loaded title with deep roots in Jewish expectation and Greek vocabulary.

Israel's Language: Hebrew

Most of the Old Testament was written in biblical Hebrew, an ancient language that evolved over centuries. What makes biblical Hebrew fascinating is the way it forms words, almost like a family tree of meanings. At its core are short "root words," typically three consonants long, read from right to left. These roots create a basic meaning from which many related words grow:

- M-L-K (מלך) carries the basic idea of royalty. From this single root springs an entire family of related words: melech (king), malkah (queen), and malchut (kingdom).

Imagine trying to read English without vowels. A word like "bt" could mean "bat," "bit," or "but," and you would have to rely on context to figure it out. Ancient Hebrew worked the same way. Readers depended on memory, tradition, and the flow of the text to interpret meaning correctly.

To preserve the accurate reading of the Hebrew Scriptures, Jewish scribes called the Masoretes (6th–10th centuries CE) developed a system of vowel points and cantillation marks. The name "Masoretes" comes from the Hebrew word *masorah*, meaning "tradition" or "transmission." Their work resulted in the *Masoretic Text*, the standard version of the Hebrew Bible used today.

Thanks to their painstaking efforts, the Hebrew Bible has remained remarkably consistent for over a thousand years.

The Tetragrammaton

YHWH is the transliteration of God's name in Hebrew. Scholars call it the Tetragrammaton, meaning "four letters." This name was considered too sacred to speak aloud. Instead, when reading Scripture or talking about God, people would say *Adonai*, a Hebrew word meaning "Lord," as a way of honoring God without pronouncing the actual name YHWH. This ancient tradition continues to shape modern Bible translations:

- LORD (in all capital letters) is used to represent YHWH, the personal name of God. This is the name by which God made Himself known in covenant relationship with Israel.

- Lord (with only the first letter capitalized) usually translates Adonai, which means "Master" or "Lord." It is a title, not a personal name, and is used to emphasize God's authority, rule, and majesty.

- God is most often used to translate Elohim, a general Hebrew term for God or gods. When referring to the God of Israel, Elohim emphasizes His power, sovereignty, and role as Creator.

Multiple Sources

Scholars began to wonder if there was something more at play when the Bible sometimes uses YHWH and sometimes Elohim. The more they analyzed the text, the more convinced they became of what is now called the Documentary Hypothesis. This idea suggests that the Torah, or first five books of the Bible, was not written by just one person but was put together from different sources over time. Each source had its own writing style, way of describing God, and focus on different aspects of Israel's history and laws.

According to this theory, four main sources were combined to form the Torah:

- J (Yahwist) source - uses YHWH as God's name
- E (Elohist) source - uses Elohim as God's name
- D (Deuteronomist) source - primarily in Deuteronomy
- P (Priestly) source - focuses on ritual and genealogy

We see this most clearly in the opening chapters of Genesis. There are two creation stories: One in Genesis 1, where Elohim creates the world in six days with structured order, and another in Genesis 2, where the YHWH Elohim forms humans first and shapes creation around them in a more personal, intimate way. The flood narrative also unfolds in two layers, sometimes saying the flood lasted 40 days, other times 150, and alternating between whether Noah took two of every animal or seven pairs of the clean animals. Even the Ten Commandments are given twice, first in Exodus 20, then again in Deuteronomy 5, with subtle but significant differences in wording and emphasis.

These repetitions are not careless mistakes but intentional reflections of Israel's rich and layered tradition. Rather than erasing different voices, the Torah holds them together in tension, allowing multiple perspectives on God, covenant, and creation to exist side by side. This is not just a historical curiosity but a theological statement.

The Septuagint

When the New Testament quotes the Old Testament, it often draws from the *Septuagint*. This is because many New Testament writers and early Christians were more familiar with Greek than Hebrew. While there are instances where the Hebrew Bible is referenced directly, the *Septuagint* was the primary source for many scriptural quotations and allusions in the New Testament.

Understanding the *Septuagint* helps us see why some Old Testament quotes in the New Testament don't match exactly when compared to modern translations of the Hebrew Bible. Since many New Testament writers used the Greek *Septuagint* instead of the Hebrew Scriptures, their quotations often reflect the *Septuagint's* wording rather than the original Hebrew text. This is why, when you look up an Old Testament passage quoted in the New Testament, it may read slightly differently from the version found in your Bible today.

For example, in Hebrews 10:5, the writer quotes Psalm 40:6, saying:

> Hebrews 10:5
> Consequently, when Christ came into the world, he said,
> "Sacrifices and offerings you have not desired,
> but a body you have prepared for me."
> NRSVue

However, if you turn to Psalm 40:6 in most modern Old Testament translations, which are based on the Hebrew text, it reads:

> Psalm 40:6
> Sacrifice and offering you do not desire,
> but you have given me an open ear.
> NRSVue

The difference occurs because the author of Hebrews is quoting from the *Septuagint's* interpretation of Psalm 40:6, which renders the phrase "given me an open ear" as "a body you have prepared for me." Theologically, this shift is significant.

In the Hebrew text, "opened ears" refers to a person's willingness to listen to and obey God, often understood as a metaphor for submission. However, the *Septuagint* translation expands this idea by emphasizing bodily obedience, interpreting it as God preparing a physical body for sacrifice. The author of Hebrews applies this directly to Jesus, using it to reinforce the idea that Christ came into the world not to offer traditional sacrifices but to give Himself as the ultimate, obedient sacrifice.

This difference highlights how the *Septuagint* shaped early Christian theology, particularly in its understanding of Messianic fulfillment. By following the *Septuagint's* wording, Hebrews presents Jesus as the perfect fulfillment of God's plan, one whose entire body and life were prepared for the redemptive work of salvation. This also demonstrates how early Christians saw Jesus' sacrifice as the true and final offering that surpassed the Old Testament system of sacrifices.

Recognizing these translation differences helps us see how the early Church interpreted Old Testament prophecies and how Scripture itself testifies to Christ's mission in ways that might not be immediately obvious when reading only the Hebrew text.

Common Hebrew Words

Many Christians encounter Greek and Hebrew words through their study of the Bible, hymns, prayers, or theological discussions. Here are some examples of common Hebrew words:

- Amen (אָמֵן) – So be it
- Hallelujah (הַלְלוּיָהּ) – Praise the Lord
- Manna (מָן) – What is it?
- Messiah (מָשִׁיחַ) – Anointed One
- Ruach (רוּחַ) – Spirit or breath
- Shalom (שָׁלוֹם) – Peace
- Shema (שְׁמַע) – Hear
- Torah (תּוֹרָה) – Law or instruction

Jesus' Language: Aramaic

Some parts of the books of Daniel and Ezra were written in Aramaic, the everyday language of international trade and diplomacy in the ancient Near East. These sections usually switch from Hebrew to Aramaic when the topic turns to global affairs or messages meant for non-Jewish audiences. For example, in Daniel 2:4, the text suddenly shifts to Aramaic when Babylonian advisors begin speaking to King Nebuchadnezzar. From that point through chapter 7, much of the narrative continues in Aramaic, reflecting the broader, more international setting of the story.

By the time of Jesus, Aramaic was still commonly spoken across the region. However, Greek had become the dominant written language, which is why the New Testament was originally written in Greek. Even so, the Gospels preserve several of Jesus' Aramaic phrases, giving us rare, vivid glimpses into how he actually spoke. One well-known example comes from the Gospel of Mark, where Jesus raises a young girl from the dead and says, Talitha koum, which means "Young woman, get up." The Gospel writers translated these phrases for their readers, allowing modern audiences to experience a deeper connection to the original language, culture, and historical setting.

> Mark 5:41
> Taking her hand, [Jesus] said to her, "Talitha koum," which means, "Young woman, get up."
> CEB

The World's Language: Koine Greek

While Jesus spoke Aramaic daily in ancient Israel, his followers needed to share his message far beyond their local region. Therefore, they chose to write in Koine Greek because it was like the English of their time, a language that merchants, travelers, and ordinary people across the Mediterranean could understand. They simply wanted as many people as possible to be able to read and understand Jesus's teachings. So, while Jesus spoke and taught in Aramaic, writing his story in Greek meant that his message could spread across the entire ancient world instead of staying limited to one small region.

Since the New Testament was written in everyday Koine Greek rather than formal Classical Greek, modern translators face an interesting challenge: they must understand the casual, street-level language of ancient marketplaces and homes, not just the polished Greek of philosophy books and poetry. It's like trying to understand 2,000-year-old slang and everyday expressions rather than formal literature. And while that's no small feat, trust me, trying to do this in Greek is like a warm hug compared to the rollercoaster that is biblical Hebrew.

Common Greek Words

You may often hear these Greek terms in Christian contexts without realizing their origins. These words have seamlessly integrated into religious language and carry deep significance:

- Agape (ἀγάπη) – Unconditional love
- Baptizo (βαπτίζω) – To wash
- Charis (χάρις) – Grace
- Christos (Χριστός) – Anointed One
- Doxa (δόξα) – Glory
- Ekklesia (ἐκκλησία) – Church or assembly

Why Translate?

- Eucharistia (εὐχαριστία) – Thanksgiving
- Kairos (καιρός) – Divine time
- Koinonia (κοινωνία) – Fellowship
- Kyrios (Κύριος) – Lord
- Logos (λόγος) – Word
- Pneuma (πνεῦμα) – Spirit or breath

Lexicons and Concordances

If you've ever wanted to dig deeper into the Bible, you've probably come across tools like lexicons and concordances. They can be incredibly helpful, but they're not perfect. It's important to understand both how to use them and where their limits are.

A lexicon is like a dictionary for the original languages of the Bible. It helps you understand what a word meant in its original setting, including shades of meaning that may not come through in English translations.

A concordance is more like an index. It shows you every place a certain word appears in the Bible, helping you see patterns, themes, or how a word's meaning might shift depending on the context.

One of the most well-known tools is *Strong's Exhaustive Concordance*, created by James Strong in 1890. It indexes every word in the *King James Version* (KJV) of the Bible and assigns a number, to each original Hebrew or Greek word. For example:

- Word: Love
- Verse: John 3:16 – "For God so loved the world..."
- Strong's Number: g0025.
- Greek Word: ἀγαπάω agapaō
- Definition: to love (in a social or moral sense): — (be-)love(-ed).

But Here's the Catch. *Strong's Concordance* is tied to the *King James Version*, which was translated in 1611 from the *Textus Receptus*, a limited set of Greek manuscripts available at the time. Since then, scholars have discovered many older and more reliable manuscripts. Today, modern translations like the NRSVue, CEB, NIV, and others are based on much broader and more accurate collections of ancient texts.

For the Old Testament, modern scholars use sources like the *Biblia Hebraica Quinta*, the Dead Sea Scrolls, and the *Septuagint*. They also draw from the Hebrew University Bible Project, which offers the most detailed comparison of all known Hebrew variations.

For the New Testament, critical editions like the *Nestle-Aland 28th Edition and the Greek New Testament* (UBS 5th Edition) are created by comparing thousands of manuscripts using powerful digital tools to get as close as possible to the original text.

So, what does this mean for you? Tools like *Strong's* can still be useful, especially for word studies or quick lookups, but they don't always reflect the most accurate or up-to-date biblical scholarship. Just because a word appears in *Strong's* doesn't mean it fully captures what the original authors meant.

If you're serious about Bible study, use lexicons and concordances as part of a broader toolkit. Pair them with a good modern translation, and don't be afraid to check multiple sources. The goal isn't just to find the definition of a word. It's to understand the meaning behind the message.

Translation Word Choices

Have you ever read a Bible verse and thought, what on earth does that mean? You're not alone. Some verses are clear, but others (like Romans

5:18) can leave you scratching your head. Let's compare how different translations handle this same verse:

> **Romans 5:18**
> Therefore just as one man's trespass led to
> condemnation for all, so one man's act
> of righteousness leads to justification and life for all.
> NRSVue

> **Romans 5:18**
> So now the righteous requirements necessary for life
> are met for everyone through the righteous act of one person,
> just as judgment fell on everyone
> through the failure of one person.
> CEB

> **Romans 5:18**
> Therefore, as one trespass led to
> condemnation for all men, so one act of righteousness
> leads to justification and life for all men.
> ESV

> **Romans 5:18**
> Nor can the gift of God be compared with the result
> of one man's sin: The judgment followed one sin
> and brought condemnation, but the gift followed
> many trespasses and brought justification.
> NIV

Confused? You're not alone. Romans 5:18 is deep, layered, and honestly, pretty tough to grasp. But this isn't the only verse like that. The Bible is full of texts that are nuanced, complicated, and sometimes just plain messy. So what's going on?

Imagine trying to understand an ancient text message, but it's from 2,000 years ago. That's what Bible translators deal with when working with Romans 5:18. Here's how it's paraphrased in The Voice:

> **Romans 5:18**
> So here is the result: as one man's sin
> brought about condemnation and punishment
> for all people, so one man's act of faithfulness
> makes all of us right with God and brings us to new life
> The Voice

It's clearer, but still complex. Why? Because understanding verses like this takes more than just knowing the words. You need some context. Namely, Romans 5:18 is part of a bigger argument.

Paul, the writer, is comparing Adam (from Genesis) to Jesus. Adam gave in to temptation, bringing sin and death. Jesus resisted temptation, bringing life and redemption. Paul isn't talking about two individuals only; he's showing how Jesus reverses the damage Adam caused. This Adam-versus-Christ idea is a core part of Paul's theology. It's more than fixing a mistake—it's about revealing what God ultimately wants for humanity through Christ.

But even with that context, the verse still raises questions. One of the trickiest parts of this verse is the Greek word *pantes*, usually translated as "all" or "everyone." But what does that mean in practice?

- **All** - The NRSVue reflects the idea of universality, emphasizing that the effect of Christ's righteousness applies to all people.

- **Everyone** - The CEB is a more specific rendering to make the concept of inclusion clear in modern English.

- **All men** - The ESV is like saying mankind. The Greek word, while grammatically masculine, was commonly used in a gender-inclusive way to refer to all people. The ESV is emphasizing the connection between Adam (as the first man) and the universal human condition.

- **Many** - The NIV highlights the contrast between Adam's disobedience (affecting all) and Christ's act of righteousness (applied to many). This wording can be confusing because it sounds like Christ's saving work only applies to some people.

These differences aren't just linguistic. They reflect theological choices. Some translations lean toward a more inclusive view of salvation. Others emphasize salvation as something for believers specifically. This is why reading multiple translations is so helpful. It shows you where translation ends and interpretation begins. Of course, no translation is perfect. Every translation involves choices, about tone, word meaning, grammar, and theology. That's why no single version of the Bible gives you the full picture. Take Job 13:15 as an example:

> Job 13:15
> See, he will kill me; I have no hope;
> but I will defend my ways to his face
> NRSVue

> Job 13:15
> Though he slay me, yet will I hope in him;
> I will surely defend my ways to his face.
> NIV

Same verse. Totally different tone. Here's what's happening: Job 13:15 exists in two different forms in the Hebrew manuscripts, and both English translations are correct because they're translating different versions. The NRSV follows one Hebrew reading that expresses despair ("I have no hope"), while the NIV follows another that expresses defiant trust ("yet will I hope in him").

This difference comes from an ancient Jewish scribal tradition called *ketiv* and *qere*, meaning "what is written" and "what is read."

Sometimes the Hebrew text had one word written down, but scribes had a tradition of reading it differently out loud. Rather than choosing one version and erasing the other, they preserved both. In Job 13:15, this creates two legitimate ways to understand the verse: one emphasizing Job's despair, the other his stubborn faith. Ancient scholars didn't see this as a problem to solve but as a richness to preserve.

What Should You Do?

Here's a few tips for dealing with these overly complex verses:

- **Compare Multiple Translations.** No single version captures everything. Comparing translations side by side can help you see what's consistent and where things differ.

- **Explore with Curiosity.** If a verse feels confusing, you're not doing it wrong. You're doing it right. Dig into the context. Look at the surrounding verses. Use study tools when needed.

- **Analyze Translators' Choices.** Examine how different translators choose words, tone, and style. Reflect on how these decisions shape your understanding of the text.

- **Lean into the Complexity.** The Bible isn't meant to be flat or one-dimensional. It's layered, rich, and written across cultures and centuries. That's what makes it powerful. Instead of looking for quick answers, learn to appreciate the questions.

Types of Translations

When choosing a Bible translation, people often refer to Eugene Nida's categories: Word-for-Word, Thought-for-Thought, Meaning-for-Meaning, and Paraphrase. These labels are commonly used to describe different translation styles, but they can actually be more misleading than helpful.

In reality, there are only two main categories: translations and paraphrases. A translation works directly from the original languages (Hebrew, Aramaic, and Greek) to convey the meaning as accurately as possible. A paraphrase, on the other hand, is more of a rewording or interpretation of Scripture, often for readability rather than precision. The problem with trying to classify translations into rigid groups is that no translation perfectly fits into just one category. Even so-called "Word-for-Word" translations, like the NASB, still have to make interpretive choices because languages do not always align one-to-one. Likewise, "Thought-for-Thought" translations, like the NIV, still aim to be faithful to the original text rather than just paraphrasing.

Instead of relying on broad categories, it is more helpful to compare translations directly and see which one works best for you. Looking at how different versions handle key passages can give you a better sense of their strengths and weaknesses. Ultimately, the best translation is the one that helps you understand and apply Scripture while remaining faithful to the original text.

The New Revised Standard Version

The *New Revised Standard Version Updated Edition* (NRSVue) stands as the gold standard of Bible translations. It is used by top theological schools and endorsed by scholars across denominations. Unlike other so-called "literal" translations, it refuses to play interpretive games. It is also the only translation that was overseen by the esteemed Society of Biblical Literature (SBL).

The biggest drawback of the NRSVue is its limited print options, making it difficult to find a well-designed edition that matches the quality of the translation itself. Unlike the NIV or ESV, which offer a wide range of study Bibles, premium editions, and reader-friendly formats, the NRSVue's selection is relatively sparse, often leaving readers with fewer appealing choices in layout, design, and study features.

The Common English Bible

More than 120 biblical scholars from 22 faith traditions contributed to the *Common English Bible* (CEB), which is based on the most up-to-date original texts. While the CEB is praised for its accuracy and accessibility, it is not without its quirks. Some of its wording choices are surprisingly edgy, occasionally departing from traditional phrasing in ways that can feel either refreshingly modern or unexpectedly jarring, depending on the reader's perspective.

> Judges 11:3
> So Jephthah ran away from his brothers
> and lived in the land of Tob.
> Worthless men gathered around Jephthah
> and became his posse.
> CEB

> Acts 17:5
> But the Jews became jealous and brought some thugs
> who were hanging out in the marketplace
> CEB

Using words like "posse" and "thugs" gives these passages a contemporary, almost streetwise feel. While this makes the text more relatable, it can also feel jarring to those familiar with more traditional phrasing, and to be quite honest, I'm not sure I like it.

Another notable example is how the CEB translates one of Jesus' most frequent self-references. In the Gospels, Jesus calls himself the "Son of Man" more than 50 times. The Greek phrase *ho huios tou anthrōpou* means "someone like me." In this case, the CEB opts for what is arguably the most literal translation: "The Human One." Nearly every other Bible retains "Son of Man" because it has been ingrained in Christian teaching for centuries, carrying deep theological significance. While "The Human One" may be technically the most accurate translation, it feels weaker. However, a serious student of the Bible can't deny the CEB's accuracy and scholarship.

The New English Translation

For those curious about the translation process, the *New English Translation* (NET) is an invaluable resource. With extensive footnotes, it explains why specific words were chosen, highlights manuscript differences, and unpacks theological implications. In an era when many assume their Bible translation simply reflects what the text says, the NET serves as a crucial reminder that every translation involves interpretation.

Some evangelicals have raised concerns that the NET leans too liberal, but these claims don't hold up under closer examination. If anything, its narrowly evangelical translation team at Dallas Theological Seminary might have benefited from broader theological input. Still, for those who value transparency in translation, the NET stands out as perhaps the third-best English Bible available today, behind only the NRSVue and CEB.

The New International Version

The *New International Version* (NIV) is the most widely sold Bible in print. I was excited when the NIV team released the TNIV (Today's New International Version), but it was quickly discontinued after public outcry over its inclusive language. As a result, we now have the NIV 2011 update.

The NIV is a good translation, easy to read, and deserves respect simply because of its popularity. However, it sometimes makes interpretive decisions for the reader rather than allowing the text to speak for itself. For example, consider how the NIV translates the Greek word *sarx*:

> Romans 7:18
> For I know that good itself does not dwell in me, that is, in my sinful nature. For I have the desire to do what is good, but I cannot carry it out.
> NIV

The Greek word *sarx* is literally "flesh" or "body." However, instead of saying this, the NIV choses to translate it "sinful nature." This is a theological shift that places Paul within a Calvinist reading of total depravity that he may or may not have intended. Psalm 51:5 follows a similar pattern:

> Psalm 51:5
> Surely I was sinful at birth,
> sinful from the time my mother conceived me.
> NIV

Other translations recognize that the psalmist is expressing the reality that we are all born into a broken world already marked by sin.

However, the NIV shifts this poetic lament into a doctrinal statement about original sin, one that the Hebrew text does not explicitly require. Psalm 51 does not say we were born as sinners, but you wouldn't know that from reading the NIV.

Despite its criticisms, the NIV remains a solid Bible translation that effectively balances readability and accuracy. Its widespread popularity means that it has one of the largest selections of print editions available, including study Bibles, devotional formats, large-print editions, and even creative journaling Bibles.

The New American Standard Bible

The *New American Standard Bible* (NASB), last updated in 2020, is widely regarded as one of the most literal English translations of the Bible. It is known for its precise word-for-word translation style, making it a favorite among those who prioritize textual accuracy over smooth readability.

The *Legacy Standard Bible* (LSB) is a more recent revision of the NASB. It was designed to refine the NASB's literal approach even further, emphasizing consistency in rendering key terms. Notably, the LSB restores the divine name YHWH (but spells it out as Yahweh, which is contradictory to Jewish tradition) rather than using LORD, and it seeks to maintain rigid fidelity to the original languages.

The LSB was developed primarily within a Reformed evangelical framework, and both the LSB and NASB 1995 rely on a relatively narrow set of textual traditions. They rarely highlight textual variants or manuscript differences, which can limit a reader's understanding of the complexities in biblical translation. While these versions are popular in some circles, they are less widely recognized in academic biblical scholarship and are seldom used as standard reference texts.

The English Standard Version

The English Standard Version (ESV) is one of the most widely popular modern translations. However, it is not without its flaws. While it aims for word-for-word accuracy, some of its translation choices reflect theological bias, particularly in areas related to gender and church leadership. Additionally, its readability can be stiff, making it less accessible than translations like the NIV or CSB. Despite its popularity, the ESV is not necessarily the best choice for every reader, especially those looking for a more neutral or widely accepted scholarly translation. Let's consider Genesis 3:16:

> Genesis 3:16
> To the woman he said,
> "I will surely multiply your pain in childbearing;
> in pain you shall bring forth children.
> Your desire shall be contrary to your husband,
> but he shall rule over you."
> ESV

The ESV translation states that a woman's desire will be contrary to her husband's, which is an interpretive choice that differs from the original Hebrew text. Instead of accurately reflecting the wording of the original scripture, the ESV modifies it. This change aligns with a theological agenda suggesting that women will inherently resist male leadership, thus supporting a complementarian view (the belief that men are divinely designated leaders in both marriage and the church).

Why Translate?

This perspective is not found in the original text of Romans either, yet the ESV still alters its translation in a similar manner, which is an example of how theological agendas, rather than textual fidelity, can shape a translation:

> Romans 16:7
> Greet Andronicus and Junia, my kinsmen and my fellow prisoners. They are well known to the apostles, and they were in Christ before me.
> ESV

What the ESV does with Romans 16:7 is deeply problematic. Junia is undisputedly a feminine name, and scholars overwhelmingly agree that Junia was a woman. Yet the ESV disregards this by referring to her as Paul's "kinsmen," a masculine term that obscures her identity.

But it does not stop there. The ESV also alters Paul's clear statement that Andronicus and Junia were "prominent among the apostles" (episēmoi en tois apostolois), changing it to suggest that they were merely "well known to the apostles." This shift subtly but deliberately denies that Junia, and perhaps Andronicus as well, were counted as apostles.

While the ESV claims to be a faithful translation, it reshapes the text to fit a particular doctrinal perspective, emphasizing a male-only apostolic tradition that the original Greek does not support. This approach goes beyond mere translation choices, representing a theological revision that prioritizes ideology over accuracy.

The King James Version

The separation between the Church of England and the Roman Catholic Church was one of the most significant turning points in Christian history. In the 1500s, political and religious tensions reached a breaking point when King Henry VIII broke away from the authority of the Pope. This split was driven in part by Henry's desire to annul his marriage, which the Catholic Church refused to approve. As a result, the Church of England was established, with the king as its supreme head.

Decades later, under the reign of King James I of England (who became king in 1603), another major shift occurred, this time in how the Bible would be read and understood by English speakers. In 1604, King James authorized a new English translation of the Bible. His goal was to create a unified and official version that would be acceptable to both Anglican and Puritan factions. The result, completed in 1611, became known as the *Authorized King James Version* (KJV).

Written in a Shakespearean-like style, it prioritized elegance over literal accuracy. It stands alongside Shakespeare's writings and has introduced countless words and phrases still in use today. Its impact extends beyond religious discourse and has shaped everyday speech, literature, and culture. Expressions such as "eye for an eye," "by the skin of my teeth," "a thorn in the flesh," "the powers that be," "cast the first stone," "a house divided against itself," "signs of the times," "from strength to strength," "labor of love," "by the sweat of your brow," "rise and shine," "go the extra mile," "the writing on the wall," "pride goes before a fall," "a fly in the ointment," "at their wit's end," and "forbidden fruit" all have their roots in the KJV.

Through its majestic prose and timeless wisdom, the *King James Version* has deeply influenced the way people speak, think, and tell stories. Its impact remains significant in both sacred and secular contexts. But for all its beauty and cultural importance, the *King James* is also a product of its time. Its translators worked with limited manuscript evidence, its language is now outdated, and many of its choices favor style over clarity or accuracy. While it deserves respect as a historic document and literary treasure, the *King James Version* remains a deeply flawed translation.

Paraphrases

Beyond translations, there are paraphrases, which focus less on grammatical structure and more on capturing the essence and emotion of Scripture. *The Good News Bible* and *The Voice* fall into this category, as does the *New Living Translation* (NLT), by simplifying and using storytelling to make biblical themes more accessible. While they are not substitutes for deep study, they serve as helpful companions that bring fresh perspectives.

Then there is Eugene Peterson's *The Message*, which is not a traditional translation but a vibrant and contemporary rendering that breathes new life into Scripture. As a pastor, Peterson aimed to make the Bible speak with immediacy and warmth. The Message reminds us that God's Word is meant to be lived, wrestled with, and proclaimed.

Translating God's Gender

Most people refer to God as "He." I do too. Not because I'm making a theological statement about God's gender, and honestly, it's not always my first choice. But sometimes, it's just the easiest way to stay connected to the language I grew up with. English picked up this habit from the King James Bible. Its poetic weight and wide reach helped cement "He" as the default pronoun for God in English.

I understand why that matters. Saying "He" can suggest that God is male, or that being male brings you closer to the divine. That's not what I believe. If you actually read Scripture, the image of God goes far beyond that: a woman in labor (Isaiah 42:14), a midwife (Psalm 22:9), a nursing mother (Isaiah 49:15), a hen gathering her chicks (Luke 13:34). God speaks through all kinds of metaphors, not just the masculine ones.

So why do I still say "He"? Not because it's more accurate, and not because "She" would be wrong. It's just the language that feels natural after a lifetime of speaking it. Jesus called God "Father." People called God "King." Those words shape the rhythm of my faith. But I don't think the real issue is theological. I think it's linguistic. English is clumsy when it comes to the divine. Hebrew doesn't have a neutral pronoun like "they." So I stick with what I inherited, even as I leave space for others to speak differently. And if one thing about translation should stay with us, it's this: language may shape how we talk to and about God, but it doesn't limit how God speaks to us.

chapter 4

Where Do I Begin?

There's something about the weight of a hardback book in my hands; it feels solid and grounded like it's meant to hold up the truths that change you. The right font matters, too. It's clear, readable, inviting, gesturing, "Come on in, stay a while." For study, I mostly use the Bible app on my laptop these days, but my favorite physical Bible? It's a beast. Over two thousand pages, nearly four pounds, a text so massive it's almost laughable. And yet, it feels exactly right because the Bible is supposed to feel a little overwhelming, right?

I remember a professor in Divinity School who used to place his thin-line Bible on the podium beside a microphone. Every time he turned a page, the sound of that delicate, crackling paper would echo through the room, sharp and distinct, like nails on a chalkboard. The pages of the Bible can be comforting, but sometimes they ought to drive us crazy, too.

Where Do I Begin?

Sometimes, I find myself simply holding one of those hefty study Bibles. I don't always read it. Sometimes, I just thumb through the thin pages, letting its weight rest in my hands, almost like holding a trusted companion. It makes me think that perhaps the Bible's physical weight is a metaphor for the spiritual gravity of its content and its pages a metaphor for its fragility.

After all, a book so vast, brimming with ancient wisdom, unsettling truths, and stories that have shaped empires and broken hearts, isn't something to skim lightly. It demands reverence. It's the kind of book that makes you pause, maybe even wonder, where do I begin?

And that's the paradox of the Bible. It doesn't start with us finding the perfect entry point. It starts with the God who's already found us. It's not about whether we can handle its weight or unravel its complexity. The real question is: are we willing to step into its story and let it reshape us? Because the Bible is a book that refuses to sit quietly on a shelf. Though, tragically, in many homes, it does, gathering dust instead of stirring hearts. But when you open it, truly open it, something shifts. It moves and disrupts. It challenges the comfortable, confronts the complacent, and calls out to the searching. It's not content to stay confined within the covers; it breaks into your thoughts, priorities, and life.

Ten Tips on Where to Start

The Bible is indeed a vast and complex book, and it can be intimidating, especially for those unfamiliar with its many genres, contexts, and voices. And guess what? That's exactly as it should be. It's not a rulebook or a manual for living; it's a diverse collection of writings from different people in different times, all wrestling with the big questions about God, life, and what it means to be human.

But let me assure you—there is no wrong place to begin. The key is to approach it not as a text to conquer but as a living conversation into which you are being invited. With this in mind, here are ten quick tips to get you started.

1 - Don't Worry About "Getting It Right"

The Bible wasn't written to be approached like a riddle to solve or a textbook to master. It's an invitation into a lifelong journey of exploration and faith. It's okay if certain parts don't immediately make sense or feel strange, because that's part of engaging with something as vast and sacred as Scripture. These moments of uncertainty are opportunities to ask questions, wrestle with meaning, and connect with God and others. The Bible invites you to engage, reflect, and have conversations about what it means to live faithfully in this complex and demanding world.

2 - Start with the Gospels

If you're new to the Bible, the best place to start is with the Gospels: Matthew, Mark, Luke, and John. These books are the centerpiece of Scripture, offering a direct window into the life, teachings, death, and resurrection of Jesus. Each Gospel offers something unique. Matthew presents Jesus as the fulfillment of Old Testament promises, highlighting His role as the long-awaited Messiah and teacher. Mark is short and action-packed, perfect for those wanting a direct introduction to Jesus' ministry. Luke is rich with detail and narrative depth, beautifully connecting Jesus' life with the larger story of humanity. John, meanwhile, is deeply theological and poetic, drawing us to reflect on Jesus as the living Word of God. These accounts ground us in the heart of Christian faith and help us understand the rest of the Bible.

3 - Embrace the Psalms

From the Gospels, consider diving into the Psalms, a collection of prayers, songs, and reflections that echo the full spectrum of human emotion. The Psalms remind us that our faith doesn't have to be polished or perfect; it's about honesty. Whether you're experiencing joy, anger, despair, or hope, there's a psalm that mirrors your heart's cry. These writings give us permission to bring every part of ourselves to God, showing us that even doubt and frustration can be acts of faith.

4 - Go to Where it all Begins

The early books of the Bible, Genesis and Exodus, are foundational stories that explore the nature of God, humanity, and the covenant relationship between the two. Instead of getting bogged down in debates over literal history, approach these texts with curiosity. What do these stories teach us about who God is? What do they reveal about human purpose, struggles, and redemption? These books lay the groundwork for understanding the rest of Scripture.

5 - Read Romans for Theology

When you're ready to go deeper, the book of Romans stands as an invitation to explore what it truly means to live by faith. Here Paul weaves together themes of grace, sin, salvation, and community, deeply rooted in the narrative of the Old Testament. Throughout history, Romans has ignited transformative moments in the lives of some of Christianity's greatest figures. Augustine was famously converted after encountering Romans 13. Martin Luther found revolutionary clarity in Romans 1:17, sparking the Protestant Reformation. John Wesley's heart was "strangely warmed" during a reading of Luther's preface to Romans. Karl Barth's groundbreaking commentary, *The Epistle to the Romans*, reshaped modern theology. Corrie ten Boom, who risked her life to shelter Jews during the Holocaust and later forgave her captors, lived out the defiant hope of Romans 8, that nothing, not even death or despair, can separate us from the love of God. Time and again, Romans has proven to be a wellspring of theological insight and a catalyst for personal transformation, speaking across centuries to those who seek deeper understanding and a closer walk with God.

6 - Read Slowly, Reflect Deeply

The Bible isn't meant to be rushed, and practicing slow reading isn't just helpful for engaging with Scripture. Slow reading is a practice we should embrace more broadly. Reading slowly helps with retention, allowing ideas to settle and take root in our minds. More than that, it reduces anxiety by creating a moment of stillness in our busy lives. When approaching the Bible, take it one passage at a time. Pause to reflect on the words and let them resonate. Ask yourself, what is God saying to me here? Or, how does this apply to my life? By reading at a deliberate pace, you create space for reflection, understanding, and peace.

7 - Read in Community

Reading Scripture in community is essential because the Bible forms and sustains the Church as a people set apart by God. Reading and hearing the Scripture read aloud at worship or a Bible study is about more than sharing perspectives. It's about being shaped together into a countercultural body that lives out the story Scripture tells. Reading it together reminds us that faith is not a private affair but a shared journey of discipleship, where we are formed into a people capable of embodying the gospel in the world. Engaging with others in Scripture is how the Church learns to narrate its identity and mission faithfully. It's about more than learning new insights; it's about becoming a people who embody what they read and proclaim.

8 - Expect to Wrestle

The Bible isn't always easy to understand or straightforward to navigate. You may find yourself asking, why is this passage included? Or, what does this mean in today's world? And that's okay. Wrestling with Scripture is not a sign of weak faith—it's part of growing deeper in it. Faith isn't about having every answer neatly tied up; it's about trust, relationship, and learning to hold questions with open hands. Even some of the most faithful people in history have doubted deeply and wrestled intensely with Scripture. Dietrich Bonhoeffer grappled with what it meant to follow Christ in the face of Nazi tyranny. James Cone struggled with God's seeming silence in the midst of racial injustice in America. And Mother Teresa, known for her unwavering service to the poorest of the poor in Calcutta, endured decades of spiritual dryness and doubt, wondering where God was even as she continued to pour herself out for others. Wrestling with God and with

Scripture isn't a flaw. It's healthy. It's where faith becomes real, personal, and alive.

9 - Widen Your Frame

The Bible tells a story of people trying to understand God, often fumbling through. It's not a story of perfect people or easy answers. It's a story of grace, struggle, and faith. As you read, focus on the big question: How does this story or passage invite me into God's story today? And as you do, be sure to consider what came before and after the passage. Place it in the context of the surrounding scripture at the very least, as this can provide deeper insight into its meaning and relevance.

10 - Understand the Context

Understanding the Bible's historical and cultural background is crucial. You don't need to be a historian or an anthropologist to achieve this; having a basic understanding of life during biblical times is sufficient to grasp the context. To assist with this, I've compiled a list of key points that build on the contextual overview provided in earlier chapters. As you will see, life was challenging, and understanding the everyday struggles of these ancient people, though often overlooked, is essential for understanding their stories.

Agrarian Society	Many biblical stories are set in farming and shepherding contexts, making agricultural imagery essential for understanding parables and metaphors.

Subsistence Farming	People relied on what they could grow themselves, which shaped their deep dependence on God for provision and weather.
Overcrowded Cities	Cities like Jerusalem were packed, especially during festivals, which helps explain public tension, disease spread, and the urgency in Jesus' teachings.
Political Instability	Constant warfare, invasions, and political upheaval destabilized daily life and made security precarious in biblical times and caused people to long for peace and security, deepening the hope for a coming Messiah.
Construction and Rebuilding	Ongoing destruction and rebuilding of cities like Jerusalem created a transient and weary population, emphasizing the need for lasting restoration.
Oppressive Empires	The Israelites and early Christians lived much of their history under the sway of powerful empires including Egypt, Babylon, Persia, Greece, and Rome. Living under empires shaped how people understood authority, resistance, and the longing for divine justice.
Geopolitical Hotspot	Due to their strategic location and religious significance, Jerusalem and its surrounding regions were often the center of geopolitical tensions, highlighting the tension between worldly power and spiritual promise.
Weather and Climate	The region's climate, including its hot, dry summers and mild, wet winters, affected food supply, which gave urgency to prayers, feasts, and famines described in Scripture.
Trade Routes	Israel's crossroads location allowed cultural, religious, and economic exchange, which influenced both conflict and opportunity.

Economic Systems	Trade and labor, including slavery, were everyday realities, which makes biblical justice and liberation deeply countercultural.
Social and Economic Inequality	Wealth was unevenly distributed, giving context to Jesus' teachings on the poor, generosity, and kingdom values.
Monotheism	Believing in one God set the Israelites apart, often bringing conflict with surrounding polytheistic cultures.
Prophetic Tradition	Prophets challenged injustice but were often misunderstood, so Jesus' prophetic role carried both authority and controversy.
Religious Tensions	Internal and external conflicts shaped faith practice and made unity among early believers a radical idea.
Patriarchal Society	Men dominated public life, making Jesus' inclusion of women and the early church's countercultural communities stand out.
Non-traditional Sexual Practices	Sex outside traditional marriage was strongly condemned, but not because of identity or orientation. The concern was usually about power, domination, or exploitation (such as in slavery, rape, or temple prostitution). The ancient world had no concept of sexual orientation, so modern LGBTQ+ identities weren't in view. What Scripture challenges is abuse, not loving, consensual relationships.
Victim Blaming	Sexual assault victims were often blamed, showing why Jesus' compassion toward the marginalized was so revolutionary.
Lack of Modern Infrastructure	Poor sanitation and daylight-dependent schedules shaped rhythms of life, vulnerability to disease, and the need for communal support.

Limited Education	Most people were illiterate, which makes the oral transmission of Scripture and communal memory especially important.
Early Death	Short life expectancy shaped urgency around family, legacy, and faith in eternal life.
Health and Medicine	Disease was misunderstood and stigmatized, which reveals the radical compassion of Jesus when he healed and touched the sick.

The list above is extensive, but understanding the historical, social, and cultural realities of the time helps readers to engage with biblical texts more thoughtfully and sensitively. The Bible was written within specific contexts that shaped its stories, laws, and teachings, often mirroring the challenges and complexities of ancient life. By considering these factors we gain a richer understanding of the struggles and resilience of the people who lived in those times. This insight, in turn, deepens our appreciation for the Bible's timeless calls for justice, compassion, and faith, messages that often stood as bold, counter-cultural responses to the hardships of the ancient world.

Models of Reading the Bible

When approaching the Bible, having a model or framework can make your reading more focused and meaningful. Navigating this complex and ancient text can feel overwhelming, but a helpful model provides a lens through which to examine its various layers. A good model illuminates different dimensions of scripture, guiding you to uncover its deeper significance and apply its lessons to your life. By adopting a structured approach, you can engage with the text in a way that enriches both understanding and personal growth, fostering a deeper connection with God's word. Below are some popular frameworks to help shape your reading.

Devotional Model	Think of it as savoring a delicious meal rather than wolfing it down. The devotional approach to Bible reading is about slowing down and connecting with God on a personal level. You might focus on a few verses, meditating on their meaning and praying for understanding. It's less about covering a lot of ground and more about deepening your relationship with God through scripture.
Contemplative Models	Imagine sitting by a quiet stream, letting the gentle sounds wash over you. Contemplative Bible reading is similar. It's about experiencing God's presence through the text, often in silence or through prayer and visualization. Practices like *Lectio Divina*, where you read, meditate, pray, and contemplate, can help you connect with God on a deeper, more intuitive level.
Narrative Models	Picture yourself engrossed in a captivating novel, following the main characters and plot twists from beginning to end. The narrative approach to the Bible does something similar. It focuses on the overarching story of the Bible, from creation to new creation, highlighting the key themes and connections between different parts. It helps you see the Bible as one grand narrative, rather than a collection of isolated stories.
Lectionary Models	The lectionary approach follows a pre-planned cycle of readings used in many churches. It connects you with the wider church community and helps you explore the Bible in a structured way, often tied to the church year and liturgical seasons.

Thematic Models	Imagine researching a specific topic, like "forgiveness," and gathering information from various sources. The thematic approach to Bible reading is similar. You choose a theme or topic and then explore all the passages in the Bible that relate to it. This allows for in-depth study and helps you understand the Bible's teachings on issues that are important to you.
Chronological Models	Imagine opening a history book only to find the chapters jumbled and out of order. A chronological approach to the Bible fixes this. It's like putting the Bible's stories on a timeline, reading them in the sequence they actually happened. Instead of going straight from Genesis to Revelation, you might jump around a bit, piecing together the narrative as it unfolded historically. This helps you see the bigger picture of God's interaction with humanity and understand the context of each book within its historical setting.
Reading Plans and Lists	Think of a reading plan as a roadmap for your journey through the Bible. These structured plans provide a schedule for reading through the entire Bible or specific portions, making the task less daunting and helping you stay on track. They can be tailored to fit your individual needs and goals, whether you want to read the whole Bible in a year or focus on a particular section.
Book-by-Book Models	Think of it as taking a deep dive into a single book. The book-by-book approach involves focusing on one book of the Bible at a time, exploring its historical context, literary style, and key themes. It's like a focused study, allowing you to gain a comprehensive understanding of each book's unique message and contribution to the overall biblical narrative.

Justice-Oriented Model	Think of reading Scripture with your eyes wide open to the cries of the oppressed. The justice-oriented model highlights how the Bible speaks to issues like poverty, racism, inequality, and systemic injustice. It challenges readers to not just learn from the Word, but to live it out through action, advocacy, and compassion. This model resonates deeply with the prophetic tradition and the life of Jesus, who consistently sided with the marginalized.
Inductive Models	Imagine being a detective, carefully examining the clues to solve a mystery. The inductive approach to Bible study is similar. It involves careful observation of the text, followed by interpretation and application. You start by asking, "What does the text say?" Then, "What does it mean?" And finally, "How does it apply to my life?" It's a disciplined approach that encourages you to discover the meaning of the text for yourself.

part 2

Enter Its Story
Explore the Heart of Scripture

chapter 5

What Is God's Story?

In my first theology class at Duke, the legendary Geoffrey Wainwright assigned us sixteen books for a single course. Sixteen. One of them was his own masterpiece, *Doxology*, which came in at nearly six hundred pages. Another, a bit smaller but every bit as dense, was C. FitzSimons Allison's *The Cruelty of Heresy*. It traced the history of heretical teachings that threatened the early Church. Even though the book is considered a theological classic, our whole class found it tough to love because it was just profoundly tragic, and reading it felt like carrying a heavy weight around all semester.

Heresy in the early Church was not just a theoretical problem; it was a big deal. From the beginning, the Church saw itself as the guardian of divine truth. Whether you were looking at the Roman Catholic Church in the West or the Greek Orthodox Church in the East, every group that claimed to be the true Church also believed it had the exclusive right to interpret that truth. Any belief that challenged their teaching was branded as heresy.

Heresy basically means a belief that goes against the core teachings of Christianity, and in those early days, it was seen as a serious threat. The fear was that it could mislead people about who God is and what salvation means. Still, labeling someone a heretic was and still is a serious move. Deciding what counts as true and what counts as false demands deep wisdom, careful study, and a good dose of humility, because getting it wrong can hurt not just individuals but the Church as a whole.

Church councils played a major role in sorting all this out. They helped define orthodoxy, meaning the official set of teachings the Church recognized as faithful to the message of Jesus and the apostles, and they condemned teachings they saw as dangerous. During the early Middle Ages, often called the "Dark Ages" (roughly from the fall of Rome in the 5th century to around the 10th century), the Church became the central authority in much of Europe. In the Western Church, no doctrinal decision was considered final until the Pope approved it. Some individuals who were declared heretics were excommunicated, meaning they were officially cut off from the life of the Church. Others, however, faced far worse. Beginning in the 12th century, during the period of the Inquisition (which formally started around 1230), some heretics were imprisoned, tortured, and even executed under Church authority.

Killing someone in the name of truth feels, to put it mildly, extreme. The Church's violent past is not something we can brush aside or pretend did not happen. Taking faith seriously means being willing to wrestle with these darker chapters of our story, not to excuse them, but to understand where we have come from and how it shapes where we are going. The truth is, whether we are comfortable with it or not, our inheritance is deeply Catholic. Protestantism did not emerge in a vacuum. It grew out of Catholicism.

The Church has always been messy. It has made mistakes. It has been complicit in injustice and often slow to repent. And yet, for all its flaws, it remains our family. Families cannot erase their history and start over. They struggle with it. They tell the whole story. They reform where they must and carry forward what is still worth passing down. And for us, there is a lesson tucked inside all that tragedy. If bad theology once led to so much damage, it should remind us to be careful with our theology today. Not because we fear another Inquisition but because wisdom, truth, and love still matter. They always have, and they always will.

The Long Struggle for Truth

The need to guard truth is not something that suddenly appears in Church history. Even in the Old Testament, we see prophets confronting false visions of God and calling the people back to faithfulness. In the Gospels, Jesus himself challenged the religious leaders of his day when their interpretations twisted the heart of God's law. From the beginning, Scripture has shown that bad theology is not just a problem of information; it can lead entire communities away from the life God intends.

Even Paul was determined to make sure his teachings lined up with those of the other apostles. When he spoke to the leaders in Ephesus, Luke records Paul's urgent call for unity among believers and his warning about the dangers of letting distortions of faith take root:

> **Acts 20:29**
> I know that, after my departure,
> savage wolves will come in among you
> and won't spare the flock.
> CEB

I love that Paul does not hold back. He straight up calls false teachers savage wolves. But if I am being honest, I think his warning is not just about them. It is about us too. Paul cared a lot about protecting the Church from wrong ideas, but he also knew that danger could come from inside the community, not just outside. The real threat was not only people out there somewhere. It was also the temptation we all face to hold onto our own ideas so tightly that we end up hurting faith instead of helping it grow.

This is why we need to be careful. Theological boundaries are important, but they should not be used like weapons. Instead, they should be held with wisdom, humility, and a willingness to admit when we are wrong. Words like "orthodoxy" and "heresy" matter, but they should be used carefully. History shows that sometimes what one generation calls "orthodox" might later be seen as too narrow or even harmful. The Church is not immune to making mistakes either. It can become rigid, exclusive, and too focused on holding power if it is not careful.

Bad Theology

Sometimes I hear a preacher on TV railing against other churches, confidently declaring himself right while condemning everyone else as misguided. But the irony is hard to miss because the theology they preaches is, at best, shallow and, at worst, deeply flawed. Sometimes it is just plain wrong.

As a university minister, I see firsthand the real-world consequences of theology in people's lives. What does it say about the Church when people absorb and repeat harmful beliefs without question? Too often, churches fail in their task of forming disciples. They trade deep theological reflection for catchy quotes that can be easily posted or shared. Even worse, I see theology used to tear down rather than build up and to manipulate rather than liberate.

Bad theology is often born from woundedness. A term I have adopted recently is that sometimes God is "misnarrated." Certain interpretations of Christianity emerge from pain, fear, or an identity that requires an enemy. When preachers stand in pulpits and define their righteousness over and against other churches, they are often protecting themselves from deeper questions. The pain bad theology causes is real, but those who perpetuate it are often trapped in cycles of inherited fear, suspicion, and control.

So yes, I get the irony in calling something "bad theology." But the truth is, bad theology still exists. At its core, a lot of it comes from failing to see the Bible as one unfolding story. You cannot slice it into pieces and expect to understand what is really going on.

The Bible is not a dictionary or an instruction manual. Its format can sometimes make it look that way, but that is not how it was meant to be read. Verses were never meant to be pulled out as quick proof for whatever point we are trying to make.

This is called prooftexting. Prooftexting happens when someone takes a verse out of its original context to support a theological idea or argument. It often involves quoting one line without paying attention to the bigger story around it. It is like grabbing a single sentence from a long novel and using it to explain the entire plot. It almost always distorts what the author meant.

That is why it is so important to know the whole story of God, not just a few isolated parts.

Good Theology

The Bible unfolds the story of a God who refuses to remain distant and continually draws nearer, breaking every barrier to meet humanity face-to-face. It is a narrative of relentless intimacy, where divine love seeks us out in deeper and more personal ways. This isn't merely an ancient account; it's the living story of God's movement toward a world transformed by love and justice. From the garden of creation to the promise of a new creation, the story is always moving forward, pointing us toward an ultimate vision: a world where all are gathered into an all-embracing community of love, united in purpose and harmony. It's a story of hope, connection, and a God who will stop at nothing to restore what is broken.

The Biblical Storyline
Finding Our Place in the Grand Story

The stories we live by shape our daily lives. They come from the culture around us, the communities we are part of, and our own personal experiences. But beyond all of our individual stories, there is a bigger story at work. This bigger story is often called a "metanarrative." It is the large, overarching story that connects everything together and gives deeper meaning to life.

The Bible tells us that there is a divine story running through all of history. It does more than explain where we came from. It shows us how to live with purpose and meaning. The pattern of God's actions in the world becomes the key to understanding our own lives. The Bible's story is not just a set of instructions or wise sayings. It is a story we are actually invited to step into and live out.

When we start to see the world through this lens, we realize that the stories we believe shape who we are and how we live in community with others.

The Bible's meta narrative unfolds in six main acts:

Act 1: The Garden of Belonging

Imagine a beautiful and peaceful place where everything is full of life and connection. In the book of Genesis, the story of the Garden of Eden tells us that humans walked closely with God and lived as his companions. This story is the foundation of the Bible and shows us three important truths.

- **We were created for a direct relationship with God.** In the Garden of Eden, people walked and talked with God personally (Genesis 3:8). There was no separation, no shame, and no fear. This close relationship is at the heart of what it means to be human.

- **Life was meant to be good.** The Garden shows us life as God intended, full of harmony between God, humans, and creation (Genesis 1:31; 2:15). Everything had its place and purpose, and God called it "very good."

- **We were given a purpose.** Humans were made in God's image and given the responsibility to steward the earth and reflect His character (Genesis 1:26-28; 2:15). They were called to walk with God and work alongside him in the world he made.

Genesis reveals more than the beginning of the world. It offers a powerful picture of humanity's purpose within creation. The world was formed through God's creativity, wisdom, and love. He shaped chaos into order and gave life meaning and direction. Humans, made in God's image, were placed in creation with a special role. God entrusted us with the care of his world, calling us to reflect His goodness and to work alongside Him. Our work was designed to be an act of worship, a way of living in harmony with God's leadership and love.

When humanity chose to disobey God, we broke the trust that had defined their relationship. Instead of relying on God's wisdom, we chose to follow our own way. Even then, God remained faithful. He did not abandon His creation. The longing for Eden, for that closeness with God, continued to echo through the generations.

God made a covenant with Noah, promising to preserve life. Later, he made a new covenant with Abraham, promising to bless the world through Abraham's family.

Abraham's calling directly connected back to God's original plan in the garden. Through Abraham and his descendants, God continued His work to bring blessing, order, and hope into the world. The hope first planted in Eden lived on in Abraham's story and points forward to the day when God and humanity will walk together once again.

Act 2: A Nation Called to Faithfulness

Beginning in Genesis 12, the biblical narrative takes root in Abraham and his family, through whom God's covenantal promises begin to unfold. The focus later shifts to his grandson Jacob, who wrestles with God one night and receives a new name: Israel. This struggle is more than a personal moment. It foreshadows the identity of an entire people, a nation destined to wrestle with God throughout its history. One of Jacob's sons, Joseph, carries the story to Egypt and sets the stage for one of the Bible's most formative narratives.

Some approach these events as literal history, but a wider lens reveals their deeper theological and symbolic significance. Egypt, for example, is more than just a geographical location. It represents a paradigm of foreign domination and a recurring symbol of oppression throughout Scripture. Biblical texts frequently reuse earlier traditions, and Egypt's role as a place of enslavement is later mirrored in Babylon and Rome. The Exodus story is not merely a one-time event. It is an archetype, a pattern of suffering, displacement, and divine deliverance that recurs in Israel's history and echoes through generations.

God's response to oppression is always redemptive. At Sinai, He establishes a covenant with Israel that is built upon two central elements: The law and the tabernacle. The law provides moral, social, and religious guidelines, not as arbitrary rules but as a framework for Israel's identity as a holy people. The tabernacle is more than a sacred tent. It signifies God's presence dwelling among His people, a portable sanctuary that embodies divine nearness and faithfulness. Both elements reflect God's desire for relationship, not just regulation.

Yet as history unfolds, Israel struggles to live out its calling. Kings chase power. Prophets are ignored or silenced. Worship grows hollow.

Sound familiar to today? Israel's failure is not merely external disobedience but a deeper forgetting of the covenant's heart. Even so, despite repeated failures, God remains faithful. From this cycle of disobedience and restoration, the hope for a Messiah emerges. A true king who will embody the covenant and bring ultimate liberation. The story that began with Abraham and was shaped by Egypt, Babylon, and Rome does not remain static history. It is a living tradition that speaks to every generation's struggle with exile, oppression, and the longing for redemption.

Act 3: Faith and Failure Between Exodus and Exile

Fascinating and powerful stories fill the space between Exodus and Exile. They are well worth reading. But spoiler alert, Israel follows the same pattern of faithfulness and failure, trust and betrayal, renewal and forgetfulness. Yet this is no ordinary cycle. It is a metanarrative that speaks to the deepest human condition. Israel is learning again and again what it means to be God's people.

- **Closeness with God**: The Exodus was not just an escape from slavery. It was a radical redefinition of Israel's identity. They were no longer subjects of Pharaoh. They were a covenant people under YHWH. In moments like King David's reign, this identity flourished. The Davidic covenant planted hope for a Messiah, an everlasting reign of righteousness and peace. Yet even then, Israel often misunderstood the covenant. Instead of seeing it as a calling, they treated it as an entitlement.

- **God's Patience Amid Decline:** As Israel grew comfortable, they drifted. They turned to idols, sought security in alliances rather than in God, and treated worship as ritual instead of relationship. Yet God did not abandon them. Through prophets, He issued a call. He did not simply expose their sin but invited them to return with power and poetry. The prophets disrupted their illusion of control, shook them from complacency, and reminded them that their true calling was to be a countercultural people of justice, mercy, and faithfulness.

- **The Cycle of Faithfulness and Failure**: Blessing followed obedience, but complacency led to collapse. This was not just a mechanical cause and effect. It was a deeper reality. When Israel abandoned its covenant identity, it lost itself. The fall of the kingdom and the destruction of the Temple were not just national tragedies. They were existential crises. Yet even in exile, punishment became possibility. One way of life had ended. Something new was beginning.

Far from their homeland, their institutions, and their sacred spaces, Israel discovered that God was still with them. The prophets, especially Ezekiel, had radical visions that shattered old assumptions. The Temple had been the symbolic center of God's presence, yet Ezekiel saw the glory of God leave the Temple in Ezekiel 10. Later, in Babylon, he saw visions of God appearing there. This was unsettling and even scandalous. God was not confined to Jerusalem. His presence was not bound to geography or institutions. He could be encountered even in exile.

Stripped of power, Israel was forced to see God in a new way. This is where hope begins, not in returning to the past but in embracing the fresh work of God. The exile birthed new theological insights, a deeper awareness of God's faithfulness, and a renewed longing for a Messiah who would bring true restoration.

Israel's story is not just one of failure. It is a story of transformation. It does not belong only to the past. It is alive today, speaking into every place where people feel uprooted, wandering, and longing for home. Just as in ancient exile, God is still calling His people beyond old certainties into something deeper and something new.

Act 4: The Fulfillment of Every Promise

Jesus fulfills the promises made to Abraham and David, although not in the way many people expected. They were looking for a political leader, someone who would defeat their enemies and build an earthly kingdom of power and control. But Jesus had a different plan. Instead of building a kingdom through domination, He brought God's reign through self-giving love.

He invited people into a new way of living, one shaped not by status or control but by humility, service, and the costly work of reconciliation. In His teaching and in His actions, Jesus showed what the kingdom of God truly looks like. He welcomed outcasts, healed the sick, and challenged the powerful. These were acts of radical love. They were signs of a deeper truth: God's kingdom stands against the broken systems of the world.

Jesus' mission was never just about personal change or spiritual escape. It was not about avoiding pain or hiding from suffering. His mission was to redeem all of creation, to restore what had been broken, and to invite us to join Him in that work. Following Jesus means taking up that same mission, even when it costs us something.

The kingdom Jesus announced does not move forward through easy victories. It grows through faithfulness, even when life is hard. To follow Him is to live in the tension between the world as it is and the world as it will one day be. It means holding onto hope, without pretending suffering is not real.

Thus, the resurrection is not a reversal of the cross. It is God's way of vindicating Jesus' sacrifice. It shows that God's power is made perfect in weakness, and it proves that even in a world that often resists His reign, God's kingdom is still breaking through.

Act 5: A People Set Apart

Born through Jesus' resurrection, the Church emerged as a countercultural community. It isn't a religious club or a loose collection of spiritual individuals but a people called to embody God's love, justice, and holiness in a world that often prefers power, control, and self-interest. Followers of Jesus aren't simply saved as individuals. They are reborn into a new identity as God's people and are set apart not for privilege but for service, witness, and suffering. Texts like Matthew 5–7, Romans 12, and 1 Peter 2 don't offer ethical advice. They describe a way of life so radically different from the world that it can only be sustained by the power of the Spirit and the shared practices of the Church.

One of the most profound marks of this new identity is the celebration of communion. But this isn't a sentimental ritual. In breaking bread and sharing wine, the Church makes a bold proclamation: our true King is Christ, not Caesar. Our loyalty belongs to His kingdom, not the kingdoms of this world. The Eucharist is an act of defiance against all false allegiances. It's a declaration of a new order, a new community, and a new way of being in the world. To eat at this table is to renounce the world's ways of division and self-preservation. It's to embrace the foolishness of God's grace, the scandal of undeserved love, and the reality that we belong to one another because we belong to Him.

As we often say at the communion table, "we are called to be the body of Christ, redeemed by His blood." But this is no easy calling. The Church, if it is to be faithful, must not blend into the culture but must bear witness to an alternative kingdom. Through this act of remembrance and renewal, we are not just proclaiming who we are but who we are becoming. We are a people transformed not for our own sake but to show the world what God's boundless love looks like. To take communion is to accept the cost of discipleship, the risk of faithfulness, and the joy of a new creation breaking into the present.

Act 6: Toward the New Creation

The final act is not an ending but a new beginning. God's ultimate vision is not destruction but reconciliation. It is a world healed, creation made whole, and humanity restored to its intended harmony. Revelation offers a stunning image of this future. A beloved community gathered from every nation, worshiping in eternal joy, where every tear is wiped away and death is no more. But this is not mere escapism. It is the hope that remakes the world.

This hope is not passive but active. It shapes how we live in the present. It compels us to love boldly, to forgive even when it costs us, and to work for justice in the face of suffering. True reconciliation, whether personal or cosmic, requires more than good intentions. It demands that we open ourselves to the radical power of God's grace, which heals not only victims but also perpetrators. It breaks cycles of vengeance and violence. To hope in God's future is to refuse to be imprisoned by the past.

This is the heart of Christian eschatology (the study of last things). It's a call to participate in God's ongoing work of redemption. The cross and resurrection show that suffering leads to something greater. They reveal a God who suffers with us and leads creation toward resurrection life. Hope is forged in the struggle and in the groaning of creation longing for renewal. Because God's promised future is certain, we are empowered to live differently now. We resist injustice, proclaim peace, and embody the love of Christ in a broken world.

The biblical metanarrative is an invitation. It calls us to live with purpose as co-laborers in God's mission. Creation, redemption, and restoration are the pattern of our own lives. When we discover our place within God's unfolding future, we find who we truly are.

Plot Twists
Ways the Biblical Narrative Continues to Surprise Us

A plot twist is an unforeseen turn of events that reshapes the story. The Bible is crammed with such moments, hundreds probably. Trust me when I say narrowing it down to just eight was no easy task. From the groundbreaking concept of covenant to what I call subversive selection, these twists showcase a God who delights in defying expectations. Time and again, we see a divine narrative that prioritizes love and justice, challenging traditional ideas of power and control at every turn.

Plot Twist 1: Covenant

Covenant is one of the most important ideas in the Bible, but it can feel a little strange at first. Simply put, a covenant is an agreement that creates a relationship based on promises and responsibilities. It is like a serious, binding commitment between two parties.

What makes the biblical idea of covenant so revolutionary is that God chooses to bind Himself to human beings through a relationship like this. In the ancient world, most religions believed that the gods were distant and mostly concerned with being worshiped or appeased. These gods demanded sacrifices, but they did not offer love or make promises to people.

But the God of the Bible is different. He initiates a relationship based on love, trust, and mutual commitment. Through a series of covenants with Noah, Abraham, Moses, and David, and finally through His Son Jesus, God voluntarily ties Himself to humanity. He makes promises to us and even accepts limits on His own freedom in order to stay faithful to the relationship.

This was a radical idea in the ancient world. No one would have expected a god to show empathy, much less unconditional love. Yet the story of Scripture shows that even when people fail and break their side of the covenant, and they do often, God remains faithful. He does not simply abandon humanity or destroy creation. Instead, He continually finds ways to restore the relationship and to keep His promises.

The covenant, then, is not just a legal contract. It is a deep, relational commitment based on love. It shows us what kind of God we worship, a God who stays faithful even when we are not.

Later in the New Testament, the apostle Paul explains how Jesus fulfills and transforms the covenant relationship. In 2 Corinthians 3, Paul says that Jesus brings a "new covenant." He does not mean that the old covenant was bad. In fact, Paul calls the covenant given through

Moses "glorious" because it revealed God's will, shaped the identity of Israel, and pointed toward God's plan to save the world.

But Paul also says that the glory of the old covenant was only a glimpse of what was coming. In Jesus, the full glory of God's plan is revealed. The law that was once written on stone tablets is now written on human hearts by the Holy Spirit. Instead of following God by external rules alone, God's people are now being transformed from the inside out.

This does not mean throwing away the Old Testament. It means stepping into the fullness of what the old covenant was always pointing toward. God's presence is no longer confined to a building or a single nation. It now lives in the Church, in a people who are being shaped by the Spirit to reflect Christ's glory to the world.

- [ ] Noah: Genesis 9:8-17 - God's covenant to preserve life
- [ ] Abraham: Genesis 15:1-21 - God's promises to Abraham
- [ ] David: 2 Samuel 7:12-16 - God's promise of an eternal kingdom
- [ ] Jesus: Hebrews 8:6-13 - The new covenant
- [ ] Church: 2 Corinthians 3:7-18 - Ministers of the new covenant

Plot Twist 2: Shalom

Shalom is the Hebrew word for peace, but it's so much bigger than we usually think. *Shalom* describes everything working the way it's supposed to. It's life as God dreamed it: people thriving, relationships healed, creation flourishing, everything in its right place.

When people talk about ultimate peace or the healing of all things, they're really talking about *shalom*. It's the vision where all brokenness gets mended and everything finds its way home again.

We often think of the Bible as a straight line pointing toward Jesus. But *shalom* runs throughout the whole story like a golden thread. It moves in spirals, circling back again and again to God's dream for the world.

In Genesis, we learn that humans are created in God's image. *Shalom* is deeply connected to this truth. It's about becoming more fully human and living into the image of God we were made to reflect. *Shalom* means seeing life as sacred and recognizing God's presence in every person and all of creation. It invites us into a lifelong journey of letting go of our need for power and control. Instead, it calls us to embrace the deep connections that tie all of existence together in God's design.

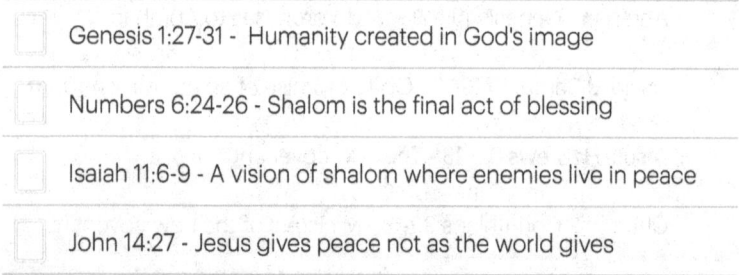

- [ ] Genesis 1:27-31 - Humanity created in God's image
- [ ] Numbers 6:24-26 - Shalom is the final act of blessing
- [ ] Isaiah 11:6-9 - A vision of shalom where enemies live in peace
- [ ] John 14:27 - Jesus gives peace not as the world gives

Plot Twist 3: Exodus

The story of the Exodus appears in Scripture as a real event, and it may well be rooted in actual history. However, its theological meaning is even more important. The Exodus stands as an archetype, a foundational pattern that reveals how God moves in the world.

It shows us that God chooses to identify with people in captivity rather than working through powerful rulers. Liberation, not domination, becomes a core theme of the Bible. Divine power is redefined as standing with the oppressed, not with empires.

The way God acts in this story changed how people thought about what it meant for a god to be powerful. Instead of supporting kings and maintaining the status quo, the God of Israel hears the cries of slaves and acts within history to free them. Justice and liberation become central to His character.

This was revolutionary. In ancient cultures, gods were usually associated with rulers and maintaining social order, not overturning systems to help the powerless.

Throughout Scripture, writers continue to return to this story as the model of how God moves. The themes of freedom, justice, and rescue that flow from it have shaped not only Israel's history but also liberation movements across the world.

When we treat the Exodus as just an old Bible story, we lose its power. This is not dusty history. It is the living heart of Scripture, a primal cry against oppression and a declaration that God sides with the marginalized, liberates the enslaved, and challenges the powerful.

We see the same pattern later as the Israelites flee Pharaoh's tyranny, as the prophets denounce injustice, and as Jesus himself stands with the outcast. The story reminds us that God remains faithful to the poor, the widow, the orphan, and the stranger.

And it is not just about ancient history. It is about us today. We are called to recognize the systems of oppression that still exist, such as poverty, racism, violence, and environmental destruction, and to join God's ongoing work of setting people free.

- [ ] Exodus 3:7-12 - God hears the cries of the Israelites
- [ ] Isaiah 43:1-2 - A promise of God's deliverance
- [ ] Micah 6:4 - Connects the Exodus to ultimate deliverance
- [ ] Luke 4:18-19 - Jesus declares liberation

Plot Twist 4: Diaspora

Diaspora means scattering. It refers to when the Jewish people were forced to leave their homeland and live among foreign nations.

Today, we usually think of Israel as a nation with a land of its own, but for much of history, Israel existed without a secure place to call home. Even before the Israelites took Jerusalem, the land belonged to the Canaanites (Genesis 12:6; Deuteronomy 7:1; Joshua 3:10). The Bible records a long history of the land passing through many rulers: Canaanite, Israelite, Assyrian, Babylonian, and Persian. Although the Bible does not record it directly, history tells us that after Persia, the region came under Macedonian control through Alexander the Great and then under the Seleucid dynasty. Finally, the Romans conquered the land, setting the stage for the world Jesus was born into. After the biblical period, other powers like the Byzantines, Crusaders, Ottomans, British, and Jordanians also ruled the land.

The Diaspora marked a major shift in the Jewish faith. It moved from being centered around a specific land and a single Temple to a way of life that could survive and thrive anywhere.

The first major scattering happened with the Assyrian conquest in 722 BCE, when the northern kingdom of Israel was captured and its people were dispersed. Later, the Babylonian exile in 586 BCE saw Jerusalem fall and the First Temple destroyed. Many Jews were forced to live in Babylon until Cyrus the Great allowed them to return about fifty years later.

The most dramatic moment came during the Roman period, especially after the destruction of the Second Temple in 70 CE. This was around the same time that much of the New Testament was being written and the early Christian church was taking shape.

For Jews, losing the Temple required a complete transformation of their religious life. Faith shifted from Temple sacrifices to prayer, study, and gathering in synagogues. This new way of life led to the development of rabbinic Judaism and the writing of the *Talmud*, which was a text that preserved Jewish law and teachings without depending on a central Temple.

For early Christians, the Diaspora created an opportunity. Jewish communities spread throughout the Mediterranean became starting points for Christian missionaries like Paul. These communities were already familiar with the Scriptures and the idea of God's promises, making them a natural place to begin sharing the story of Jesus.

The destruction of the Temple also helped shape early Christian theology. Christians began to see God's presence not tied to a building but to Jesus himself, and later to the community of believers, the Church.

The Diaspora reminds us that belonging to God is not about having a homeland. It is about carrying faith wherever life takes us. It is about resilience, community, and holding on to hope even in exile. It reminds us that our true home is not a piece of land but the Beloved Community God is forming among His people.

- [ ] 2 Kings 17:6-23 - The Assyrian exile of Israel
- [ ] 2 Kings 24-25 - The Babylonian exile of Judah
- [ ] Ezekiel 11:14-25 - God will gather the scattered
- [ ] Acts 2:1-11 - The Church's birth at Pentecost
- [ ] James 1:1 - James addresses to the scattered believers

Plot Twist 5: Unexpected Messiah

With such turmoil, it is no surprise that Israel longed for a Messiah, someone anointed by God to rescue them. A close reading of the Old Testament shows they expected a king like David, a mighty ruler who would defeat their enemies and restore Israel's power and independence. By the time of Jesus, many hoped this Messiah would overthrow Rome and bring political freedom.

But the Gospels reveal a shocking twist. Instead of sending a conquering king, God sent a suffering servant. Jesus fulfilled the promises made to Abraham and David, but not in the way anyone expected. Rather than building a political kingdom through force, Jesus redefined God's kingdom around humility, service, and self-giving love.

This unexpected Messiah was not a rejection of Israel's hopes but their radical fulfillment. The people wanted a ruler who would bring justice by using power and might. Instead, Jesus came as a humble teacher and healer, fulfilling Isaiah's prophecy of the Suffering Servant who bears the pain of others (Isaiah 53).

His battle was against sin, death, and the spiritual powers that enslave the world (Colossians 2:15). Rather than calling down armies of angels to destroy His enemies, Jesus willingly went to the cross. He took upon Himself the suffering of the world and established God's kingdom through sacrifice and love.

This redefinition of the Messiah created a crisis, not only for first-century Jews but for us today. We still long for leaders who will fight for our causes, win our battles, and use power on our behalf. We are tempted to claim that God endorses our wars, our politics, or our pursuit of control.

Sometimes, Christians even excuse brutal and unfaithful leaders by comparing them to Cyrus, the Persian king God used in the Old Testament, even though Cyrus did not know or worship Him (Isaiah 45:1). But this kind of reasoning misuses Scripture.

Jesus redefines what real power looks like. He kneels to wash the feet of His followers. He welcomes the outcasts. He heals the broken. His kingdom does not operate by the world's standards, but it has true authority. In Jesus, true strength is found not in domination but in self-giving love, humility, and the cross-shaped victory of God's justice.

- [ ] Psalm 2:1-9 - The expectation of enemies shattered
- [ ] Isaiah 9:6-7 - Expecting a military defeat
- [ ] John 13:12-17 - Jesus washing feet
- [ ] Philippians 2:5-11 - Jesus' humility and exaltation

Plot Twist 6: The Gentile Inclusion

One of the most surprising developments in the biblical story is that non-Jews, called Gentiles, are fully included among God's people. This was a massive shift in understanding God's plan for humanity. Many in Israel expected that God's covenant blessings were meant primarily, or even exclusively, for the descendants of Abraham through bloodline and cultural tradition. Early believers struggled with the idea that Gentiles could be welcomed without first adopting Jewish customs like circumcision, dietary laws, and Sabbath observance.

But the message of Jesus, and later the mission of the early Church, made it clear. God's plan had always been bigger than one nation. The promise made to Abraham included a vision that "all nations on earth will be blessed" through him (Genesis 12:3).

The full inclusion of Gentiles shattered long-standing assumptions about election, identity, and religious boundaries. It showed that God's love and salvation were meant for all people, not just one ethnic or cultural group.

This caused major conflicts in the early Church, as recorded in places like Acts 15 during the Jerusalem Council, where leaders debated whether Gentile converts needed to follow the Jewish law. Ultimately, the decision was that faith in Jesus, not cultural conformity, was what made someone part of God's family.

The inclusion of Gentiles is a radical act of grace. It tears down walls of exclusion and reminds us that God's love knows no boundaries. It challenges us even today to break down the divisions that separate people and to build communities that reflect the wideness of God's welcome.

The story of Gentile inclusion invites us into a vision of the Church as a place where all are welcome, not because they fit a certain mold, but because God's grace is for everyone.

- Acts 10:34-48 - Peter's vision and the inclusion of Cornelius
- Romans 11:17-24 - Gentiles grafted into the covenant
- Galatians 3:28-29 - All are one in Christ Jesus
- Ephesians 2:14-16 - Creating a new humanity

Plot Twist 7: The Already and Not Yet Kingdom

As noted, Israel waited for the Messiah to establish a powerful kingdom that would defeat their enemies and set up a new world order. Surprisingly, many Christians today still imagine God's kingdom only as a place we go after death, like heaven somewhere far away. This is strange when we realize how contrary it is to the Bible's actual vision of the kingdom, which is described as both a present reality and a future hope.

The reality presented in the Bible of the kingdom of God is both a present reality and a future hope. When Jesus said, "The kingdom of God is at hand" (Mark 1:15), His followers expected a political and military revolution that would immediately overthrow Roman rule. Instead, Jesus introduced a very different kind of kingdom, one that had already begun to arrive but was not yet fully completed.

The kingdom grows by a different logic. It spreads quietly, like a mustard seed planted in a field, not through armies or political power

(Matthew 13:31-32). It advances through love, compassion, justice, and sacrifice, not domination or conquest.

This creates what theologians call the tension of the "already and not yet." God's reign has started through Jesus' ministry, through the presence of the Holy Spirit, and through the witness of the Church. Yet the full completion of God's kingdom, the day when every tear is wiped away and justice reigns completely, still lies ahead (Revelation 21:1-4).

Rather than a simple march toward a perfect world, we live in a reality where God's kingdom is quietly growing within and alongside broken systems that still exist. Jesus teaches us to live faithfully in this tension, to hold onto the victory that has already begun, while patiently enduring the struggles that remain.

We experience glimpses of God's reign here and now when we love our neighbors, work for justice, offer forgiveness, and live with hope. Yet we still long for the day when the kingdom is fully realized, when all creation is restored and God's will is done on earth as it is in heaven. This tension shapes how we live today, because we are called to be people of hope, working for God's purposes even in the face of hardship, trusting that what has already begun will one day be completed in full.

- [ ] Matthew 4:17 - Jesus announces the kingdom at hand
- [ ] Mark 1:14-15 - The kingdom of God is at hand;
- [ ] Luke 17:20-21 - The kingdom is among you
- [ ] Romans 8:18-25 - Hope for the full realization of redemption

Plot Twist 8: Subversive Selection

God's choices throughout the Bible continually overturn human expectations. Again and again, He works through those whom society overlooks or rejects.

God often chooses the younger over the older, as seen with Jacob being chosen over Esau and David being chosen over his older brothers. He elevates women as key agents in a world that often marginalized them, highlighting figures like Sarah, Rebekah, Rachel, Miriam, Ruth, and Mary. He calls outsiders and foreigners, such as Ruth the Moabite and Rahab from Jericho. He even works through deeply flawed leaders like Moses the murderer, David the adulterer (and worse), and Peter the denier.

But this is not just about flipping human hierarchies upside down. It is something deeper. God is not simply disrupting the world's power structures. He is redefining what true community looks like. Belonging to God's family is no longer based on status, strength, or social standing. It is based on God's calling and grace.

This pattern reaches its high point in Jesus Himself, the crucified Messiah from Galilee. He does not come from a place of power and prestige. He comes from the margins. He gathers to Himself the people the world casts aside, including fishermen, tax collectors, women, sinners, and outcasts.

The story does not end there. The Church is born from this same radical movement. Fishermen become apostles. Enemies become brothers. People who would have never shared a table are now family in Christ.

God is not just working through unexpected people. He is forming a new kind of belonging where the old divisions no longer hold. In

Christ, the barriers that once divided people, whether by ethnicity, status, gender, or past mistakes, are broken down. The Church becomes a new community, defined not by human achievement but by God's mercy and love.

- [ ] Genesis 25:23 - Jacob chosen over Esau
- [ ] Judges 4:4-5 - The leadership of Deborah
- [ ] Ruth 1:16-17 - Ruth, an outsider, becomes part of God's story
- [ ] 1 Samuel 16:7-13 – David, the youngest, chosen as king
- [ ] John 20:17-18 - Mary Magdalene, the first Christian preacher
- [ ] Matthew 4:18-22 - Fishermen called as the first apostles
- [ ] Acts 9:1-19 - Saul becomes an apostle

Theology of the Narrative
The Core Themes That Shape the Biblical Story

Christian theology is kind of like a living language. It has grown and changed over time as people have wrestled with Scripture, culture, and big ideas about life and faith. Different communities, in different places and times, have developed their own ways of talking about God based on their experiences and questions.

One important voice in this story is Anselm, a medieval theologian. He believed that faith leads us to want to understand more about God. His approach is often summed up as "faith seeking understanding." At the core, it means that loving and trusting God naturally makes us curious about who God is. Anselm also believed that wisdom from the wider world, like philosophy and reason, could help us, not hurt us, in learning about God.

As we explore the Bible's big themes, keep in mind that theology is not something frozen in time. It is more like ocean waves, always moving and reshaping as people across generations respond to God's call. Theology grows, changes, and stretches as we reach toward a deeper understanding of God. It is always bigger than human words can fully capture.

My role here is not to give you all the answers or close the conversation. It is to step into the journey with you. I will outline some important ideas from the Bible and explain what they mean. But think of this as a starting point, a way to launch into your own learning, questions, and discoveries.

The Bible's Theology

Atonement 2 Corinthians 5:21	Atonement signifies reconciliation with God. In the Old Testament, Yom Kippur, the Day of Atonement, was a time for Israel to confess sins and seek renewal. Jesus fulfills this reconciliation through His life, death, and resurrection, breaking the power of sin and death to bring new creation. His atonement offers not just forgiveness, but freedom, inviting us into a transformed way of life.
Blessing Numbers 6:24-26	Blessing is the gracious outpouring of God's favor and a tangible assurance of divine peace and protection.

Calling Romans 8:30	Calling is the divine initiative that draws individuals into a life shaped by God's purposes, a holy invitation to participate in the unfolding story of redemption.
Communion John 15:5	Communion is more than bread and wine. It is our participation in the life of God. In the Eucharist, we are drawn into the love shared eternally between the Father, Son, and Spirit. It is not merely a meal of remembrance or an act of personal devotion. It is where we are reshaped as the body of Christ, and thus communion reminds us that we are made for connection.
Cross 1 Corinthians 1:18	The cross, Rome's brutal instrument of execution, becomes God's ultimate act of embrace. Divine love enters the depths of human sin and death not to destroy but to transform. In this place of state-sanctioned humiliation and suffering, Christ meets the world's violence with forgiveness, turning an instrument of terror into a call to costly discipleship. This way of love does not mirror the powers of domination but overcomes them.
Discipleship Mark 8:34	Discipleship is the journey of learning and following as a student of the rabbi (teacher) Jesus. It is a countercultural path embodying His radical call to justice, peace, and the renewal of creation. To follow Jesus is to unlearn the world's lies and live as if the gospel is true.
Divine Revelation Hebrews 1:1-2	God reveals Himself through prophets, creation, and most fully in Jesus, who shows us His heart of compassion and forgiveness. This revelation continues in prayer and transformed lives.
Election Deuteronomy 7:6	Israel is considered God's chosen people, or the elect, through whom God demonstrates His purposes and blessings. This concept is central to understanding God's covenantal relationship and His plan to extend grace to all nations.

Faith Galatians 2:20	Faith is more than what we believe. It is who we trust and how we live. People often place faith in country, money, power, or status, but God invites us to trust in Him only. Thus, faith is not just believing in Jesus. It is walking in His way with courage, kindness, and a heart open to His transforming love.
Glory Exodus 40:34	Glory is the weight and beauty of God showing up so real you can't ignore it, the kind of presence that leaves you humbled, wide-eyed, and changed.
Grace Ephesians 2:8-9	Grace is God's unearned love, transforming our brokenness into beauty and calling us to extend the same mercy to others.
Heaven Luke 17:21	Heaven is not just a future destination but the reality of God's presence with us.
Holy Spirit Acts 2:17-18	The Holy Spirit enlivens creation, reshaping communities into spaces of belonging and binding us to God's work of renewal.
Hope Revelation 21:4	Hope is God's assurance that despair is not the end. Scripture points to a future of healing, justice, and peace, urging us to live in this promise.
Imputation Romans 4:24	Imputation means God gives you what you could never earn. Christ's goodness becomes yours. You are clothed in a holiness you didn't make, buy, or deserve, but that covers you anyway.
Incarnation John 1:14	The term Incarnation originates from the Latin word that means "to become flesh." In the Incarnation, the Word of God took on human nature, uniting divine and human realities. This union allows humanity to be drawn into the divine life, signifying God's tangible and intimate presence in the world.

Intercession Romans 8:26	Intercession is when Jesus and the Spirit step in for us, praying and pleading, even groaning when we cannot find the words, standing in the gap between our weakness and God's strength.
Justice Amos 5:24	Justice is love in action, flowing from God's heart to lift the oppressed and challenge injustice. It calls us to build a world where all creation flourishes.
Justification Romans 3:23-24	You can think of justification as "just if I'd" never sinned. While Paul describes it as Jesus' death covering our sins, it's more than a legal pardon; it's an invitation to a changed life in Christ.
Love 1 Corinthians 13	Love is the radical, inclusive force of God that calls us to embrace others as they are, breaking down walls of division and fear.
Praise Psalm 150:6	Praise is our response to God's goodness, expressed not just in worship but in everyday acts of love and hope.
Providence Romans 8:28	Providence simply means God provides, and thus illustrates God's continuous involvement with creation, guiding and caring for all things.
Redemption Ephesians 1:7	Redemption is God's liberating act through Christ, rescuing humanity from sin's bondage and restoring belonging, echoing ancient images of ransom and freedom.
Repentance Acts 3:19	Repentance is the Spirit-led turning from sin toward the living God, a reorientation of heart and life that opens the way for forgiveness and renewal.
Resurrection and New Life 2 Corinthians 5:17	Resurrection proclaims that death and despair do not have the final word. It invites us to live transformed lives in the light of God's victory.
Righteousness Matthew 6:33	Righteousness is living in harmony with God, others, and the world by aligning our lives with His love and justice

Salvation Titus 3:5	Salvation is God's merciful rescue of humanity from sin and death, a divine gift of new life accomplished not by human effort, but by the cleansing and renewal of the Spirit.
Sanctification 1 Thess. 4:3	Sanctification is the ongoing work of the Spirit shaping believers into Christ's likeness, a transformative journey of holiness that unfolds within the life of the Christian community.
Sin and Forgiveness Romans 6:23	Sin is not just personal failure. It is a brokenness that affects our relationship with God, one another, and the world. Yet through Jesus, God does more than mend what is broken. He steps into our struggles, offering forgiveness that is not only a fresh start but an invitation to a new way of living.
Trinity Matthew 28:19	Trinity is a dynamic and relational expression of God's nature, emphasizing that the Father, Son, and Holy Spirit reveal God's being as communion, inviting believers into a life of shared love and participation in God's redemptive work

chapter 6

What Matters Most?

Imagine standing at a turning point, a place where big ideas about history, belief, and meaning come together. The choices made in moments like this affect what happens next and shape how people live, think, and believe for generations. That is the kind of moment we explored earlier, and now we return to it with fresh eyes.

Picture the earliest Christian leaders facing a challenge that would shape the future of faith. In front of them was a wide collection of scrolls, letters, and stories. Some were familiar, others unfamiliar, and many deeply moving. Each one spoke in a different voice and offered a unique perspective on who Jesus was and what it meant to follow him.

But their task was not simply to sort through them and decide what to keep. It was much more than that. They had to ask deep, guiding questions. What speaks to the heart of what we believe? What points us toward something real and lasting? This was not about making quick or random choices. Without a thoughtful and grounded approach, their decisions would have lacked meaning.

Asking the Right Questions

We may not know every question the early church leaders asked, but we can get a good sense of what guided them. They likely asked things like: Does this writing reflect what Jesus taught? Does it stay true to the message shared by the apostles? Has this already been embraced by the broader community of believers?

Their answers to questions like these shaped the Bible as we know it today. But those questions did not fade away once the Bible was finalized. Hundreds of years later, during the Protestant Reformation, Martin Luther found himself asking them again. He held the Bible in high regard, but he also understood that not every part carried the same weight. He pointed to books like the Gospel of John, the letters of Paul (especially Romans) and 1 Peter as essential to understanding the Christian message. On the other hand, he gave less attention to writings like Leviticus or even the book of James.

Why? Because Luther saw something important. He recognized that Jesus wasn't simply reinforcing the details of ancient religious law. Jesus was bringing that law to completion, drawing people into its heart and purpose. This doesn't minimize the Old Testament. It brings it into focus. Jesus steps fully into the tradition, embodying it, interpreting it, and carrying it forward. He lives within it and brings out its deepest intent.

Luther understood what the Gospels make clear when we pay attention: Jesus engages the law not to repeat it word for word, but to show what it was always pointing toward. He moves through the Torah with a sense of purpose that deepens its meaning. Not by adding more rules, but by uncovering the spirit behind them.

Jesus Asked Tough Questions Too

This tension runs deep in the Gospels. It's there in the details of Jesus's life and the choices he made. Over and over, he brought people back to what really matters. When he healed on the Sabbath, he was giving someone their life back, showing that the Sabbath was meant to help people, not hold them down. When his disciples picked grain because they were hungry, he didn't shame them. He saw their need and reminded everyone that tradition should lift people up, not weigh them down. When he spoke to the religious leaders, he didn't hold back. He called out what was off track and pointed everyone back to the heart of the law.

For Jesus, the Torah wasn't a list of restrictions. It was a living guide, shaping a community to look more like God's character. It was about covenant, about learning justice, mercy, and real relationship. Jesus stepped right into that story, honoring its depth and showing what it was really about.

Jesus didn't just talk about the law. He didn't just talk about religion or faith. It's fascinating to encounter so many Christians who talk a good faith but don't seem to live it, which is totally contrary to the way Jesus lived. Listen, I'm guilty of this too. Instead, Jesus brought the Jewish scriptures to life by loving people, by living out its vision, always pointing back to what matters most: the heart of God. And that heart is full of compassion, faithfulness, and justice.

What Questions Should We Ask

I've heard a metaphor that really helps me make sense of the Bible. Imagine the Bible as a dartboard. Every time someone quotes a verse, it's like they're tossing a dart at the board. Sure, if it's from the Bible, it lands somewhere. But the real thing to pay attention to isn't just whether it's on the board, it's where it lands.

Some verses hit right at the center, and those are the ones that get to the heart of what Christianity is all about. Take John 3:16, for example: "God so loved the world that he gave his only Son." That's the bullseye. It sums up the core of the faith. But then you have verses like the one where Paul asks someone to bring him his coat and some books (2 Timothy 4:13). That's still in the Bible, but it's not shaping anyone's life in the same way. Both are there, but they don't matter equally.

This comes up a lot. Sometimes people will throw a verse at you and act like that settles everything because it's "in the Bible." But not all verses carry the same weight. And sometimes, people even quote things that aren't in the Bible at all, like "God helps those who help themselves." That one doesn't even make it onto the dartboard.

So, here's how I think about it: the closer a verse is to the center (the bullseye) the more it tells us about who Jesus is and what he cared about. The stuff at the edges is still part of the story, but it's not the main point. It all has to be understood in light of what's at the center.

That's how I try to read Scripture. I start with Jesus at the center and let that shape how I see everything else. Some verses just hit closer to home, and others are more on the edges. When I'm not sure where something lands, I ask myself a few questions to help figure it out. Here's the questions I try to ask:

- **Does this line up with the good news of Jesus?** If Jesus shows us what God is really like, then anything that clashes with how he lived and loved needs a second look.

- **Does this shake up what I already think?** The Bible isn't here just to make us comfortable. It's supposed to challenge us, get under our skin, and even mess with our assumptions.

- **Does it catch me off guard with grace?** God keeps picking the outsiders, breaking the rules, and flipping the script. If something in Scripture surprises you with mercy, you're probably near the bullseye.

- **Does it put love at the center?** When a teaching is all about selfless love, compassion, and caring for others, it's echoing what Jesus was all about.

- **Does it lean toward mercy instead of judgment?** Jesus often pushed back against harsh, rule-heavy readings of Scripture that forgot about kindness.

- **Does it lead us into real worship?** For centuries, Christians have gathered to worship and be changed by these teachings. If something doesn't move us toward deeper awe, real praise, or a life shaped by Christ's love, it's worth questioning.

These six guiding questions are the criteria I used to select the 52 chapters that matter most, as well as the additional chapters that are also important. The same criteria can be applied to individual verses. For example, you could use the framework I developed or create your own, assigning a point value to each verse. Those with the highest scores would be at the center of your dartboard, ensuring that texts reflecting Jesus' core message of selfless love-especially for the outcast and vulnerable-remain central.

This approach does not diminish the value of scripture or attempt to create a new biblical canon. Rather, it helps us discern what matters most. Not all scripture is equally relevant to the life of faith, nor should every verse be given the same weight in shaping our understanding of God. Fundamentalists, like those who challenged Jesus and those who challenge us today, often love to hurl verses at people as weapons, citing passages that prop up exclusion, injustice, and rigid legalism while ignoring the sweeping biblical narrative of God's relentless grace.

The Bible is massive, so it's understandable that biblical and Christlike don't always mean the same thing. The Pharisees had plenty of scripture on their side when they condemned Jesus, yet they entirely missed the heart of God.

When scripture is used to harm rather than heal, to bind rather than liberate, or to enforce human agendas rather than reveal God's mercy, we must ask whether we are reading the Bible in the light of Christ or for our own gain. Jesus himself reinterpreted scripture, prioritizing love over law and mercy over sacrifice. If our reading of the Bible does not lead us deeper into the self-giving love of Jesus, then we may need to read it again.

The 52 Chapters that Matter the Most

Genesis 1 - The Creation of the World

Genesis 1 opens with one of the most powerful lines in all of scripture: "When God began to create the heavens and the earth." This ancient story pulls us right into the drama of creation-step by step, God turns emptiness and darkness into something alive, ordered, and beautiful. Every act of creation is intentional, and after each one, God steps back and sees it's "good." It's a reminder that everything in this world has value and purpose, that nothing is just random or worthless.

What's striking about Genesis is the sense of calm and order. Unlike other ancient stories about the world's beginnings, which are often full of violence and chaos, Genesis just quietly insists that one God made it all, on purpose, with care. The steady rhythm of the seven days gives the story a kind of peace, almost like a heartbeat, and shows us creation as an outpouring of God's creativity and love.

The high point comes when God makes people. "In the image of God," it says. That's huge. It means every person carries something of God's own character, every single one of us has dignity and worth. We're made to reflect God, to care for the world, and to look out for each other. This truth pushes back against any idea that some people matter more than others. Genesis is clear: we all count.

So, Genesis 1 tells us more than how everything started. It reveals who God is: powerful, intentional, and good. And it shows us who we are: people with a special place in the world, loved by God, and called to live with purpose.

Exodus 3 - God's Call to Moses

Exodus 3 is the story of Moses and the burning bush, a moment that changed everything for him. Moses is just out there, working as a shepherd, when he spots a bush that's on fire but not burning up. Well, that's different. Curious, Moses goes to check it out, and suddenly, God speaks. God tells Moses He's seen the suffering of His people and wants Moses to lead them out of slavery in Egypt.

Moses doesn't feel up to it. In essence he asks, "Who am I to do this?" God basically responds, "I'll be with you." That's it. God doesn't give Moses a pep talk about his strengths or skills. He just promises His presence.

Then God tells Moses His name: "I Am Who I Am." It's mysterious, but it means God is always present, always steady. The burning bush that isn't consumed is a sign of God's power to sustain and protect.

Moses is scared and full of doubts. He's not a great speaker. He's not confident. He has a past. But God chooses him anyway. That's the point. God doesn't need us to be perfect. He just wants us to be willing. Moses' journey from a hesitant, insecure shepherd to a leader shows what can happen when we say yes to God, even when we feel unqualified. It's a reminder that God's presence and calling can change our lives, no matter how ordinary or unsure we feel.

Exodus 20 - The Ten Commandments

The Ten Commandments, given in Exodus 20, are more than a list of rules-they're a framework for living a life that reflects God's character. These aren't just arbitrary restrictions; they're a gift, meant to help people live well with God and with each other.

The first four are about our relationship with God: don't chase after other gods, don't make idols, respect God's name, and keep the Sabbath. These are still relevant. We're always tempted to put other things first or forget to rest and honor what matters. The Sabbath command, in particular, is radical-it says everyone deserves rest and dignity, no matter their status.

The other six are about how we treat people: honor your parents, don't murder, don't cheat, don't steal, don't lie, don't covet. These aren't about controlling people-they're about creating a community where everyone can thrive.

Obedience isn't about fear or coercion. It's about being drawn into a life of love. Too often, people use the commandments to judge or exclude others, but that's not the point. They're meant to bring people together, to foster dignity and reconciliation.

For the Israelites, the commandments were a guide to living as free people-people who show God's justice and mercy. Even now, they remind us that real freedom comes with responsibility, and they help us figure out where our deepest loyalties lie.

Deuteronomy 6 - The Shema

Just as central to Jewish faith as the Ten Commandments is the *shema*, from Deuteronomy 6. The word *shema* means "hear," and it's not just the first word of Deuteronomy 6:4, it's the heartbeat of Jewish belief: "Hear, O Israel: The Lord our God, the Lord is one. Love the Lord your God with all your heart, with all your soul, and with all your strength." Observant Jews recite it daily; it's the first thing a child learns and the last words many hope to say before death. It's woven into every part of life.

The *shema* isn't just about believing in God's oneness, it's about living it out. Jewish tradition takes this seriously: teach it to your kids, talk about it at home and on the road, from morning to night. It's a call to let faith shape everything.

Jesus later said the *shema* was the greatest commandment, and he added, "Love your neighbor as yourself." After all, love for God and love for people is the core of both Jewish and Christian faith. The *shema* calls us not just to know God is one, but to live in a way that shows it, every day.

2 Samuel 7 - David's Prayer

In 2 Samuel 7, David wants to do something big for God. He's settled in as king, and it bothers him that God's Ark is still in a tent while he lives in a nice house. He tells the prophet Nathan he wants to build a permanent temple. But that night, God sends Nathan back with a different message: David isn't the one to build God a house. Instead, God says He's going to build David a "house," and this house won't be a physical building, but a family line, a dynasty that will last forever.

God's promise goes way beyond David's own life or even his son Solomon, who would eventually build the Temple. God says David's throne will be established forever, and that promise points forward to something much bigger-the arrival of the Messiah, Jesus, who comes from David's line and whose kingdom never ends. This isn't about David earning anything; it's about God's faithfulness and grace, choosing David and sticking with him even when things get messy.

David's reaction is honest and humble. He's floored that God would pick him, a former shepherd, for something so huge. He prays, not with pride, but with gratitude and awe, admitting he doesn't deserve it and asking God to keep His promise, not for David's sake, but for God's own name and for the people.

1 Kings 8 - Solomon Dedicates the Temple

This chapter is a turning point. It shows that sometimes our dreams for God aren't what He actually wants from us. David wanted to build a temple, but God had a bigger plan, one that would outlast David and change everything. The story is a reminder to hold our own plans loosely and trust that God's vision is bigger and better, even if it doesn't look like what we expect.

In 1 Kings 8, Solomon finally finishes the Temple his father David dreamed about, and it's a huge deal for Israel. The Ark is brought in, the cloud of God's presence fills the place, and everyone knows something holy is happening. Solomon stands before the people and prays. He knows God can't be contained in a building, no matter how grand. The temple is just a place to focus their prayers, a symbol that God is with them, but not limited to four walls.

Solomon's prayer is honest and wide-ranging. He asks God to hear people's prayers when they're in war, drought, disaster, or even when they mess up and need forgiveness. He doesn't just pray for Israelites, but for anyone who comes seeking God, showing that God's heart is bigger than just one nation. Through all of it, Solomon keeps coming back to God's faithfulness and the hope that, no matter what, God will keep listening and forgiving when people turn back to Him.

Psalm 22 - A Plea for Deliverance

Psalm 22 opens with a gut-wrenching cry: "My God, my God, why have you forsaken me?" The writer feels abandoned and crushed, surrounded by enemies, mocked, and alone. But even in the middle of all that pain, he doesn't let go of God completely. The psalm is raw and honest, holding nothing back.

The details of pierced hands and feet and divided clothes are eerily similar to what happens to Jesus on the cross, and Christians see this as prophetic. But for the original audience, it was a song for when life was falling apart, a way to bring their pain to God. As the psalm goes on, something shifts. The writer starts to remember God's faithfulness and ends up praising Him, even before things get better. It's a reminder that God can handle our honesty, and that hope can break through even in the darkest moments.

Psalm 23 - The Lord Is My Shepherd

Often read at funerals and memorial services, Psalm 23 is a favorite passage and an anchor of peace and promise in the midst of sorrow. It is more than poetic comfort; it is a lifeline. "The Lord is my shepherd; I lack nothing." These opening words breathe calm into chaos.

The psalmist invites us into a vision of God as a faithful shepherd, one who guides, provides, and protects. There are green pastures, still waters, and the gift of real rest. Even in the darkest valley, the "valley of the shadow of death," fear does not triumph because God is present.

Then the imagery shifts from fields to a feast. God prepares a table, even in the presence of enemies, and anoints with oil, a sign of sacred care. The cup overflows. It's a promise that grace will not run out.

Psalm 23 closes with certainty, not just hope: "Surely goodness and mercy shall follow me all the days of my life, and I shall dwell in the house of the Lord forever." It's a psalm of presence, of peace, and of promise, declaring that God's love is relentless and our home with God is eternal.

Psalm 51 - A Prayer for Forgiveness

Not all the psalms are attributed to David, but Psalm 51 is. It stands as his heartfelt plea for mercy following his adultery with Bathsheba and his orchestration of Uriah's death in battle. This dark chapter in David's life, recorded in 2 Samuel 11–12, prompted one of Scripture's most moving prayers of confession and repentance after the prophet Nathan confronted him with his sin.

David openly acknowledges his sin, asking for cleansing and transformation: "Create in me a clean heart, O God, and renew a right spirit within me." His prayer reflects repentance as more than seeking pardon; it is a desire for complete renewal.

David also recognizes the communal consequences of sin. His restoration is both personal and meant to restore relationships and inspire others. He promises to teach others of God's mercy, turning his failure into a testimony of grace.

Psalm 51 reminds readers that no sin is beyond God's forgiveness. It highlights the power of genuine repentance and offers hope that God's mercy can transform even the most broken hearts.

This psalm is traditionally read on Ash Wednesday, the beginning of the Lenten season in many Christian traditions. Its themes of confession, repentance, and spiritual renewal align perfectly with Lent's focus on self-examination and preparation for Easter. The psalm's plea for cleansing and restoration resonates with Ash Wednesday's emphasis on mortality and the need for reconciliation with God, making it a powerful liturgical text that guides believers into a season of penitence and spiritual discipline.

Isaiah 6 - Isaiah's Call and Commission

Isaiah 6 tells about a vision that turned Isaiah's world upside down. He sees God on a throne, surrounded by angels calling out, "Holy, holy, holy is the Lord Almighty; the whole earth is full of his glory." The scene is overwhelming.

Seeing this, Isaiah is terrified and says, "Woe to me! I am ruined! For I am a man of unclean lips." He knows he doesn't belong in this moment. But then something unexpected happens: an angel touches his lips with a burning coal, cleansing him. When God asks, "Whom shall I send?" Isaiah finds himself saying, "Here am I. Send me!" It must have been confusing. One moment he's convinced he's going to die, the next he's volunteering for whatever God has in mind.

But God's assignment isn't easy. Isaiah will deliver a message of judgment to people who won't want to hear it. Isaiah 6 shows us what happens when we truly encounter God's holiness. It strips away our pretenses, cleanses us, and calls us to something bigger than ourselves. It helps us trust God's plans, even when we can't see where they're leading.

Isaiah 40 - Comfort for God's People

Isaiah 40 opens with a liturgical summons: "Comfort, comfort my people," says your God. This double imperative carries covenantal weight. It is a call to speak tenderly to Jerusalem, signaling that exile is ending and God's faithfulness still holds. For a people whose temple lies in ruins and whose story feels broken, this is not sentiment, it is theological reorientation.

The chapter shifts Isaiah's tone from judgment to restoration, from dislocation to return. Its imagery reshapes the landscape: valleys lifted, mountains leveled, a highway prepared for God's glory to be revealed. Renewal comes not through denial of suffering, but through God's decisive action to bring His people home. Verses like "they shall mount up with wings like eagles" speak of restored capacity, strength to move forward, to endure, to hope again.

Human frailty appears in the line "all people are like grass," but it is held beside the enduring power of God's word: "the word of our God will stand forever." Isaiah presents God as both Creator and Sustainer, the one who stretches out the heavens and calls the stars by name. This same God strengthens the weary and renews the powerless. Divine majesty and personal care are not opposites; they belong together. Isaiah 40 anchors hope in the character of a God who is both mighty enough to deliver and near enough to heal.

Isaiah 53 - The Suffering Servant

Isaiah 53 introduces the suffering servant, who endures rejection, pain, and injustice to bring healing and redemption. He is described as "despised and rejected," carrying the weight of humanity's sin and suffering. His wounds become the means of restoration: "By His stripes we are healed."

This chapter reveals that suffering can be redemptive. The servant's sacrifice brings peace and salvation, a message Christians see fulfilled in Jesus. Jesus embodies the suffering servant through His crucifixion, demonstrating God's victory through humility and self-giving love.

Isaiah 53 redefines power and justice, showing that God's grace often works through what the world views as weakness. For readers today, this passage offers hope that even amid pain, God is at work, bringing healing and restoration. It is a profound reminder of the depth of God's love and willingness to bear suffering to redeem humanity.

Jeremiah 18 - The Potter's House

In the book of Jeremiah, there's an incredible scene where God tells the prophet to go watch a potter at work. Jeremiah sees the potter shaping a lump of clay on the wheel. But when the clay doesn't form the way he wants, the potter presses it down and starts over. Still using the same clay. Still with purpose.

That's how God works with us, Just like clay in a potter's hands. This isn't about control in a cold or distant way. It's about care. It's about the patience of a Creator who doesn't give up on what he's shaping. If a life gets off course, he doesn't toss it aside. He reshapes it. This story says something real about God. He's powerful, yes, but also personal. He pays attention. He responds. When we're willing to be reshaped, he gets to work again. And even when we've made a mess of things, he can still form something meaningful from the same raw material.

It's hopeful, but also honest. We're not here to impress God with how put-together we are. What he wants is humility. Openness. A heart that says, "I'm willing to be changed." When we trust him with that, he turns our broken places into something beautiful.

Jeremiah 31 - The New Covenant

Jeremiah goes on to speak of something even deeper. A new kind of connection between God and his people. He describes it like this: instead of laws written on stone tablets, God will write his ways directly on people's hearts.

This is about relationship, not just religion. The people had failed over and over again. They had tried and failed to live up to the rules. But God didn't give up on them. He made a new promise. A new covenant. One that wasn't based on perfection but on grace. Not about earning but about knowing him.

This promise wasn't just about ancient Israel returning home. Christians see it as something bigger. Something fulfilled in Jesus. He makes the connection personal. Through his life, death, and resurrection, the barrier between us and God comes down. And the kind of change God wants to bring doesn't start with guilt or pressure. It starts with love. From the inside out.

Ezekiel 37 - The Valley of Dry Bones

One of the most haunting and powerful images in the Bible is a vision Ezekiel had. A valley full of bones. Dry. Lifeless. Scattered. It was a picture of total despair. A people who had lost everything and felt forgotten.

God asks Ezekiel, "Can these bones live?" And then, piece by piece, the bones come together. Muscles. Skin. Flesh. But they're still not alive. Not until breath enters them. That breath represents God's Spirit.

The point is clear. Real life, real restoration, takes more than just fixing the outside. It's not just about structure or appearance. It's about God breathing something new into us.

This wasn't just a metaphor. For Israel, it meant hope in exile. But for us, it speaks even louder. It points to Jesus. The one who overcame death itself and brings life where it looks like nothing is possible anymore.

If you've ever felt like the light went out, like the bones in your soul are dry, this is for you. God hasn't given up. And he knows how to bring life back to places that feel long gone.

Micah 6 - Requirements of the Lord

Micah 6 addresses what God truly desires from His people. It rejects the notion that elaborate sacrifices can substitute for a life of integrity and devotion. Instead, it presents a profound and simple call: "To act justly, to love mercy, and to walk humbly with your God."

Acting justly means standing for what is right and treating others fairly. Loving mercy calls for kindness and compassion in all relationships. Walking humbly with God requires dependence on Him and a rejection of arrogance or self-reliance.

This passage critiques hollow religious rituals and emphasizes that true worship is expressed in ethical living. It challenges us to align our priorities with God's values and demonstrate faith through justice, mercy, and humility.

Micah 6 reminds us that God desires a transformed heart and a life that reflects His character. True faith is a way of being. God cares less about the show and more about the substance. He wants a life that reflects his heart. And that means how we treat people matters. How we live matters. Our faith isn't proven by what we say. It's shown by what we do when no one's watching.

Matthew 5-7 - The Sermon on the Mount

The word "Beatitude" comes from a Latin word that means "blessed." In the Bible, the Beatitudes are Jesus' way of flipping the script, one bold blessing after another about who's really got it good in God's eyes. In the opening lines of Matthew 5, He delivers one bold blessing after another, revealing who's really got it good in God's eyes.

This moment kicks off what we now call the Sermon on the Mount, Jesus' revolutionary vision of God's kingdom. Picture Him on a hillside, surrounded by a diverse crowd. Farmers. Fishermen. Skeptics. Seekers. He begins not with commands, but with compassion. The Beatitudes celebrate the humble, the merciful, and those who ache for justice.

Each line turns the world's values upside down. Power takes a backseat. Privilege is not the goal. Instead, Jesus lifts up qualities like humility, integrity, and compassion, the very traits most people overlook.

Jesus teaches that obeying God is not just about following rules on the outside but about having a changed heart on the inside. He calls

His followers to love their enemies, forgive freely, and live with integrity. Using metaphors like "salt of the earth" and "light of the world," Jesus challenges His disciples to reflect God's character and bring hope to a broken world.

These blessings and the sermon declare the core principles of God's kingdom: a realm where the marginalized are elevated, strength is found in humility, and love is the highest calling. This teaching invites us to align our lives with God's purposes, living with radical love and unwavering faithfulness.

Matthew 25 - The Least of These

In Matthew 25, Jesus tells a story that puts everything on the table. He describes a future moment when people are separated, not by belief statements, but by how they treated others, specifically, the most overlooked and vulnerable. He says that when we feed the hungry, welcome the stranger, or visit someone in prison, we are doing it for Him. And when we ignore those needs, we are ignoring Him too.

This teaching breaks down the barrier between the spiritual and the everyday. Faith, in Jesus' words, is not a private or abstract thing. It is lived out in how we respond to real people in real need. Jesus places Himself not on a distant throne, but in the lives of those the world tends to forget.

Matthew 25 pushes us to rethink what it means to follow Christ. It is not about religious performance or checking the right boxes. It is about love made visible through mercy, generosity, and compassion. These are not optional extras. They are at the core of what it means to live out the gospel.

Matthew 26 - The Passion Begins

Matthew 26 begins the final stretch of Jesus' life. At the Last Supper, He shares a meal with His closest followers. But this is no ordinary meal. He redefines it, saying the bread and wine now represent His body and blood, given for the forgiveness of sins. This moment ties back to the Jewish celebration of Passover and points forward to a new kind of covenant, a new kind of relationship with God.

Later, in the Garden of Gethsemane, we see Jesus deeply troubled. He prays for another way, but ultimately chooses to stay faithful to what He knows must happen. It is a raw, human moment that reveals both His vulnerability and His commitment. He is not detached from suffering; He steps fully into it.

Even when betrayed, arrested, and abandoned, Jesus does not resist. He willingly chooses the path of sacrifice. Matthew 26 invites readers to reflect on the profound significance of that decision. The cross became a powerful symbol of hope and transformation. By offering Himself, Jesus opened a new way for people to be reconciled with God.

Mark 8 - Peter's Confession

Mark 8 confronts us with the uncomfortable realization that we have no idea what we mean when we say "Messiah." After doing miracles and feeding crowds, Jesus asks His disciples, "Who do you say I am?" Peter says, "You are the Messiah." That sounds like the right answer, but Peter doesn't understand what it means.

Peter thinks the Messiah will be strong, maybe even a fighter who will defeat enemies and take charge. But Jesus says the opposite. He says He will suffer, be rejected, and die. Then He says something even harder. If you want to follow Him, you have to take up your own cross. That means giving up comfort and pride and being willing to trust God, even when it's hard (or nearly impossible).

Jesus is not a leader who relies on force or control. Instead, He chooses to suffer for others and calls His followers to do the same. Mark 8 reveals not only who Jesus is, but also what it means to follow Him. Being His disciple is not about success or popularity; it is about remaining faithful, even when it requires sacrifice.

Mark 15 - The Crucifixion Narrative

Mark 15 reaches its climax in what looks like failure. Jesus is crucified, mocked by soldiers, abandoned by His disciples, and dies in public shame. Yet this is not defeat. For Mark, this is the moment when the story of Israel reaches its surprising fulfillment.

This is not just a tragedy. It is a revelation. Jesus, the true King, refuses to rule through domination. He accepts suffering rather than respond with violence. In this, He fulfills the pattern of the suffering servant from Isaiah. His silence before Pilate, His refusal to save Himself, and His death on a Roman cross reveal the character of a God who works through weakness.

Then the temple curtain tears in two. This moment happens right after Jesus dies on the cross (Mark 15:38). It's just one verse, but it's loaded with meaning. In the Jewish Temple in Jerusalem, there was a thick curtain (sometimes called a veil) that separated the innermost room called "the Holy of Holies" from the rest of the Temple. That room symbolized God's direct presence, and only the high priest could enter it, and only once a year, on the Day of Atonement.

The curtain symbolized a division between God and humanity, a visible sign that God's presence was not fully accessible to people because of sin. Because of Jesus's death, there is now a new way to be in relationship with God. Not through animal sacrifices, not by entering a special building, and not by relying on a priest to act on your behalf. The curtain's tearing shows that Jesus's death has made direct access to God possible. No more barrier. In the letter to the Hebrews, we actually see this same point explained more directly (look up Hebrews 10:19-20).

Mark 15 calls us to see power differently. It redefines kingship in terms of love rather than control. What looks like humiliation is the very moment God's kingdom arrives. The cross does not end the story. It opens the way for us to understand the whole story as one shaped by self-giving love.

Luke 2 - The Christmas Story

Luke 2 tells the beloved story of Jesus' birth in the simplest of settings. As the time drew near for Jesus to be born, a mandatory Roman registration made it necessary for Joseph to return to his ancestral home of Bethlehem. There, Mary gave birth to Jesus, and He was placed in a manger. This act reveals both His deep humility and His full participation in the human experience. In stark contrast to rulers who flaunt their power, Jesus enters the world in vulnerability and embodies God's presence in a way that redefines kingship.

The first to hear the announcement of His birth are the shepherds. They were ordinary and often marginalized people, precisely the kind of individuals God shows favor for throughout Luke's Gospel. The angelic proclamation of good news of great joy for all people signals that Jesus' mission is universal and extends beyond social and political boundaries.

Later, wise men from the East came to worship Jesus and recognized Him as the true King. Their arrival unsettles Herod and the religious establishment in Jerusalem. Like many rulers before and after him, Herod sees Jesus as a threat to his fragile grip on power. His violent response mirrors the world's resistance to God's kingdom, and this theme unfolds throughout Jesus' life and ministry. To escape Herod's wrath, Joseph and his family flee to Egypt. This echoes Israel's own journey in and out of exile. When they return to Palestine, they settle in the remote district of Galilee, where Jesus grows up in the village of Nazareth, far from the power players in Jerusalem. In doing so, He continues the pattern of God's work being revealed among the humble and the overlooked.

Luke 4 - The Mission of the Kingdom

In Luke 4, Jesus begins His public ministry with a powerful declaration of purpose. After enduring forty days of testing in the wilderness, resisting temptations of power and pride, He returns filled with the Spirit. In the synagogue of His hometown in Nazareth, Jesus stands to read from Isaiah, boldly declaring His mission: "to bring good news to the poor, freedom for the oppressed, and healing for the brokenhearted."

This statement sets the tone for His ministry, focusing on justice, compassion, and inclusion. Yet, Jesus' message challenges His audience, who struggle to accept its implications for those outside their community. Their resistance underscores the radical nature of His mission.

Luke 4 is a theological key to understanding the Gospel of Luke as a whole. Jesus' proclamation in Nazareth is a decisive moment that reveals the nature of His mission and the cost of faithfulness to it. The resistance He faces foreshadows the larger rejection that will culminate in the cross, reinforcing that the kingdom of God does not advance through human approval but through the work of the Spirit. To read Luke 4 rightly is to recognize that Jesus' call to justice, compassion, and liberation is not merely a past event but an ongoing reality in which the faithful are summoned to participate.

Luke 10 - The Good Samaritan

Luke 10 includes some of Jesus' most memorable teachings, each revealing a different aspect of kingdom living. First, He sends out 72 disciples to proclaim the kingdom of God, instructing them to travel lightly and trust in God's provision. Their mission reflects a life of dependence and dedication to spreading peace. This sending is significant because it extends Jesus' ministry beyond the twelve apostles, showing that the mission of God's kingdom involves the whole community of faith, not just a select few.

The parable of the Good Samaritan confronts prejudices and redefines what it means to be a neighbor. A man is beaten and left for dead, ignored by a priest and a Levite who represent the religious establishment. A Samaritan, despised by Jews as a religious and ethnic outsider, becomes the unlikely hero, showing compassion and providing care. Through this story, Jesus teaches that a neighbor is anyone in need, regardless of societal or cultural divisions. The parable cuts to the heart of how God's kingdom values mercy over ritual purity and love over religious status.

The chapter concludes with Mary and Martha hosting Jesus. While Martha is preoccupied with preparations, Mary sits at Jesus' feet, choosing spiritual attentiveness over busyness. Jesus affirms Mary's choice, reminding us of the importance of prioritizing time with Him. This scene reveals a tension that every follower of Jesus faces: how to balance active service with contemplative devotion.

Together, these stories emphasize the holistic nature of discipleship. They show us that following Christ involves both going out in mission and sitting at His feet, both crossing cultural boundaries to serve others and creating space for spiritual formation. Luke presents a vision of faith that is both deeply personal and radically communal, rooted in prayer and expressed in love.

Luke 15 - The Lost Sheep, Coin, and Son

Luke 15 shares three parables that reveal God's deep love for the lost: a shepherd searching for one lost sheep, a woman rejoicing over a recovered coin, and a father welcoming home his wayward son. The story of the prodigal son is especially moving, showing a father who runs to embrace his repentant child and celebrates his return, while the older brother struggles with resentment. Together, these parables invite us to embrace God's boundless grace and to rejoice in the restoration of others, challenging us to let go of self-righteousness and share in God's joy over every person who returns home.

These three parables are important because they give a vivid picture of God's boundless mercy, personal care, and unconditional love. They show that no one is beyond God's reach, and that every individual is precious to Him. The joy and celebration in each story reveal that God delights in restoring and forgiving those who are lost, offering hope and welcome to all who turn back to Him

John 1 - The Word Became Flesh

John doesn't waste time with shepherds or mangers. He doesn't open his Gospel with sentimental Christmas stories or family drama. He starts with a big, audacious claim: "In the beginning was the Word."

When John says "Word" (in Greek, *Logos*) he's using a term loaded with meaning for both Jewish and Greek listeners. For ancient Jews, the Word of God wasn't just speech. It was the active, powerful force through which God created the world. Think Genesis: "And God said, 'Let there be light.'" God speaks, and things happen. The Word is God in motion.

For Greek thinkers, *Logos* meant something like the rational structure behind the universe. The logic or reason that holds everything together. The principle that makes sense of all this chaos.

John takes both ideas, Hebrew power and Greek reason, and then upends expectations. "And the Word became flesh." We also learn that the *Logos* is not just with God; He is God. He is face to face in relationship, fully part of the divine life. Through this Word, everything came into being. And through this Word, life and light entered the world, light the darkness cannot overcome.

John moves fast, from cosmic beginnings to human history. Suddenly, John the Baptist appears, a man sent to bear witness to the light (verses 6–8). His role matters. He isn't the light. He just points to it. Then comes a shift in tone (verses 9–13). The Word steps into the world He made, but the world doesn't recognize Him. He comes to His own people, but most turn Him away. And yet, to those who receive Him, who believe in His name, He gives a new identity: children of God. Not born of blood, or human will, but born of God.

And then, the turning point: "The Word became flesh and lived among us" (verse 14). Eugene Peterson paraphrases this in *The Message* as "The Word became flesh and blood, and moved into the neighborhood." This verse changes everything. God didn't stay distant. He moved in next door.

John 3 - Jesus Teaches Nicodemus

In John 3, Nicodemus, a Pharisee (a member of a Jewish religious group devoted to strict observance of the Law), approaches Jesus at night. Indirectly, he suggests that the miracles Jesus performs can only be done by someone with God's power. He seems to want Jesus to confirm this. Jesus responds and says that unless a person is "born from above," what Nicodemus is suggesting won't be entirely clear.

When Jesus tells Nicodemus that one must be born *anōthen*, He uses a Greek word that carries a beautiful double meaning: "from above" or "again." The ambiguity is intentional. Nicodemus hears only one side of it, interpreting it as a literal second birth, while Jesus is pointing to a spiritual rebirth that comes from God. Some English translations choose "born again" to match Nicodemus's confusion, while others prefer "born from above" to capture what Jesus really means. Jesus goes on to clarify that this rebirth has nothing to do with the physical. Instead, it's spiritual, accomplished by the Holy Spirit, unpredictable and mysterious, and beyond human control.

This chapter also contains one of the most well-known verses in Scripture, John 3:16: "For this is how God loved the world: He gave His only Son so that whoever has faith in Him will not be lost forever, but will have eternal life." This verse encapsulates the heart of the Gospel, reminding us that God's love and gift of salvation through Jesus invite us into a relationship that transcends mere understanding.

The Jesus we encounter in John's Gospel is deeply philosophical, challenging rigid thinking with spiritual truths that transcend human reasoning. Nicodemus struggles to grasp what Jesus is saying because he is accustomed to structured, logical answers. Yet Jesus invites him to see that faith is not merely about understanding; it is about transformation.

John 11 - Jesus Raises Lazarus

In John 11, we find the story of Lazarus, the brother of Mary and Martha, who had died. News of his death had reached Jesus, their friend, yet he did not come right away. This delay, as the narrative unfolds, was part of a greater divine purpose. Up to this point, John's Gospel had built a series of signs, each unveiling more of Jesus' identity. But the raising of Lazarus, the seventh and climactic sign, was different. It revealed who Jesus was and shifted the Gospel's focus from the "Book of Signs" to the approaching "Book of Glory," where the cross and resurrection take center stage.

When Jesus finally arrived, Martha came to meet him, her words full of both grief and faith: "Lord, if you had been here, my brother would not have died." Jesus responded with a declaration that echoed the divine name spoken in Exodus 3:14: "I am the resurrection and the life." This was a word of comfort and a profound statement of his divine identity. Martha's response, "Yes, Lord, I believe that you are the Messiah," became a pivotal confession of faith.

John emphasizes that Lazarus was undeniably dead, even noting the stench of the tomb after four days had passed. In Jewish tradition, some believed the soul lingered near the body for three days before departing. By four days, death was seen as completely irreversible.
This moment contrasts Jesus' divine power, already revealed to Martha, with his deeply human grief as he wept for his friend. This tension between Jesus' divinity and humanity lies at the heart of the Gospel of John. Jesus, the one who would conquer death, also entered fully into human pain and suffering.

The raising of Lazarus was more than a miracle; it was a turning point. While it demonstrated Jesus' power over death, it also set in motion the events leading to his crucifixion. What brought Lazarus out of the grave would ultimately send Jesus to His own grave.

John 14 - Jesus' Farewell Discourse

John 14 opens a window into the intimate dialogue between Jesus and His disciples. It offers both profound theological insight and a glimpse into Jesus' deep appreciation for their candor and curiosity. He knows they love Him, and He uses this as the foundation for a challenge. They must take that love and extend it to others.

It is a difficult conversation because Jesus understands that His time is short. For His message to take root, He must entrust it to these disciples. They are flawed and uncertain yet capable of great things. Though they wrestle with doubt, He believes they are up to the challenge. Evangelicals often interpret John 14 as a cosmic duel between God and the Devil. Yet neither Satan nor the Devil is mentioned here. Instead, Jesus contrasts the Kingdom of God with the ruler of this world who is coming. This ruler is not a supernatural adversary but the violent and self-serving Roman imperial system that will soon execute Him.

It is no surprise that Jesus' message is misunderstood. Even Thomas and Philip take His words literally, failing to grasp that He is speaking theologically. Yet Jesus reassures them that although His days on earth are numbered, they will not be left alone. Another Advocate, the Holy Spirit, will be with them. This implies that Jesus Himself is also their Advocate. In this trinitarian promise, He guarantees that the love of the Father and the Son will endure.

John 20 - The Resurrection of Jesus

John 20 celebrates the resurrection of Jesus, marking the turning point of the Gospel story. It begins with Mary Magdalene arriving at the tomb early in the morning, only to find the stone rolled away. At first, she believes someone has taken Jesus' body. Confused and grieving, she runs to tell Peter and John, who come to see the empty tomb for themselves. Yet it is Mary who lingers, and it is to her that Jesus first appears.

At first, she does not recognize Him. But when He calls her by name, everything changes. Her sorrow turns to joy. In that moment, the risen Christ is not just a theological truth; He is a living presence. Mary becomes the first witness to the resurrection and the first messenger of the good news, sent to tell the disciples, "I have seen the Lord." Her role underscores the inclusive and world-turning nature of the Gospel. The first person entrusted with the news of the resurrection was not a man of influence or a religious authority. It was Mary Magdalene, a woman often overlooked and often misunderstood. She was the one Jesus chose to carry the most important message in history. Her role reminds us that the Gospel has always advanced through those willing to say yes, not just those in positions of power. And from the very beginning, that has included women.

Jesus then appears to His disciples, entering a locked room and speaking peace over them. He shows them His hands and side, anchoring their belief in the reality of His resurrected body. He commissions them to carry on His mission and breathes the Holy Spirit upon them, a symbolic act that echoes the creation of Adam and anticipates Pentecost. What began in fear turns into bold purpose.

Thomas, absent at Jesus' first appearance, expresses doubt when told of the resurrection. But a week later, Jesus appears again. This time, Thomas sees and believes, declaring, "My Lord and my God." His words are the climax of the chapter and a profound confession of faith, one that echoes down through the ages to every believer who has not seen, yet still believes.

John 20 is an invitation to encounter the risen Jesus, to receive the peace only He can give, and to join in the mission He entrusts to His followers. The resurrection is not the end of the story; it is the beginning of new creation. Mary's witness reminds us that God often chooses the unlikely to carry the most world-changing news.

Acts 2 - The Day of Pentecost

The name "Pentecost" comes from the Greek word *pentēkostē*, meaning "fiftieth." It refers to the Jewish festival celebrated on the fiftieth day after Passover, known as the Feast of Weeks or Shavuot. According to Acts 2, on this day, the Holy Spirit arrived dramatically. As the apostles gathered, "tongues of fire" rested upon them, filling them with the Spirit and enabling them to speak in various languages. People from diverse nations heard the Gospel in their own language, a powerful sign of God's inclusive message.

Peter delivers a bold sermon, declaring that this event fulfills Joel's prophecy about the Spirit being poured out on all people. He proclaims the resurrection of Jesus and calls for repentance, leading to about 3,000 people being baptized and added to the Church. And by the way, in the New Testament, it's clear that when someone was baptized, their whole household joined in. There's no example or even a hint of Christian families waiting to baptize their children until they could decide for themselves or express their own faith.

Pentecost marks the birth of the Church and the beginning of its mission to the world. It parallels the Jewish festival of Shavuot, commemorating the giving of the Law. Still, now the Spirit replaces the Law as the guiding force for God's people. This chapter reminds us that the same Spirit empowers believers today to share God's love across all barriers.

Acts 7 - Stephen Addresses the Council

In Acts 7, Stephen delivers a bold, Spirit-filled speech before the Jewish Sanhedrin. His recounting of Israel's history not only emphasizes God's faithfulness despite the people's repeated disobedience but also provides an excellent summary for us to reflect on today. At issue is how he exposes their persistent refusal to live as a holy people.

Stephen's rebuke strikes at the heart of the Sanhedrin's idolatry. They have reduced faithfulness to a fixation on the Temple as if God's presence could be contained within the walls of a human institution. But the God of Israel is never a possession to be managed. He is the One who called Abraham before there was a temple, who met Moses in a burning bush far from any sacred space, and who now makes Himself fully known in the crucified and risen Christ. Stephen's words expose the Sanhedrin's fundamental failure. They have not merely rejected Jesus. They have always resisted the work of the Spirit, who calls God's people into a new way of life.

Their rage is not surprising. The Gospel has always been a scandal to those who wish to keep power on their own terms. In response, they cast Stephen out and stone him, proving his point that they, like their ancestors, are not rejecting a man but rejecting the very presence of God among them. Yet Stephen does not meet their violence with resistance. In his dying breath, he does what the world cannot comprehend. He prays for his executioners. In this act, he does not merely imitate Christ. He embodies the crucified life to which all who follow Jesus are called.

The early Church did not survive because it was strong in the way the world measures strength. It survived because it was willing to die. Stephen's martyrdom reminds us that faithfulness is not about preserving religious structures or securing our place in the world. It is about being a people so transformed by the Spirit that even death itself loses its power over us. His death, like Christ's, reveals the only true victory, which is the victory of a life given entirely to God.

Acts 9 - The Conversion of Paul

Acts 9 recounts Saul's dramatic transformation into Paul, one of Christianity's greatest apostles. Initially from what is now Turkey, Saul, a relentless persecutor of Christians, never encountered Jesus during His earthly ministry. However, his encounter with the risen Christ profoundly transformed him, leading him to become a central figure responsible for writing much of the New Testament.

On the road to Damascus, Saul was blinded by a vision of the risen Jesus. Jesus asked, "Why are you persecuting Me?" and Saul's life was forever changed. Led into Damascus, Saul met Ananias, a reluctant disciple who had been sent by God to heal and baptize him. Saul regained his sight, received the Holy Spirit, and began boldly proclaiming Jesus as the Messiah.

Saul's conversion is a powerful testament to God's grace, showing His ability to transform even the most unlikely individuals and repurpose their lives for His use. Once a fierce persecutor of Christians, Saul undergoes a profound transformation and receives a new identity in Christ, becoming Paul, a devoted apostle called to spread the Gospel to the Gentiles. Saul was his Hebrew name, while Paul (*Paulus* in Latin) was his Roman name, which he used to connect more effectively with the Gentiles and the broader Roman world, a key focus of his mission. His story underscores the inclusivity of God's kingdom. It challenges us to trust in God's power to redeem any life for His purposes.

While Paul's dramatic conversion tends to overshadow other aspects of the chapter, Ananias also plays a crucial part. Despite his initial fear and reluctance, Ananias obeys God's command to seek out Saul. This act of obedience and compassion is remarkable, considering Saul's reputation as a fierce persecutor of Christians. Ananias's willingness to heal and baptize Saul underscores the power of faith and forgiveness, as well as the importance of lesser-known figures in the early Christian community.

Romans 3 - Justification by Faith

Romans 3 reveals the universal condition of humanity, confronting both Jews and Gentiles with the profound reality of sin and the utter inability to achieve righteousness through their own efforts. This shared predicament exposes the frailty of the human condition, our estrangement from the Creator, and our complete dependence on divine grace.

In this chapter, Paul proclaims a radical and world-changing truth. Through Jesus Christ, God has acted decisively, offering redemption as a gift rather than as a reward for human effort. Justification is not earned by merit. It is pure grace, an extravagant act of divine love that dismantles human pride and self-reliance. Faith is not about intellectual agreement or moral success. It is trust, a deep and relational trust in the God who keeps promises and reconciles us not through our striving but through His initiative.

By pointing to Abraham, Paul reminds us that faith has always been a trusting response to God's call, a life oriented not by adherence to the law but by the promise of the One who is faithful. This faith, uniting all people in God's redemptive plan, is not something we possess or achieve but an ongoing posture of dependence, gratitude, and hope.

Romans 3 invites us to confront the truth of our brokenness, not with despair, but with the freedom to relinquish the exhausting burden of self-justification. It calls us to embrace the gift of being justified by grace through faith and to live lives shaped by humility, gratitude, and joyful participation in God's work of reconciliation.

Romans 6 - New Life in Christ

Romans 6 declares who we truly are: alive, free, and fully embraced by God. Paul presents baptism as more than just a ritual. It is a decisive, symbolic moment where we are united with Jesus, stepping into His story, dying to the old way of life, and rising into something entirely new. It is about identity. It is about transformation.

Paul confronts a twisted version of the gospel that happens when grace gets separated from the story of Christ. Some might think: if grace covers everything, then how we act doesn't matter. But for Paul, this kind of thinking shows a basic misunderstanding. Grace isn't a free pass to do whatever we want; it's God's power that transforms our lives. It doesn't accept us as we are and leave us there. Instead, grace kills our old way of living and raises us to new life in Christ. To live "under grace" means following the pattern of Jesus' own faithfulness. It's not freedom from responsibility but freedom for obedience.

This is not about following rules or managing behavior. It is about waking up to the truth that sin no longer has the final say. You are no longer bound by shame, guilt, or the patterns that kept you stuck. You have been set free, free to live fully alive, fully human, and fully present in the beauty and purpose of this new life.

Romans 8 - Life Through the Spirit

Romans 8 offers one of the most powerful reflections in all of Scripture on what it means to live a life shaped by the Spirit of God. Paul speaks of freedom from condemnation and of a deeper transformation, one that redefines identity, belonging, and purpose. Life "in the flesh," driven by fear and self-interest, gives way to life "in the Spirit," marked by renewal, courage, and hope.

It is the Spirit that confirms our adoption into God's family, making us not just followers but heirs, participants in Christ's suffering and sharers in His future glory. That glory is not about status or reward. It is about the full restoration of who we were always meant to be.

Even in our weakest moments, when we cannot find the words to pray, the Spirit is present, interceding, guiding, and aligning our lives with the will of God. Paul is reminding us that the Spirit is not a distant force but God's active presence, always working and always leading throughout the story of His people.

And then, in one of the most unshakable promises ever written, Paul declares that nothing (not hardship, not loss, not even death) can separate us from the love of God in Christ Jesus. These are not just comforting words for individual hearts. They are a call to the Church, across generations and across the world, to hold fast to the truth that our faith is not fragile. It endures. And so do we.

Romans 12 - Marks of a Christian

Romans 12 shift gears. Paul, having opened the floodgates of God's mercy in the preceding chapters, now turns with urgency to the question: What does a life touched by such mercy actually look like? He does not offer abstraction. He offers bodies. Minds. Daily decisions. He brings theology to the ground, to the body, to the grit of real life.

Paul speaks of sacrifice, reclaiming it as life poured out. This is a summons to inhabit the world with a new posture. The holy offering is the self, wholly given, expressed in the language of love, written in acts of mercy, and visible in lives shaped by a deeper sense of worth and purpose.

This is more than moral adjustment. It is a re-creation of vision. Paul asks us to see with renewed minds, minds no longer shaped by cultural scripts of power, domination, and performance. These are minds awakened to God's reconciling work in the world. Renewal begins not with effort, but with grace.

Paul refuses to let this vision stay personal. The transformation he describes is always communal. This is a body made of many parts, a people who belong to one another. Love is not a sentiment here; it is the architecture of a new humanity. Each gift matters. Each voice counts. Each life leans toward the common good because mercy has gathered us into one.

Paul is casting a vision of what it means to be alive, fully alive, in response to God's overwhelming mercy. A life that is free to give. A people drawn into the mysterious and beautiful work of becoming what God has always intended: a holy people, living love in public.

1 Corinthians 12 - Unity and Diversity

1 Corinthians 12 celebrates the unity and diversity of the Church, comparing it to a body where every part has a unique and indispensable role. Paul explains that the Holy Spirit gives various spiritual gifts, all designed to benefit the community and serve the common good. These gifts are not for personal pride or gain but for building up the Church as a whole.

Addressing divisions within the Corinthian Church, Paul emphasizes that no member or gift is more important than any other. Each believer's contributions are essential for the health and mission of the Church, whether they are visible and celebrated or quietly working behind the scenes. The metaphor of the body reminds us that the Church thrives when its members value one another's roles and work together in harmony.

Paul concludes with a critical reminder that love is the foundation for using spiritual gifts. Without love, even the most impressive gifts lose their meaning and purpose. Paul calls his readers to honor one another, value the unique gifts God has given, and prioritize love and mutual care in every aspect of Church life.

1 Corinthians 13 - The Chapter of Love

1 Corinthians 13 offers a timeless and profound reflection on the nature of love, elevating it as the greatest of all virtues. Paul declares that without love, even the most extraordinary spiritual gifts or sacrifices are ultimately meaningless.

He describes love as patient, kind, selfless, and enduring, emphasizing that it "never fails." This chapter critiques spiritual pride and urges the pursuit of maturity in faith by centering their lives on love. It also points to the truth that God is love. Try reading it with 'God' in place of 'love,' and you'll see that God is patient. God is kind. God never fails.

Paul portrays love as the essence of true discipleship, mirroring the self-giving love of Christ, who demonstrated perfect love through His life and sacrifice. His vision calls us to make love the defining mark of our faith, transforming how we relate to one another and shaping communities into reflections of Christ's love.

1 Corinthians 15 - Resurrection Theology

1 Corinthians 15 is a defense of the resurrection. It is a bold proclamation of the hope and power at the very center of the Christian faith. For Paul, the resurrection is not just a future promise; it transforms the present. If Christ is not raised, then faith is not only empty; it is powerless to change anything. But because Christ has been raised, everything changes. The resurrection is God's definitive declaration that sin, death, and all forces of destruction will not and cannot have the final word.

Paul describes Christ's resurrection as the "first fruits," a foretaste of what is to come for all of God's people. This hope extends beyond individual salvation. It points to the renewal of all creation, fulfilling God's promise to make everything new. The resurrection is the victory of God's justice and the liberation of humanity from every force that dehumanizes, divides, and destroys. It is not just a theological concept; it is a transformative reality that reshapes how we live and engage with the world.

This chapter calls us to live in light of this hope, not by retreating from the world but by stepping into it with courage, joy, and perseverance. The resurrection empowers us to work for justice, love our neighbors, and trust that no labor done in the Lord is ever wasted. Even in the face of suffering and death, we can stand firm, knowing that God's purposes will prevail.

For Paul, the resurrection is more than a historical event or a distant promise. It is the climax of God's redemptive plan and the source of the Church's mission. It weaves together the biblical narrative, from Israel's hope for renewal to the Church's call to embody the good news of God's reign. In the resurrection, we witness the triumph of God's love, a love that brings life out of death, hope out of despair, and a new creation out of the old. It is the ultimate assurance that God is making all things new.

2 Corinthians 5 - Ministry of Reconciliation

2 Corinthians 5 celebrates the power of the Gospel, which heals the broken relationship between people and God through Christ. Paul says

that in Christ, believers become new creations: "The old has gone; the new is here!"

This personal change affects how believers live. Jesus' followers are called to be ambassadors of Christ, sharing the message of reconciliation with the world. Paul explains that through Christ's sacrifice, God has mended the divide caused by sin, offering restoration and unity to everyone.

Reconciliation is a key part of the Gospel, reflecting the promises of renewal and faithfulness from the Old Testament. This chapter encourages readers to practice reconciliation in their relationships and join God's work in making everything new. Christians are called to embrace the hope and renewal offered through Christ, becoming living examples of His love.

Galatians 5 - Freedom in Christ

Galatians 5 is about the freedom believers have in Christ and Paul's call to stand firm against the chains of legalism. This freedom is not an excuse for selfishness but a call to love and serve one another. To illustrate this, Paul uses the metaphor of fruit. Fruit does not appear overnight. It starts as a seed, small and unnoticed. However, given the right conditions, such as having water, sunlight, and time, it grows. It becomes something you can see, hold, and taste. The fruit of the Spirit works the same way. It is evidence that something deep inside you is changing, growing, and transforming.

Paul explains how this change happens. He says believers have crucified the flesh, meaning they have a choice. They are not just a collection of impulses ruled by instinct. They can choose to put selfishness, greed, and division to death. When they do, something new grows from within. Love, joy, peace, and kindness.

For Paul, restoration is the most powerful of the fruits. When someone stumbles, the instinct may be to judge or condemn. But Paul pushes back. The real test of transformation is not how perfectly you avoid mistakes. It is how well you help others recover from theirs.

Paul also rejects the idea of exclusivity. He makes no distinction between so-called Spirit-filled Christians and everyone else. Inner circles and elitism have no place. If you are in Christ, you are in. Period. Unity over division.

Some view Galatians 5 as a checklist, but it is not. It is not a contract, a rule, or a set of boxes to check. It presents an entirely new way of being, giving, and growing in Christ. In doing so, we become something bigger than ourselves.

Ephesians 2 - Made Alive in Christ

In Ephesians 2, Paul tells us that we are saved by grace through faith and not by works, highlighting the overwhelming generosity of God's grace. This reality disrupts any attempt to control or manage our relationship with God. Salvation is not something we accomplish; it is something God has done for us in Christ, drawing us into a new reality where we are no longer defined by sin, death, or our own striving.

This grace is neither abstract nor merely spiritual. It is revealed in the creation of a new humanity. Christ's breaking down of the dividing wall between Jew and Gentile is not simply a metaphor but the tangible work of God's reconciling love. The Church is called to be a witness to this new creation. In this community, worldly divisions are rendered meaningless, and peace is practiced as the concrete expression of God's reign.

The good works Paul mentions are not efforts to earn salvation but the practices necessary for the Church to embody its calling as a sign of the kingdom. The reconciliation accomplished in Christ requires that the Church reject the ways of violence, division, and domination, living instead as a people shaped by forgiveness, hospitality, and mutual care.

Ephesians 2 refuses to let us reduce salvation to private belief or moral improvement. It insists that grace is cosmic in scope, drawing all creation into God's redemptive work. To be saved by grace is to be drawn into the life of a people who embody the peace of Christ, a people whose very existence bears witness to the triumph of God's reconciling love.

Philippians 2 - The Christ Hymn

Philippians 2 focuses on the Christ Hymn, a powerful reflection on Jesus' journey from divine glory to humble service. Paul introduces this hymn not just as theology but as a call to action, urging believers to adopt Christ's mindset of selflessness, service, and obedience.

The hymn tells a striking story. Though fully divine, Jesus "emptied Himself," taking on human form and willingly submitting to the most shameful death, crucifixion. This dramatic descent from the highest glory to the lowest humiliation becomes the model Paul sets before believers.

By calling Jesus "Lord," Paul makes a bold and politically risky statement in Philippi, a Roman colony fiercely loyal to the Empire. This title, often reserved for Caesar, put Philippian Christians in a difficult position. The hymn challenges not only personal attitudes but also the world's power structures. Paul insists that true lordship is not about dominance and control but about self-giving love.

Paul takes it even further by applying language from Isaiah 45, words spoken exclusively about Israel's God, directly to Jesus. This is not just a claim about what Jesus did but a claim about who God is. Jesus' self-sacrificial love is not merely one of God's actions. It is His very nature.

Since Jesus' life sets the pattern for believers, Paul urges the Philippians to "work out" their salvation, not by earning it but by living it out in daily obedience and community life. He reminds them that God is at work within them, empowering their faithfulness. Drawing from Israel's wilderness failures, he warns them against disobedience. He encourages them to shine as faithful witnesses in a corrupt world.

Throughout this passage, Paul weaves profound theology into practical encouragement, calling believers to unity, humility, and sacrificial love. The Christ Hymn is not just a declaration of who Jesus is. It is an invitation to follow His example by living lives of obedience, service, and radical love.

Colossians 1 - The Image of the Invisible God

Colossians 1 unveils a stunning vision of Christ at the center of everything: creation, redemption, and the restoration of all things. Paul proclaims Jesus as the image of the invisible God, the One in whom the fullness of God dwells. This is a cosmic declaration. Through Christ, all things (every atom, every tree, every creature, and every system) were created and are held together by Him.

And here is the radical twist. This supreme Christ, above all powers and authorities, chose the path of self-giving love, reconciling all creation through His death on the cross. This reconciliation is spiritual, physical, relational, and ecological in nature. It declares that the brokenness of the world (human sin, oppressive systems, and the groaning of creation) are being restored in and through Christ.

This chapter invites us to marvel at Christ's supremacy and to consider its implications. It challenges us to live in alignment with His reign. If all things are being reconciled in Christ, then our lives, relationships, communities, and even how we care for creation must reflect that reconciliation. Paul's poetic vision confronts the powers that exploit, destroy, and divide, reminding us that true power is found in humility and sacrificial love. It calls us to join in God's ongoing work of restoration.

Colossians 1 invites us to see Christ as the sustainer of life and as the One who is actively making all things new. It is a call to trust in this reconciling work and to participate in it, to live lives rooted in hope, shaped by justice, and oriented toward the flourishing of all creation.

Hebrews 11 - Faith in Action

Hebrews 11 is a journey through the ages, revealing how faith shapes history, overcomes impossibilities, and moves God's people toward a kingdom yet to come. It begins with creation, where faith recognizes that the universe was spoken into existence by God's command. Before human effort, there was only the Creator's voice, the true foundation of faith.

One by one, early witnesses step forward. Abel's offering shows that faith is more than duty. It is devotion. Enoch's walk with God reminds us that faith is about abiding in His presence. Noah builds when judgment looms and trusts God to preserve His own. Abraham, the great pioneer of faith, leaves behind all that is familiar and longs for a city whose architect is God. He believes in the impossible, receives a son, and even trusts that God can raise the dead when that son is laid upon the altar.

Faith then passes from generation to generation. It sustains Isaac, Jacob, and Joseph as they cling to a promise they will not see fulfilled. It rises in Moses, whose parents hide him in the reeds of the Nile. He forsakes Egypt's treasures and confronts Pharaoh. He leads the people through the sea and trusts in the blood of the lamb to turn away judgment. Faith brings down Jericho's walls and welcomes Rahab, a Gentile whose trust in God secures her place in the Messiah's lineage.

Hebrews 11 then sweeps us into the great cloud of witnesses. Gideon, David, Samuel, and the prophets all stand among them. Some conquered kingdoms and saw miracles. Others suffered and were martyred, holding onto the promise they never saw fulfilled. In every case, faith anchored them beyond the present moment and fixed their eyes on a kingdom yet to come.

James 2 - Faith and Works

James 2 delivers a powerful message about what faith looks like in real life, grounded in a deeply Jewish understanding. For James, faith is not a private or abstract belief but a trust in God that is meant to be evident in how we live. He famously says, "Faith without works is dead," demonstrating that true faith and action are inextricably linked as part of a life devoted to God.

The chapter opens with a strong critique of favoritism, calling the community to follow the "royal law" of Scripture: "You shall love your neighbor as yourself." This echoes the teachings of the Torah and Jesus, urging justice and mercy, especially toward the poor and marginalized.

To make his point, James uses the examples of Abraham and Rahab, who demonstrated their faith through bold action. Their lives demonstrate that faith is not just about agreeing with ideas or making declarations but about living out trust in God through our actions.

James 2 emphasizes that living an ethical life is central to faith. He challenges his readers to align their lives with God's principles, creating a community defined by justice, mercy, and love in action. Faith and works are not opposites but are woven together as part of a life shaped by devotion to God and care for others.

This chapter reminds us that genuine faith is alive and active. It is not just about what we believe, but also about how we respond to God by living with love, justice, and mercy in every part of our lives.

1 Peter 2 - A Chosen People

1 Peter 2 presents a vision of the Church as a transformative, set-apart community. A people chosen by God, a royal priesthood, a holy nation. These are not merely titles but a calling to proclaim the mighty acts of the God who has brought them out of darkness into His light. This vision is not individualistic but deeply communal, rooted in the shared identity and mission of God's people.

Peter uses the imagery of exile to describe the lived reality of early Christians, displaced, misunderstood, and often marginalized by society. Yet this status as "strangers and foreigners" is reframed as an opportunity to bear witness. They are called to live lives of integrity, holiness, and submission, not out of weakness but as a bold declaration of their allegiance to God's kingdom. Even in the face of hostility, their actions serve as a proclamation of the Gospel, revealing the transformative power of God's grace.

This chapter challenges the Church to see their lives as a witness through their holiness, faithfulness, and unwavering commitment to justice and love. For those living on the margins or in tension with cultural powers, 1 Peter 2 offers a radical vision of hope and purpose. To embody God's reign and proclaim His goodness, even in the most challenging circumstances.

1 John 4 - God's Love and Ours

1 John 4 proclaims that "God is love," calling believers to love one another as a reflection of their relationship with Him. This is not a vague sentiment. It is the foundation of Christian identity. God's love is revealed in the sending of His Son as an atoning sacrifice, showing that divine love is not abstract or passive but deeply personal and transformative.

The chapter offers a clear warning: no one can truly love God while harboring hatred toward others. Love is not a suggestion. It is the defining mark of genuine faith. To know God is to live in His love, and to be known by Him is to be changed by it. This love forms the heart of a community shaped by compassion, humility, and shared purpose.

The passage calls believers to move beyond words into action, making God's love visible in relationships, daily choices, and acts of mercy. It invites a life not shaped by fear or division but by the steady courage of love that gives. When we live this way, we become a testimony to the world around us, evidence of God's presence, His grace, and His reconciling power.

Revelation 21 - A New Heaven and a New Earth

Revelation 21 brings the biblical story full circle. In Genesis, we see the beginning of creation as God brings order out of chaos, forms the heavens and the earth, and establishes a garden where humanity walks in communion with Him. Revelation 21 envisions the culmination of that story, where God's creation is not abandoned but renewed, introducing a new heaven and a new earth where God dwells permanently with His people.

The image of the new Jerusalem adorned as a bride powerfully recalls the primal harmony between Adam and Eve in Eden, yet now represents something greater: the perfected union between God and redeemed humanity. What was shattered in the Fall finds its complete restoration. This radiant vision stands in stark contrast to Babylon, which embodies the corrupt world system that rebels against divine authority, much as the Fall disrupted God's intended order. However, Revelation culminates in God's definitive triumph over evil. This victory restores creation to its original goodness and wholeness, fulfilling His redemptive purpose.

chapter 7

What Also Matters?

The Bible is massive, with nearly 1,200 chapters of wisdom, history, poetry, and divine inspiration. It's a staggering collection, and if the thought of reading it all feels daunting, you're in good company. Let's be honest: even among pastors, theologians, and lifelong believers, many haven't made it through every single page. Some will freely admit it, while others might skillfully sidestep the confession. But here's the beautiful thing: you don't have to read all 1,200 chapters to connect deeply with the heart of Scripture.

This all started because my students kept getting stuck. They'd start reading the Bible, get through the first few books, and then right around Leviticus they'd show up and ask me the same question: "What actually counts the most?"

Which makes sense. You start with creation, epic plagues, burning bushes, and then out of nowhere, someone touches mildew and we're sacrificing birds about it (Leviticus 14, by the way, doesn't make the list). It feels less like a spiritual journey and more like a health code violation.

Eventually, I realized I needed a better answer. I started combing through all 1,189 chapters, looking for patterns. Core themes. Repeated ideas. The places where the message of the Bible really comes into focus. It took years. Some of it was productive. Some of it was just me arguing with myself about Isaiah.

But in the end, I landed on 470 chapters that carry the heart of the whole story. The big narrative. The through-line that keeps showing up. You've already seen 52 of those. The ones I believe rise to the very top. Now we're adding 418 more. Not everything, but enough to see the Bible in a whole new way.

These aren't random selections or personal favorites. They're the foundational chapters that reveal the Bible's heartbeat, its overarching themes, and its timeless truths. With these chapters, you'll see Scripture's story come alive in a profound, purposeful, and refreshingly approachable way.

Why This Plan is Unique

- **Crafted with Purpose**: I've gone through every chapter, hand-picking the ones that matter most. It's not perfect, but its careful.

- **A Journey, Not a Marathon**: Think of this as the greatest hits of the Bible, carefully curated to avoid unnecessary repetition.

- **Comprehensive Yet Manageable**: At 470 chapters, this plan balances depth and accessibility. It offers a view of the

Bible that's comprehensive enough to give you confidence in your understanding.

Why It Works

- **Engagement, Not Exhaustion**: Many reading plans start strong but fizzle out in the long genealogies or dense history. This plan keeps the journey engaging, inspiring, and focused.

- **The Right Balance**: You'll experience the poetry of Psalms, the wisdom of Proverbs, the power of the Gospels, and the depth of Paul's letters, alongside the foundational Old Testament narratives that set the stage for it all.

- **Connecting the Dots**: By the time you finish these chapters, you'll have a clearer, richer, and deeper view of Scripture that connects the dots across God's redemptive plan.

A Bold Promise

Call me skeptical, but sometimes it feels like encouraging people to read the entire Bible can be used as a guilt trip. It's as if someone says, "read the whole thing," knowing how overwhelming it is. When people inevitably struggle, give up, and feel bad about it, the person who made the suggestion can come across as smug or judgmental, which is far from biblical living.

Instead, what if you started with smaller, manageable steps? Not trying to conquer the whole Bible in a month. Not chasing some impossible reading goal that just leads to guilt. Just one clear step at a time. And give yourself some credit. You've probably read more of the Bible than most Christians throughout history. For centuries, most believers didn't even have access to the full text. Before the printing

What Also Matters?

press, Bibles were rare, handwritten, and kept under lock and key in churches. Even after that, many couldn't read. So if you've read even a few books of Scripture, you're already engaging with it in a way most people never could.

That's why this reading plan matters. It's not about covering every single verse. It's about engaging deeply with the heart of Scripture. So I'll just say it plainly: reading these 470 chapters is enough. Enough to give you a solid grasp of the Bible's core message. Enough to challenge you, inspire you, and shape how you live out your faith. Honestly, this plan doesn't just scratch the surface. It offers more than enough to transform your understanding of Scripture.

That said, I want to affirm your desire to read the entire Bible if that's your goal. It's a worthy pursuit and one every Christian should aspire to. While I hope you'll have the time and opportunity to explore every chapter over your lifetime, this plan offers a clear and accessible place to begin. It is uniquely comprehensive without being overwhelming.

Follow it at your own pace: one chapter daily, and you'll finish in just 15 months. Double it to two chapters daily, and you'll complete it in less than 8 months. Either way, you'll experience a simple, meaningful, and transformative journey.

So why wait? If you've ever found it challenging to stay consistent in your Bible reading or weren't sure where to start, this plan is here to guide you. You'll notice that some chapters are in **bold**, as they are part of the 52 chapters that matter most. In some cases, you'll find must-read chapters, while in others, I'll encourage you to explore the entire book. No matter where you begin, this plan is designed to help you engage with Scripture in a meaningful way.

What Also Matters?

clings to hope. Each story shows faith lived in real life. Through families, tribes, and a nation, God remains connected.

Must-Read Chapters

☐ **Genesis 1 - God creates the world in six days, forming light, land, sea, creatures, and humanity, then rests.**

☐ Genesis 2 - God creates Adam and Eve, placing them in the Garden of Eden to live and work harmoniously.

☐ Genesis 3 - Humanity falls into sin as Adam and Eve disobey God, leading to their expulsion from Eden.

☐ Genesis 4 - Cain and Abel show us how jealousy and anger can turn tragic.

☐ Genesis 6 - God grieves humanity's sin and calls Noah to build an ark to preserve life through the coming flood.

☐ Genesis 7 - The floodwaters cover the earth as Noah, his family, and the animals find refuge in the ark.

☐ Genesis 8 - The waters recede, and Noah offers a sacrifice to God, who promises never to flood the earth again.

☐ Genesis 9 - God establishes a covenant with Noah, marked by the rainbow, and gives new instructions for life after the flood.

☐ Genesis 11 - Humanity's pride leads to the construction of a tower, and God scatters the nations.

☐ Genesis 12 - Abram is called by God, marking the beginning of the covenantal relationship with Israel.

☐ Genesis 15 - God formalizes His covenant with Abram, promising descendants and the land of Canaan.

☐ Genesis 17 - God's covenant with Abraham is reaffirmed and signified.

The Torah
Creation, Covenant, and Calling

The first five books of the Bible are known as the *Torah*, a Hebrew word meaning "instruction" or "teaching." They're not just a record of beginnings or a list of laws, they form a literary and theological masterpiece. The *Torah* weaves together themes of creation, covenant, and liberation into a unified narrative that reveals God's character and intentions for humanity. Its structure and artistry invite deep reflection on the balance between God's faithfulness and human responsibility. Together, these books lay the foundation for understanding what it means to live in covenant with God and in community with others.

GENESIS

Genesis opens with God bringing order to chaos, shaping a vibrant world, and breathing life into humanity. God creates the world, and within seconds (not literally) humans are blaming each other for everything. It's a story of beginnings, where beauty and brokenness intertwine as people make choices that strain their connection with God. Yet, through it all, God's relentless kindness and determination to restore what's been lost shine through.

From Adam and Eve's missteps to Noah's Ark and Abraham's journey of trust, Genesis shows how God works through one family to bring hope and healing to the world. This family is messy, complicated, and human, yet God's covenant takes shape through them. Abraham trusts the promise. Sarah laughs at its absurdity. Isaac obeys. Joseph

- [ ] Genesis 22 - Abraham's faith is tested as God commands him to sacrifice Isaac.
- [ ] Genesis 25 - The rivalry of twin brothers Jacob and Esau set the stage for God's plans through Jacob.
- [ ] Genesis 27 - Jacob deceives his father Isaac to receive the blessing intended for Esau, sparking lifelong conflict.
- [ ] Genesis 28 - Jacob's dream introduces his relationship with God and the continuation of the Abrahamic covenant.
- [ ] Genesis 30 - Jacob's messy family grows through rivalry and divine blessing.
- [ ] Genesis 32 - Jacob wrestles with a divine being, earning a new name, Israel, and a renewed covenant with God.
- [ ] Genesis 37 - Joseph's dreams of leadership spark jealousy among his brothers, who sell him into slavery.
- [ ] Genesis 41 - Joseph interprets Pharaoh's dreams and rises to power, securing Egypt's grain supply.
- [ ] Genesis 45 - Joseph reveals his identity to his brothers, showing how God used his trials to save lives during famine.
- [ ] Genesis 50 - The conclusion of Genesis reflects God's providence and the overarching theme of forgiveness.

EXODUS

Exodus is the story of a God who hears the cries of the oppressed and steps into history to set them free. God reveals His name to Moses at the burning bush as YHWH. This name appears over 6,800 times in the Bible and points to something profound; it's not just a name but a declaration. When Moses asks, "Who should I say sent me?" God responds, "I Am Who I Am." It's like God is saying, I exist. I have always existed. I will always exist. I'm here. It's a name that's less about what we call God and more about how we understand God.

Although some laws may seem tedious, the overarching story of liberation, divine power, and establishing a relationship between God and His people is foundational to understanding redemption. This narrative of deliverance lingers long after the first read, inviting us to reflect on a God who hears, acts, and remains present in the lives of His people.

Must-Read Chapters

- [ ] Exodus 1 - The Israelites grow numerous in Egypt, prompting Pharaoh to enslave them and kill their male infants.
- [ ] Exodus 2 - Moses is born, saved by Pharaoh's daughter, and flees to Midian after killing an Egyptian.
- [ ] **Exodus 3 - God appears to Moses in the burning bush, calling him to lead Israel out of Egypt.**
- [ ] Exodus 4 - God gives Moses signs and his brother Aaron to assist him in speaking to Pharaoh.
- [ ] Exodus 5 - Moses demands freedom for Israel, but Pharaoh's refusal brings more oppression.
- [ ] Exodus 6 - God reaffirms His covenant and promises to deliver Israel from slavery.
- [ ] Exodus 7 - Moses confronts Pharaoh, turning the Nile to blood as the first plague begins.
- [ ] Exodus 9 - The escalation of plagues (livestock death, boils) reveals Pharaoh's hardened heart.
- [ ] Exodus 11 - The climactic warning of the final plague, the death of the firstborn, is pivotal in Pharaoh's eventual capitulation.

Exodus 12 - God commands the Passover, sparing Israel's firstborn and initiating their liberation.

Exodus 13 - God leads His people out of Egypt, guiding them with a pillar of cloud and fire.

Exodus 14 - God parts the Red Sea, allowing Israel to escape while drowning the pursuing Egyptians.

Exodus 16 - God provides manna and quail to sustain the Israelites in the wilderness.

Exodus 19 - Israel arrives at Mount Sinai, where God prepares to give them the covenant.

Exodus 20 - God delivers the Ten Commandments, establishing the moral foundation for Israel.

Exodus 24 - Moses ascends Mount Sinai as Israel confirms their covenant with God.

Exodus 25 - God provides the blueprint for the Tabernacle, His dwelling place among His people.

Exodus 32 - The Israelites create a golden calf, leading to God's judgment and Moses' intercession.

Exodus 33 - Moses intercedes for Israel and requests to see God's glory, deepening their covenantal relationship with God.

Exodus 34 - God renews the covenant, reestablishing Israel's role as His chosen people.

Exodus 40 - Israel completes the tabernacle, and God's glory fills it, signifying His presence dwelling among them.

LEVITICUS

At first glance, Leviticus might feel like a maze of rituals and regulations, the kind of book that tests your endurance. But look again.

Beneath the detail is a daring question: What does it look like to invite God into every corner of daily life?

Leviticus is not all about sacrifice or ceremony. It's also about learning to live as God's chosen people, embodying a divine call to holiness. It's as if God is saying "you wanted a relationship with a holy God. Here this is what holiness actually costs." It reveals how the sacred can saturate the ordinary and how meals, work, relationships, and community life can all become expressions of worship.

Through precise instructions on offerings and sacred practices, God invites His people to sustain relationships even in their imperfections. Rituals like the Day of Atonement or the Bread of the Presence are not just symbolic; they serve as a bridge between heaven and earth, reminding us of forgiveness, provision, and grace.

Yes, the rules can feel dense. But they point to a God who cares deeply, not just about religion but about shaping a community marked by justice, compassion, and reverence.

Must-Read Chapters

- [ ] Leviticus 1 - Worship begins with the burnt offering, sacrifices that rise to God, symbolizing total surrender.
- [ ] Leviticus 2 - Offerings of grain serve as a fragrant reminder that all we have comes from God.
- [ ] Leviticus 8 - A priesthood is set apart through oil, obedience, and detailed sacrifices.
- [ ] Leviticus 10 - A sobering moment occurs where God's holiness demands proper worship.
- [ ] Leviticus 16 - The Day of Atonement is pivotal to Israel's understanding of sin and forgiveness.

- Leviticus 19 - Ethical laws are outlined, emphasizing the need to love your neighbor because God's love defines goodness.
- Leviticus 23 - Worship is marked through festivals, celebrating and remembering significant events.
- Leviticus 25 - God proclaims the Year of Jubilee, ensuring rest, restoration, and forgiveness.

NUMBERS

Numbers tells the story of the Israelites traveling through the wilderness. Along the way, they face challenges such as rebellion and doubt, but God provides for them in remarkable ways. The book gets its name from the census lists, but it's really about how the people learn (and struggle) to trust God. The narrative includes powerful moments, such as God's guidance through the pillar of cloud and fire and the sending of manna and quail to sustain them. It also details their failures, like their refusal to enter the land promised due to fear, which results in forty years of wandering. Alongside the drama are important lessons about leadership and community. While the lists of names and numbers can seem tedious, the heart of the story reveals God's patience, discipline, and unwavering care for His people, as well as the persistent grace of a God committed to creating a people who embody His justice, mercy, and hope in the world.

Must-Read Chapters

- Numbers 11 - The Israelites complain, leading God to provide quail and then send a plague.

What Also Matters?

- [ ] Numbers 12 - Miriam and Aaron criticize Moses, but God defends him.
- [ ] Numbers 13 - Twelve spies are sent to explore Canaan and assess the land and its inhabitants.
- [ ] Numbers 14 - The people reject God's plan and are condemned to wander for 40 years.
- [ ] Numbers 16 - The earth opens up, swallowing the rebels as God enacts dramatic judgment against rebellion.
- [ ] Numbers 19 - God commands the red heifer ritual, providing a means to cleanse impurity and restore purity.
- [ ] Numbers 20 - Moses disobeys God's command, marking a pivotal moment that alters his leadership role.
- [ ] Numbers 21 - God instructs the creation of the bronze serpent, a symbol later linked to salvation through Christ.
- [ ] Numbers 22 - Balaam's donkey sees what Balaam cannot: God's angel standing in the way.
- [ ] Numbers 23 - Balaam again blesses Israel, affirming God's protection.
- [ ] Numbers 24 - Balaam's Third and Fourth Oracles, with visions of their future greatness, despite Balak's plans for a curse.
- [ ] Numbers 27 - The appointment of Joshua as Moses' successor, setting the stage for leadership transition.

DEUTERONOMY

Deuteronomy is Moses' final address to the Israelites, a passionate and heartfelt call to remember their identity and the journey they have undertaken. Standing on the edge of the Promised Land, Moses knows he won't enter with them, so he shares everything they need to carry their legacy forward. He reminds them of their rescue from Egypt, the years in the wilderness, the manna, the water from the rock, and the pillars of cloud and fire. Throughout their journey, God was with them.

Moses doesn't only repeat the laws; he reframes them, inviting the people into a vision of life centered on love. "Love the Lord your God with all your heart, soul, and strength" (Deuteronomy 6:5). This is the heartbeat of faith. Love God and love each other. Let that love shape how we treat the widow, the orphan, and the stranger. Let it guide worship, work, relationships, and the pursuit of justice.

Deuteronomy portrays a community living under God's care and protection. In this society, leaders seek justice, everyone remembers their shared story, and faith is woven into the fabric of daily life. Moses repeatedly reminds them: teach this to your children, pass it on, keep telling the story, and don't forget.

Deuteronomy is more than Moses' farewell; it's a roadmap for living well amid God's promises and human challenges. It pulses with encouragement, urgency, and wisdom. It's not about following rules to please God; it's about living in a way that reflects the God who brought them this far. It's about remembering their past to fully understand their future.

Must-Read Chapters

Deuteronomy 5 - Moses retells the Ten Commandments, reminding Israel of God's covenant and call to obedience.

Deuteronomy 6 - God calls Israel to love Him fully and teach His commandments to future generations.

Deuteronomy 8 - Moses warns Israel not to forget God in times of prosperity.

What Also Matters?

- [ ] Deuteronomy 11 - Moses urges Israel to love God fully, promising blessing for faithfulness.
- [ ] Deuteronomy 15 - God commands the forgiveness of debts every seven years, ensuring no one is left in need.
- [ ] Deuteronomy 31 - Moses commissions Joshua as his successor and assures Israel of God's constant presence.
- [ ] Deuteronomy 32 - Moses proclaims a poetic song, reflecting on God's faithfulness, Israel's rebellion, and God's justice and mercy.
- [ ] Deuteronomy 34 - Moses sees the Promised Land from Mount Nebo before his death.

The Historical Books
Faith and Failure in the Promised Land

Don't let the word historical throw you off. These stories aren't historical in the modern sense. The notion that history should record events exactly as they happened, focusing solely on facts, is relatively recent; it emerged in 19th-century universities. In earlier times, history served a different purpose. It wasn't about capturing every detail of the past; instead, it aimed to teach valuable lessons. These lessons included how to live, how to be a good citizen, and how to follow God. Sometimes, history was crafted to enhance a king's reputation. In the ancient Near East, historical accounts were deeply intertwined with broader questions about meaning, faith, and identity.

When exploring these books, don't expect a detailed chronicle of ancient Israel's history. That wasn't their intent. The authors crafted narratives to reveal profound truths about God, Israel, and their relationship with each other. These texts were dynamic, edited, and reshaped over time to reflect the beliefs and needs of those who preserved them. While historians can extract fragments of historical information, the primary goal of these texts was to convey spiritual truths about God and His people rather than to serve as modern historical records.

JOSHUA

The book of Joshua recounts the compelling story of Israel's conquest of the Promised Land, filled with miracles and challenges. Following Moses' death, Joshua takes the helm, guiding the Israelites into their next chapter. With God's command to be strong and courageous echoing in his mind, Joshua urges the people to remember Moses' words, trust in God, and prepare for the battles ahead. Their journey begins with the miraculous crossing of the Jordan River.

What follows is a series of strategic military campaigns, highlighted by dramatic events such as the fall of Jericho, where obedience and divine power combine to bring down walls. Under Joshua's leadership, the Israelites face fierce battles, witness miraculous victories, and are continually reminded of God's faithfulness.

The early chapters of Joshua are packed with action and adventure. Each win is quickly followed by a new problem. The latter portion shifts focus to the division of the land among the tribes, emphasizing the fulfillment of God's promises and the administrative tasks necessary to establish a nation. Though these sections may test your patience, they underscore the importance of perseverance and trust.

Must-Read Chapters

- [ ] Joshua 1 - God commissions Joshua, promising His presence as he leads Israel into the Promised Land.
- [ ] Joshua 2 - Rahab, a Canaanite woman, hides Israelite spies and declares her faith in the God of Israel.
- [ ] Joshua 3 - Israel crosses the Jordan River as God stops the flow, leading them into the Promised Land.
- [ ] Joshua 6 - Obedience and faith lead to a miraculous victory as the walls of Jericho fall.
- [ ] Joshua 7 - Achan's sin brings defeat to Israel, highlighting the community's accountability.
- [ ] Joshua 10 - The sun stands still as God gives Israel victory over their enemies in an extraordinary battle.
- [ ] Joshua 11 - Joshua leads Israel in defeating northern kings, securing the land God promised.
- [ ] Joshua 20 - Cities of refuge are established as places of safety and justice for those accused of accidental killing.
- [ ] Joshua 24 - Joshua's farewell speech challenges Israel to renew their covenant with God.

JUDGES

Judges tells it like it is when it comes to the messiness of real life and faith. This isn't a feel-good story where everything works out perfectly. Instead, it's an honest look at what happens when people try to live according to their values in a complicated world. The book shows a frustrating cycle: people drift away from what they know is right, things fall apart, they desperately ask for help, get rescued, then somehow manage to forget everything and start over again.

The Israelites found themselves living among neighbors who had completely different beliefs and ways of life. Without strong leadership or regular spiritual practices to keep them grounded, they kept losing sight of who they were and what they stood for. It's something many of us can relate to. How do you stay true to your deepest convictions when the culture around you seems to be moving in a different direction?

The leaders in Judges were far from perfect. Gideon battled intense self-doubt even when he was supposed to be leading others. Samson had incredible natural talents but lacked the maturity and self-control to use them wisely, and his poor decisions eventually destroyed him. These weren't spiritual superheroes but regular people with serious character flaws in positions of enormous responsibility.

Deborah stands out as a refreshing contrast. She combined sharp intelligence with genuine courage, showing how wisdom and integrity can turn around even hopeless situations. Her story demonstrates what becomes possible when someone fully embraces both their gifts and their responsibility to serve others.

What makes Judges compelling is how it reveals something beautiful about grace and second chances. Even when leaders mess up badly and communities lose their way completely, the possibility for renewal keeps showing up. Real, lasting change requires more than quick fixes. It needs the kind of deep personal transformation that comes from genuinely committing to justice, compassion, and truth.

Must-Read Chapters

Judges 2 - Israel repeatedly falls into sin, facing oppression until they cry to God, who raises up judges to deliver them.

- [ ] Judges 3 - God raises up Othniel, Ehud, and Shamgar to deliver Israel from their oppressors.
- [ ] Judges 4 - Deborah leads Israel alongside Barak in a decisive victory over Canaanite forces.
- [ ] Judges 6 - God calls Gideon, despite his doubts and insecurities, to deliver Israel from Midianite oppression.
- [ ] Judges 7 - Gideon's army is reduced to just 300 men to ensure God receives the glory for their improbable triumph.
- [ ] Judges 13 - The angel of the Lord announces the miraculous birth of Samson.
- [ ] Judges 14 - Samson's strength and riddles begin his tumultuous journey, driven by his own desires.
- [ ] Judges 15 - Samson takes revenge on the Philistines with foxes and a jawbone, showing God's power despite his flaws.
- [ ] Judges 16 - In his final act, Samson calls on God for strength and brings down the Philistine temple.

RUTH

In the chaos of the Judges' era, Ruth's story is a quiet breath of hope, tender and unexpected. Like a well-written novel that lingers in your heart, her story weaves faithfulness into everyday life, revealing God's love through loyalty and redemption. The book of Ruth offers a glimpse into God's unfailing love, lived out through the choices and relationships of ordinary people.

Ruth, a Moabite woman on the margins of Israelite society, defies every expectation. Her unshakable loyalty to Naomi, her widowed mother-in-law, is extraordinary. When Ruth declares, "Where you go, I will go," she embodies faithfulness that mirrors God's covenantal love.

Their story reminds us that divine restoration doesn't always come with fanfare but often through the quiet, everyday choices of people who trust in something greater than themselves.

Read the Entire Book

- Ruth 1 - Naomi loses everything, but Ruth clings to her and chooses Naomi's God.
- Ruth 2 - Ruth gleans in Boaz's fields, and he protects and provides for her generously.
- Ruth 3 - Ruth approaches Boaz at night, asking him to redeem her and Naomi.
- Ruth 4 - Boaz redeems Ruth, they marry, and Obed is born, Naomi's joy is restored.

1 SAMUEL

First Samuel is a story of transition, as Israel moves from the wild, unpredictable days of the judges into the structured, yet messy, reality of monarchy. Israel asked for this change, and, to be fair, God's response was basically, "you sure about that?"

It's packed with gripping moments: Samuel, the prophet who hears God's voice as a boy; Saul, the king who begins with promise but crumbles under the weight of his ambition; and David, the shepherd boy who slays a giant and rises to greatness.

This story is like an epic drama, full of loyalty, betrayal, and redemption. With every twist, it reveals the cost of calling and the fierce faith of those who trust God in uncertain times. The Israelites' demand for a king is pivotal, driven by their desire for security and stability, even at the cost of rejecting God's way. Meanwhile, the Ark of the Covenant, symbolizing God's presence, is captured and passed around like a high-value target, reflecting the chaos of the times.

At the center of the story stands David, embodying both courage and remarkable restraint. Despite Saul's betrayal, David spares his life, entrusting justice to God's perfect timing. It is a tale of faith tested in the fires of adversity, where human frailty encounters the steadfastness of divine faithfulness, a narrative rich with tension and depth.

Must-Read Chapters

- [ ] 1 Samuel 1 - A barren woman's desperate prayer leads to the birth of Samuel, the prophet who will change Israel's history.
- [ ] 1 Samuel 3 - As a young boy, Samuel hears God's voice for the first time, setting him apart as a prophet in a time of silence.
- [ ] 1 Samuel 4 - Israel loses the Ark of the Covenant in battle, a devastating moment of defeat and loss.
- [ ] 1 Samuel 5 - The Philistines take the Ark, but God's power humbles their idols and plagues their cities.
- [ ] 1 Samuel 8 - The people reject God's leadership, demanding a king to be like the nations around them.
- [ ] 1 Samuel 9 - God grants Israel their first king, choosing Saul, a man who begins with promise.
- [ ] 1 Samuel 10 - Saul is anointed as Israel's first king, confirmed by signs, and publicly declared.
- [ ] 1 Samuel 15 - Saul's failure to follow God's instructions marks the turning point in his reign.

- **Isaiah 40 - A soaring message of hope, proclaiming God's greatness and the promise of renewal for His people.**
- Isaiah 41 - God reassures His people, declaring His power over the nations and His presence with those who trust Him.
- Isaiah 43 - God declares His love for Israel, promising redemption and a new way in the wilderness.
- **Isaiah 53 - A vivid picture of one who suffers, carrying our brokenness and bringing us peace.**
- Isaiah 55 - God invites His people to seek Him and promises that His word will achieve its purpose.
- Isaiah 58 - True fasting is about justice and compassion, not empty rituals.
- Isaiah 61 - A prophecy of liberation and restoration, vividly echoed in Jesus' ministry.
- Isaiah 65 - A vision of the new heavens and new earth, where God makes all things right.

JEREMIAH

Jeremiah's message is piercing. He is a prophet with a broken heart. His words toll like a funeral bell: slow, solemn, and heavy with grief. He speaks to a nation racing toward disaster, and yet he refuses to give up on them. This is why he is called the weeping prophet. He pleads with rebellious people on the brink of ruin, urging them to return to God with everything they have.

Despite their stubbornness, Jeremiah does more than lament. He dares to hope. He envisions a future shaped by mercy, a new covenant where God's guidance comes from within rather than from external rules you have to constantly remember and follow. In this vision, doing what's right becomes as natural as breathing because it flows from who you are at your core, not from fear of punishment. His prophecy is heavy with sorrow yet layered with the kind of hope that only comes through fire.

Though the book of Jeremiah is long and its tone often weighty, it is unforgettable. Jeremiah's raw honesty about human failure and divine faithfulness speaks across centuries. He is relentless, standing firm in rejection, weeping yet unwavering. His life becomes a living parable of the cost of carrying God's truth. It is a path marked by suffering and solitude but also by the profound intimacy of being seen, known, and upheld by God in the darkest moments.

Must-Read Chapters

- [ ] Jeremiah 1 - God appoints Jeremiah as a prophet to the nations, promising His presence despite Jeremiah's youth.
- [ ] Jeremiah 7 - Jeremiah warns that empty religious rituals cannot save Judah from judgment.
- [ ] **Jeremiah 18 - God's sovereign power to shape and reshape nations and lives.**
- [ ] Jeremiah 23 - A promise of righteous shepherds and the coming King who will bring justice.
- [ ] Jeremiah 28 - Jeremiah confronts a false prophet, affirming God's truth even in the face of opposition.
- [ ] Jeremiah 29 - God's promise of hope and a future to His people in exile, urging them to seek the welfare of their city.
- [ ] **Jeremiah 31 - A vision of a new covenant where God's law will be written on the hearts of His people.**

LAMENTATIONS

Lamentations reads like the most heartbreaking song you've ever heard, raw and beautiful in its grief. Written after Jerusalem's destruction, it doesn't shy away from the devastation and pain of exile. Lamentations captures what it sounds like when your heart breaks for people who couldn't or wouldn't hear the warnings, and let's be honest, we're usually the ones not listening.

But this isn't just mourning for mourning's sake. Scholars recognize it as "resistance literature" that refuses to let despair win, keeping faith alive even when everything seems lost. Right in the middle of the deepest darkness, the writer makes this stunning declaration: "The steadfast love of the Lord never ceases, his mercies never come to an end" (Lamentations 3:22).

Must-Read Chapters

Lamentations 1 - Sorrowful reflection on the desolation and suffering of Jerusalem after its destruction.

Lamentations 3 - Amid Jerusalem's destruction, the writer affirms God's steadfast love and mercy.

EZEKIEL

Ezekiel feels like stepping into a vivid, surreal dream that stays with you long after you wake up. His visions take us on a mind-bending journey, from God's withdrawal from the Temple, leaving Israel vulnerable to judgment, to a valley of dry bones coming to life in a stunning display of restoration. Ezekiel's strange symbolic actions underscore the urgency of his message, pulling us deeper into the meaning behind his visions.

At its core, Ezekiel reveals a God who disciplines but ultimately restores, promising to dwell with His people again one day. It is a challenging yet deeply rewarding book, full of moments that will leave you in awe of God's justice, creativity, and mercy.

Must-Read Chapters

- [ ] Ezekiel 1 - Ezekiel is called through a stunning vision of God's glory, filled with mysterious creatures and a fiery chariot.
- [ ] Ezekiel 10 - The glory of God departs, leaving the Temple in silence and sorrow.
- [ ] Ezekiel 18 - God declares that each person is accountable for their own sin, shifting away from collective blame.
- [ ] **Ezekiel 37 - A dramatic vision of God bringing life to a valley of dry bones, symbolizing Israel's restoration.**
- [ ] Ezekiel 47 - A vision of a life-giving river flowing from God's Temple, bringing renewal to the land and its people.

DANIEL

It never ceases to amaze me how Daniel's story is shared in Sunday school. His world was a waking nightmare, his faith tested in a den of monsters. Far from a bedtime story, it's pure horror. Yet, we tell it to children, as the author masterfully conceals dark truths beneath sweet, simple verses.

The first half features dramatic, almost surreal events, like Daniel's friends walking unharmed through a fiery furnace and Daniel surviving a night in a den of lions. These gripping accounts inspire courage and trust in God's power, but they are anything but tame. The vivid imagery and supernatural elements underscore the profound faith required to stand firm in the face of adversity, making these stories both compelling and challenging.

The second half of Daniel takes a sharp turn into apocalyptic literature. This genre is known for vivid, symbolic visions that reveal divine secrets about the end of time. It often emerged during times of crisis and persecution, offering hope to people facing overwhelming odds. In Daniel, the visions are filled with strange imagery and cosmic battles. They present a sweeping view of history and show God's ultimate victory over evil. These intense, otherworldly passages remind us that even when everything seems to be falling apart, God is still in control. More than anything, Daniel teaches that we can remain faithful in a broken empire without letting it break us.

Must-Read Chapters

- Daniel 1 - Daniel and his friends remain faithful to God in Babylon, refusing the king's food.
- Daniel 3 - Shadrach, Meshach, and Abednego are saved after refusing to worship Nebuchadnezzar's golden statue.
- Daniel 5 - A hand writes on the wall, and a king learns the weight of his arrogance.
- Daniel 6 - Daniel's faithfulness in prayer leads to his deliverance from a den of lions.
- Daniel 7 - A prophetic vision of kingdoms rising and falling, culminating in the rule of the Son of Man.

HOSEA

Hosea is both heartbreaking and hopeful, raw and honest. Through the prophet's troubled marriage, we see a powerful metaphor for the complex relationship between God and humanity. The story uses the intimate language of marriage and betrayal to explore themes of faithfulness, disappointment, and unconditional commitment. The prophetic poetry cuts deep, blending pain, anger, and heartbreak with a fierce promise of renewal.

Hosea's story shatters the idea of a neat, transactional faith, which views the relationship with God as a series of exchanges where good deeds are rewarded and sins are punished. It reveals a divine love that defies simple categories of justice or punishment. This is a messy, paradoxical love, filled with anguish and hope. It's the kind of love that pursues relentlessly, forgives scandalously, and refuses to give up. Hosea reminds us that God's love is not distant or detached but deeply connected to our struggles and our potential for renewal.

The book challenges us to think beyond the metaphor's surface and grapple with what it means to be in relationship with the divine, even when that relationship involves disappointment, repair, and redemption.

Must-Read Chapters

- [ ] Hosea 1 - God tells Hosea to marry an unfaithful woman, showing how Israel has turned away from God.
- [ ] Hosea 3 - Hosea is instructed by God to seek her out and purchase her back from slavery, symbolizing redemption.

- Hosea 11 - A tender depiction of God as a loving parent grieving over Israel's rebellion.

- Hosea 14 - God's forgiveness for repentant Israel, inviting them to abundant restoration and blessings.

JOEL

Joel's prophecy hits you immediately with its vivid, urgent tone, opening with a catastrophic locust swarm that devastates everything in its path. But just when the destruction feels overwhelming, Joel pivots to an extraordinary promise: that God's Spirit will be poured out on everyone, regardless of age, gender, or social status, ushering in something completely new.

The book starts by describing a rural disaster so severe that no one alive had ever seen anything like it. This crisis and the unexpected recovery that followed become the foundation for a story Joel insists must be told to children and grandchildren for generations to come. His call for people to change course is direct and uncompromising, yet it comes with genuine hope for forgiveness and restoration.

Though Joel is one of the shorter prophetic books, it packs a punch. It serves as both a stark warning about consequences and a compelling invitation to trust that mercy and renewal are possible, even after the worst devastation.

Read the Entire Book

- Joel 1 - The locusts devour everything, a vivid sign of God's judgment and the urgency of turning back to Him.

- [ ] Joel 2 - A coming day of darkness and destruction calls for repentance, but God's mercy offers hope and renewal.
- [ ] Joel 3 - God holds the nations accountable, restores His people, and establishes a future where justice reigns.

AMOS

If your faith ignores the poor, God wants nothing to do with it. At least according to Amos. Amos doesn't sugarcoat a thing. He speaks into a society drowning in wealth and comfort while the vulnerable are crushed and forgotten. He doesn't care about polished prayers or loud worship if people are still being exploited. God doesn't either.

"Let justice roll down like a river." This verse is demanding. Amos is done with religion that looks good on the outside but rots at the core. He calls out every excuse, every system built to protect the powerful and silence the weak. His words cut through the noise.

This isn't about ancient Israel alone. It's about us. Our systems. Our silence. Our faith that praises at worship, but turns away from the hungry, the unhoused, the oppressed. Amos is short, but it hits hard. It's a warning. God won't be part of worship that forgets justice. And if our faith doesn't care for the most vulnerable, it's not faith at all.

Read the Entire Book

- [ ] Amos 1 - God's judgment isn't arbitrary, it starts with the nations and moves inward, exposing Israel's complicity.
- [ ] Amos 2 - The oppression of the vulnerable and the betrayal of the covenant bring God's fierce anger.

- [ ] Amos 3 - Privilege demands accountability, Israel's relationship with God makes their injustice intolerable.
- [ ] Amos 4 - Empty rituals mean nothing when justice is ignored; God's warnings are acts of grace.
- [ ] Amos 5 - True worship is justice lived out; anything less insults God's holiness.
- [ ] Amos 6 - The complacency of the elite masks a nation on the brink of collapse.
- [ ] Amos 7 - The plumb line of justice reveals a nation out of alignment with God's purposes.
- [ ] Amos 8 - A harvest of corruption leads to a famine, not of food, but of God's word.
- [ ] Amos 9 - Judgment refines, but restoration reveals God's ultimate intention to rebuild and heal.

OBADIAH

Obadiah is short, but it doesn't hold back. It calls out pride, betrayal, and the kind of justice that sees everything, even what we try to hide. Edom, Judah's neighbor, didn't lift a finger. They stood back and watched while everything burned. This book rips apart the lie that staying neutral makes you innocent. It names the moral failure of standing by. Justice isn't a vague ideal. It shows up in real moments, in real choices. Edom's sin was doing nothing and feeling proud about it.

Obadiah won't let us off the hook. It demands that we see ourselves clearly. But it doesn't stop at judgment. There's still a thread of hope. God's justice is real, and it will bring restoration. The arrogant will fall. The wounded won't be forgotten. Just don't confuse silence with goodness.

Read the Entire Book

- [ ] Obadiah - God condemns Edom for its pride and betrayal of Israel, promising justice for His people.

JONAH

Jonah's story is predictable in the worst way and surprising in the most honest way, because it's exactly how we act when God asks us to do something we'd rather not. Jonah is called by God to warn the city of Nineveh about its impending doom. However, instead of obeying, Jonah tries to run away and ends up in the belly of a great fish. This dramatic turn of events forces Jonah to confront his fears and eventually fulfill his mission.

When Jonah finally warns the people of Nineveh, they surprisingly repent, and God shows them mercy. And Jonah becomes furious because he wanted these people destroyed. He's genuinely upset that his enemies get forgiveness instead of punishment. Jonah forces us to confront the truth that we aren't the center of the universe, and God's love for the people we can't stand exists whether we approve of it or not. Thus, Jonah's story challenges us to see the depth of God's compassion, even for those we might not think deserve it.

Read the Entire Book

- [ ] Jonah 1 - Jonah runs from God's call to preach to Nineveh, only to be caught in a storm and swallowed by a great fish.
- [ ] Jonah 2 - From the belly of the fish, Jonah prays a prayer of repentance and thanksgiving for God's deliverance.

- Jonah 3 - Jonah reluctantly preaches in Nineveh, and the city repents, prompting God to relent from sending destruction.

- Jonah 4 - Jonah is angry at God's mercy toward Nineveh, revealing the tension between human and divine wills.

MICAH

Micah's words cut deep; he exposes corruption and injustice among Israel's leaders, calling them to account for exploiting the vulnerable. His prophetic voice resonates with a demand for moral integrity and social responsibility. Yet his message also offers hope: a ruler from Bethlehem will lead with justice and peace, embodying God's intentions for the world. At its heart, Micah distills faith into three essential acts: "Do justice, love mercy, and walk humbly with your God" (Micah 6:8). Balancing judgment with restoration, Micah calls for a life aligned with God's covenant and a vision of hope beyond failure.

Read the Entire Book

- Micah 1 - The land shows the consequences of God's judgment on people who have been disloyal to Him.

- Micah 2 - Injustice has personal and communal consequences, but God promises a remnant will rise.

- Micah 3 - Leaders who exploit the vulnerable turn their backs on God's justice and invite disaster.

- Micah 4 - God's reign will transform the world, replacing war with peace and arrogance with humility.

- Micah 5 - A ruler from humble beginnings embodies God's justice and brings peace to the earth.

- [ ] **Micah 6** - God's requirements are simple yet profound: act justly, love mercy, and walk humbly with Him.
- [ ] Micah 7 - Even in the depths of failure, hope remains because God's mercy is unwavering.

NAHUM

Nahum is Israel's fierce response to the Assyrian Empire's violent rule, specifically the fall of Nineveh, once repentant in Jonah's day but now returned to its old ways of conquest and cruelty. The book reads less like divine fury and more like theological protest: a cry from the oppressed that empires don't get to win forever. When Nineveh finally collapsed, Israel saw it not just as history but as proof that injustice has limits and that faith in God's justice wasn't in vain.

Read the Entire Book

- [ ] Nahum 1 - God's character as both avenger and protector is revealed as He promises judgment on Nineveh.
- [ ] Nahum 2 - A vivid description of Nineveh's destruction, showcasing God's power over even the greatest empires.
- [ ] Nahum 3 - Nineveh's cruelty and pride are condemned, and its downfall is celebrated as a testament to God's justice.

HABAKKUK

Habakkuk's approach was somewhat different. He is known for questioning God's justice and grappling with the existence of evil and suffering in the world. Habakkuk's wrestling with doubt and his ultimate affirmation of faith in God, despite unanswered questions, provide a powerful model for navigating life's challenges and maintaining trust in God's goodness, even in the face of uncertainty. Habakkuk's brief but powerful message speaks directly to the human struggle to believe in God's goodness amid our sufferings.

Read the Entire Book

- Habakkuk 1 - The prophet questions why God allows injustice and violence to go unpunished.
- Habakkuk 2 - God promises that the wicked will be judged, and the righteous will live by faith.
- Habakkuk 3 - Habakkuk responds in worship and trust, declaring his faith in God's sovereignty even amid suffering.

ZEPHANIAH

Zephaniah captures Israel's struggle with their own failures and the chaos around them through the vivid imagery of the "Day of the Lord." This isn't so much a prediction of divine punishment as it is an attempt to make sense of a world falling apart, including their own community's battles with justice and faithfulness. The prophet's intense language about judgment reflects the real consequences Israel saw when nations, including their own, turned away from the values that held people together. Still, Zephaniah doesn't leave it there.

Behind the hardest parts of the book is a clear hope that things can be made right again, that broken communities can be healed, and that the world moves toward restoration, not ruin. Zephaniah is honest about consequences, but he doesn't believe they have the final say. This isn't about a furious God swinging between anger and mercy. It's about

Israel's deep belief that the world is built on both justice and love. People aren't called to change out of fear, but because they catch a glimpse of how good life could be when it's lived the right way.

> ### Read the Entire Book
>
> - [ ] Zephaniah 1 - A warning of coming judgment against Judah and the nations for their idolatry and rebellion.
> - [ ] Zephaniah 2 - The prophet urges the humble to seek God while foretelling judgment on neighboring nations.
> - [ ] Zephaniah 3 - After judgment, God vows to restore a faithful remnant and rejoice over them with love.

HAGGAI

In the book of Haggai, we hear a clear and urgent message to people who have returned from exile but remain spiritually unsettled. The prophet speaks in a moment when the Temple lies in ruins, and the people are more focused on rebuilding their own homes than on restoring a place for God's presence. Haggai challenges them to shift their priorities, not just to build walls and a roof, but to recenter their lives around God. His message is a wake-up call. The real blessing, lasting peace, and true prosperity come when God is at the center. Rebuilding the temple is not just about a physical structure; it is about restoring a relationship. It is a reminder that God's faithfulness invites a faithful response from His people, offering a chance to start fresh, grounded in purpose and hope.

Read the Entire Book

- Haggai 1 - Haggai challenges the people to prioritize rebuilding the Temple instead of their own comforts.

- Haggai 2 - God encourages the people, promising the Temple's future glory and blessing for their faithfulness.

ZECHARIAH

Zechariah's visions are strange and striking, filled with symbols that point to God's ultimate plans for His people. He encourages weary people to rebuild Jerusalem and the Temple, reminding them that God's Spirit, not human strength, will complete the work. Looking forward, Zechariah foresees a humble King who will bring peace and unity, offering hope beyond their immediate struggles. Complex and layered, Zechariah speaks to the long arc of God's redemptive purposes, inviting careful reflection on His far-reaching plans, not confined to the immediate restoration of Israel but unfolds on a cosmic scale, where judgment and renewal converge to establish a kingdom marked by justice, holiness, and the universal reign of God.

Must-Read Chapters

- Zechariah 1 - God's call to return is an invitation to participate in His renewing work.

- Zechariah 3 - God's restoration is transformative, cleansing the unworthy for a new beginning.

- Zechariah 4 - The rebuilding of a broken world depends on God's Spirit, not human strength.

- [ ] Zechariah 8 - God's promises bring hope, a future marked by truth, joy, and flourishing.
- [ ] Zechariah 9 - A humble king comes, reshaping power and bringing peace to the nations.
- [ ] Zechariah 14 - A grand vision of the Day of the Lord, where God reigns as King and brings justice and restoration to all creation.

MALACHI

Malachi addresses people who have grown complacent, their worship reduced to half-hearted offerings and hollow rituals. He challenges their disobedience and calls them to renewed faithfulness, reminding them of God's unchanging love. The book ends with a promise that a messenger will come to prepare the way for the Lord, bridging the silence between the Old and New Testaments. Malachi's words are sharp and direct, but they leave us hopeful: God is coming to renew and restore.

Read the Entire Book

- [ ] Malachi 1 - God declares His love for Israel but confronts their dishonor through empty worship and corrupt sacrifices.
- [ ] Malachi 2 - God condemns unfaithfulness in marriage and warns the priests for leading the people astray.
- [ ] Malachi 3 - A prophecy of a messenger who will prepare the way for the Lord, calling for repentance.
- [ ] Malachi 4 - God promises ultimate justice, where the wicked will be destroyed, and the faithful will rise in healing and joy.

The Gospels
The Life and Ministry of Jesus

The Gospels present the central figure of Scripture, Jesus Christ, in a vibrant and multifaceted way. Each Gospel offers a distinct lens through which to encounter His life, teachings, death, and resurrection, portraying Him as the fulfillment of God's promises and the embodiment of divine love. Their narratives draw readers into the reality of God's kingdom breaking into the world, challenging them to live in its light. Together, the Gospels are a powerful and transformative testimony to God's work in Christ.

The Synoptic Gospels (Matthew, Mark, and Luke) share a significant amount of their material and structure, providing a cohesive narrative of Jesus' ministry while emphasizing distinct theological themes. John, on the other hand, offers a profoundly unique perspective, focusing on the cosmic significance of Jesus as the eternal Word of God and diving deeply into His identity and relationship with the Father.

It's important to resist the temptation to view the Gospels as simply individual authors recording their personal impressions of Jesus. Rather, each Gospel emerges from and speaks to distinct early Christian communities, each wrestling with their own questions, challenges, and contexts. Matthew's Gospel reflects a community deeply rooted in Jewish tradition, grappling with how Jesus fulfills Hebrew Scripture while opening God's covenant to all peoples. Mark's community appears to be facing persecution and needs to understand a suffering Messiah. Luke writes for a more diverse, Gentile audience seeking to understand their place in God's expanding story. John's community seems to be navigating questions about Jesus' divine nature and their relationship to both Jewish synagogues and the broader world, requiring a Gospel that emphasizes the cosmic, eternal dimensions of Christ's identity. These aren't competing versions of the truth, but rather complementary witnesses to the inexhaustible richness of who Jesus is and what His life means for the world.

MATTHEW

The Gospel of Matthew is one of the most beloved books in the Bible, renowned for its rich theology and compelling storytelling. Among the four Gospels, Matthew provides a comprehensive and thoughtful portrayal of Jesus' life, ministry, and teachings. From the very beginning, Jesus is portrayed as the long-awaited King, the one who fulfills God's promises. His genealogy connects Him to Abraham and David, and His Sermon on the Mount reveals a new way of life rooted in the heart of God's law. Throughout the Gospel, Jesus' parables reveal profound truths about God's kingdom, while His miracles and healings demonstrate both His compassion and His authority, particularly toward those often marginalized by religious, social, or political systems.

Matthew invites people to live out the values of God's kingdom in real life, encouraging Jesus' followers to challenge the status quo and form communities marked by humility, service, and justice. Deeply rooted in Jewish tradition, Matthew presents Jesus as the authentic interpreter of the law and the fulfillment of God's covenant with Israel. At the same time, the Gospel expands the vision of who belongs in God's family, welcoming Gentiles and inviting radical reconciliation.

Matthew doesn't avoid conflict either. It tells of Jesus' bold ministry to the marginalized and His challenges to established religious norms. The Gospel promotes ethical leadership, critiques misplaced loyalties to power, and highlights the broad reach of God's love that transcends every barrier. These themes remain relevant today, addressing fundamental questions and tensions that Christians encounter in modern life. Matthew invites believers into a faith that holds onto tradition while also engaging the present moment with courage and compassion.

Matthew Chapter by Chapter

Matthew 1 - Connects Jesus to Israel's story through Abraham and David, culminating in His miraculous birth as Emmanuel, God with us. Unique to Matthew is the detailed genealogy and the focus on Joseph's perspective.

Matthew 2 - Foreigners honor Jesus as King, while Herod's rage and the family's escape to Egypt reveal the danger and divine protection surrounding His birth. Unique to Matthew is the visit of the Magi, the flight to Egypt, and the fulfillment of prophecies through Herod's actions and return to Nazareth.

Matthew 3 - John baptizes Jesus, marking the beginning of His public ministry and God's declaration, "This is my beloved Son." Unique to Matthew is John the Baptist questioning why he should baptize Jesus.

Matthew 4 - Jesus resists Satan's temptations in the wilderness and begins proclaiming the kingdom of God.

Matthew 5 - Jesus redefines righteousness, calling His followers to live as salt and light and to love even their enemies. Unique to Matthew is Jesus' emphasis on fulfilling the law and His radical reinterpretation of righteousness.

Matthew 6 - Jesus teaches authentic devotion through prayer, fasting, and trust in God's provision. Unique to Matthew is Jesus' detailed teaching on practicing love, prayer, and fasting in secret.

Matthew 7 - Jesus calls for humility, discernment, and obedience, warning about the narrow path. Unique to Matthew is His puzzling instruction not to throw pearls before pigs, a saying that invites reflection.

Matthew 8 - Jesus heals the sick, calms a storm, and casts out demons, demonstrating His authority over sickness, nature, and the spiritual realm.

Matthew 9 - Jesus forgives sins, heals the hurting, calls Matthew, and challenges religious leaders with His radical mission of mercy.

Matthew 10 - Jesus sends His disciples with authority, instructing them to preach, heal, and face opposition with courage. Unique to Matthew is the focus on the disciples' initial mission to Israel.

Matthew 11 - Jesus answers John's doubts, condemns unrepentant cities, and invites the weary to find rest in Him. Unique to Matthew is Jesus' personal invitation to the weary.

Matthew 12 - Jesus confronts the Pharisees' legalism, performs miracles, and declares that true family does God's will.

Matthew 13 - Jesus uses parables to reveal the nature of the kingdom of God, hidden yet unstoppable. Unique to Matthew are parables like the Weeds, Hidden Treasure, and Pearl.

Matthew 14 - Jesus feeds the five thousand, walks on water, and reveals His power to His disciples in moments of fear. Unique to Matthew is Peter stepping out in faith to walk on water.

Matthew 15 - Jesus teaches that defilement comes from the heart, not rituals, and performs miracles for both Jews and Gentiles.

Matthew 16 - Peter declares Jesus as the Messiah, and Jesus foretells His death and resurrection. Unique to Matthew is Jesus' declaration of Peter as the rock.

Matthew 17 - Jesus reveals His glory and teaches on faith, humility, and His death. Unique to Matthew is the coin-from-a-fish temple tax miracle.

Matthew 18 - Jesus emphasizes humility, reconciliation, and forgiveness. Unique to Matthew are His conflict-resolution steps and the Unforgiving Servant parable.

Matthew 19 - Jesus teaches about marriage, blesses children, and challenges a rich man to give up everything to follow Him.

Matthew 20 - Through parables and prophecy, Jesus teaches about God's upside-down kingdom. Unique to Matthew is the parable of the workers in the vineyard.

Matthew 21 - Jesus enters Jerusalem as King, cleanses the Temple, and confronts religious leaders with His authority. Unique to Matthew is the parable of the two sons.

Matthew 22 - Jesus silences His challengers with teachings about love for God and neighbor as the heart of the law.

Matthew 23 - Jesus delivers scathing rebukes to religious leaders for their hypocrisy and pride. Unique to Matthew is the extensive list of woes against the Pharisees.

Matthew 24 - Jesus prophesies the destruction of the Temple and warns about His return, urging vigilance and faithfulness.

Matthew 25 - Jesus calls His followers to be prepared for His return through faithful stewardship and acts of love. Unique to Matthew are the parables of the Ten Bridesmaids and the Last Judgment.

Matthew 26 - Jesus shares the Last Supper, prays in Gethsemane, and is betrayed, arrested, and denied by Peter.

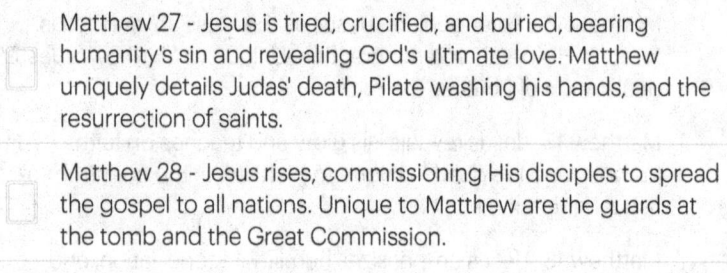

- Matthew 27 - Jesus is tried, crucified, and buried, bearing humanity's sin and revealing God's ultimate love. Matthew uniquely details Judas' death, Pilate washing his hands, and the resurrection of saints.

- Matthew 28 - Jesus rises, commissioning His disciples to spread the gospel to all nations. Unique to Matthew are the guards at the tomb and the Great Commission.

MARK

Mark's Gospel is urgent and action-packed, pulling readers into the fast-paced rhythm of Jesus' ministry. But beyond the miracles and confrontations lies a deeply subversive mission that challenges systems of power and calls for radical transformation. Mark is often underrated for its brevity and simplicity. Still, it is arguably the most radical of the Gospels, carrying a powerful undercurrent of resistance against empire and oppressive authority.

Mark gives us four characters: Jesus, the disciples, the religious and political establishment that wants him dead, and the crowds who show up for the show but don't really commit to anything. Since we can't be Jesus and we damn sure don't want to be the ones trying to kill him, that leaves us with a choice: stay in the crowd where it's safe and comfortable, or step up and follow him into the messy, costly work of actually changing the world.

This path is not easy. It is marked by suffering, resistance, and the ongoing work of transformation. It reflects God's justice and mercy in tangible ways. Jesus' actions, such as healings, exorcisms, and shared meals, are not only spiritual acts but also bold challenges to the political, religious, and economic systems that exploit and exclude.

Mark's Gospel isn't about getting people to have a personal relationship with Jesus and call it a day. It's about entire communities flipping the script on how the world works and building something different based on God's kingdom values. It's calling for organized resistance to systems that crush people and demanding we create alternative ways of living that actually prioritize compassion, fairness, and truth. This is prophetic imagination at work, grounded in the real struggles of people getting stepped on by the powerful and fueled by the audacious hope that God's love can actually remake this broken world.

Mark Chapter by Chapter

Mark 1 - Jesus bursts onto the scene, announcing the kingdom of God, calling disciples, and healing with unmatched authority. Unique to Mark is the repeated emphasis on Jesus withdrawing to pray.

Mark 2 - Jesus forgives sins, eats with sinners, and challenges religious traditions, showing that God's grace isn't bound by human rules.

Mark 3 - As tensions rise, Jesus identifies those who do God's will as His true family. Mark uniquely notes that even Jesus' own family questioned His sanity. Jesus also speaks of binding the strong man, symbolizing the defeat of oppression.

Mark 4 - Jesus uses parables to reveal a kingdom that grows quietly. Unique to Mark is Jesus' explanation of parables as both revealing and concealing the kingdom's mysteries, along with the Parable of the Growing Seed.

Mark 5 - Jesus restores a demon-possessed man, heals a woman with unrelenting faith, and raises a dead girl, proving nothing is beyond His power.

What Also Matters?

- [ ] Mark 6 - Jesus faces rejection in His hometown, sends out the twelve, and feeds thousands with just five loaves and two fish. Unique to Mark is Jesus being identified as a craftsman.

- [ ] Mark 7 - Jesus challenges tradition, teaching that what comes from the heart truly matters. Unique to Mark is the personal account of Him healing a man's deafness and speech.

- [ ] **Mark 8 - Peter confesses Jesus as the Christ, but Jesus shocks everyone by revealing the path to the kingdom is through suffering. Unique to Mark is the two-stage healing of a blind man in Bethsaida.**

- [ ] Mark 9 - Jesus is transfigured before His disciples, but then teaches that greatness in God's kingdom is found in serving others. Unique to Mark is the father's raw plea, "I believe; help my unbelief," and Jesus' teaching on salt and fire.

- [ ] Mark 10 - Jesus welcomes children, confronts the rich, and declares that true greatness comes through humility and sacrifice.

- [ ] Mark 11 - Jesus enters Jerusalem on a donkey, cleanses the Temple, and challenges the leaders who have corrupted worship.

- [ ] Mark 12 - Jesus silences His critics and declares love for God and neighbor as the heart of the law.

- [ ] Mark 13 - Jesus speaks of trials and tribulations, urging His followers to stay alert and faithful as they await His return.

- [ ] Mark 14 - Jesus shares the Last Supper, prays in Gethsemane, and is betrayed, arrested, and denied by Peter. Unique to Mark is the man fleeing naked during Jesus' arrest.

- [ ] **Mark 15 - Jesus is condemned, mocked, and crucified, but even in death, His identity as the Son of God shines through.**

> Mark 16 - The tomb is empty, and the women are told to share the news that Jesus has risen, leaving us with a call to go and tell the story. Unique to Mark are the varying endings, highlighting early efforts to address its abrupt conclusion.

LUKE

Whereas Mark is concerned with the oppressor, Luke is concerned with the oppressed. Luke's Gospel portrays Jesus as the one who restores the broken, reconciles the estranged, and reaches across every cultural, social, and economic barrier. With profound concern for the marginalized, including women, the poor, sinners, and outsiders, Luke paints a portrait of a God whose mercy knows no boundaries and whose grace reaches the furthest corners of human experience.

At the heart of Luke's narrative is an invitation to step into the unfolding kingdom of God, where justice is lifted, hospitality is extended, and hope is restored. It assures us that God's broader story is still being written, even in the midst of a fractured world. With literary beauty and theological depth, Luke draws us into the life of a Savior who not only proclaims good news but also embodies it. In doing so, he calls us to live as agents of that good news, participants in God's inclusive, redemptive mission.

The Gospel reveals a persistent theme of "the great reversal," where the last are made first and the lowly are lifted. This theme serves both as a word of hope for the oppressed and as a challenge to the powerful. For Luke, salvation is never merely personal; it is also social, political, and economic. It represents liberation not only from sin but also from everything that prevents people from becoming what God created them to be: poverty, violence, exclusion, and fear.

Luke Chapter by Chapter

Luke 1 - God's plan begins as the angel Gabriel announces the miraculous births of John the Baptist and Jesus. Unique to Luke is the detailed focus on Elizabeth and Mary's faith.

Luke 2 - Jesus enters the world in humility, heralded by angels and worshiped by shepherds, fulfilling God's promise of peace and joy for all people. Unique to Luke is the story of shepherds and Jesus' presentation in the Temple

Luke 3 - John the Baptist calls for repentance, and Jesus begins His public ministry with baptism and a genealogy that ties Him to Adam.

Luke 4 - Jesus resists Satan's temptations in the wilderness and proclaims His mission to bring good news to the poor, but His hometown rejects Him. Unique to Luke is Jesus reading from Isaiah in the synagogue.

Luke 5 - Jesus calls ordinary fishermen, forgives sins, and begins healing the sick, showing that He came to bring transformation to broken lives.

Luke 6 - Jesus teaches radical love, forgiveness, and humility in the Sermon on the Plain, flipping societal values on their head. Unique to Luke is the "woes" paired with blessings.

Luke 7 - Jesus heals the centurion's servant, raises a widow's son, and forgives a sinful woman who anoints His feet, demonstrating compassion and authority. Unique to Luke are the widow's son's resurrection and the anointing woman.

Luke 8 - Jesus calms storms, drives out demons, heals the sick, and raises the dead, revealing His authority over every realm. Unique to Luke is the mention of Mary Magdalene, Joanna, and Susanna.

Luke 9 - Jesus sends out His disciples, feeds the five thousand, and prepares His followers for His coming death and resurrection. Unique to Luke is Jesus' rebuke of His disciples.

Luke 10 - Jesus sends out seventy disciples to proclaim the kingdom, and through the Parable of the Good Samaritan, teaches radical love for neighbor. Unique to Luke is the mission of the seventy and the story of Mary and Martha.

Luke 11 - Jesus teaches His disciples to pray and persist in asking, seeking, and knocking, promising that God's response is generous and good. Unique to Luke is the parable of the persistent friend.

Luke 12 - Jesus warns about greed and calls His followers to trust God for provision, challenging them to live ready for His return. Unique to Luke is the Parable of the Rich Fool.

Luke 13 - Jesus calls for repentance, heals a woman on the Sabbath, and shares the Parable of the Fig Tree, urging people to bear fruit before it's too late. Unique to Luke is the healing of the woman on the Sabbath.

Luke 14 - Through parables and teachings, Jesus emphasizes humility, hospitality, and the costly but worthy call of following Him. Unique to Luke is the parable on choosing the lowest seat at the banquet and counting the cost of discipleship.

Luke 15 - Jesus shares parables of the lost sheep, lost coin, and the prodigal son, celebrating God's relentless pursuit of the lost. Unique to Luke are the Parables of the Lost Coin and the Prodigal Son.

Luke 16 - Jesus warns of the dangers of greed. Unique to Luke is the story of the rich man and Lazarus.

Luke 17 - Jesus heals ten lepers, but only one, a Samaritan, returns to give thanks, highlighting faith and gratitude. Unique to Luke is the story of the grateful leper.

Luke 18 - Through parables of the Persistent Widow and the Tax Collector, Jesus teaches the importance of persistence and humility in prayer. Unique to Luke is the Parable of the Persistent Widow and the Tax Collector.

- [ ] Luke 19 - Jesus transforms the life of Zacchaeus, weeps over Jerusalem, and enters the city as King, knowing the cost of what's ahead. Unique to Luke is the story of Zacchaeus.
- [ ] Luke 20 - Jesus answers challenges to His authority with wisdom, exposing the hypocrisy of religious leaders.
- [ ] Luke 21 - Jesus warns of trials and persecution before His return, urging His followers to stay vigilant and faithful.
- [ ] Luke 22 - Jesus celebrates the Last Supper, prays in Gethsemane, and is betrayed and denied, preparing to face the cross. Unique to Luke is Jesus forewarning Peter.
- [ ] Luke 23 - Jesus is mocked, declared innocent, and crucified, but even on the cross, He forgives and promises paradise to a repentant thief. Unique to Luke is Jesus' forgiveness of His executioners and assurance to the thief.
- [ ] Luke 24 - Jesus rises, appears to His disciples, walks with followers to Emmaus, and ascends to heaven, promising the Spirit to continue His mission. Unique to Luke is the Emmaus Road story and Jesus' ascension.

JOHN

John's Gospel is both profound and deeply theological, offering a unique and reflective portrait of Jesus as the Word of God, the eternal Logos through whom all things were created, now bringing light and life into the world. Through signs and miracles that reveal His true identity, and the powerful "I am" declarations, John presents Jesus as the eternal Son of God who makes the Father known and offers salvation to all who believe in Him. This revelation is not merely informative but transformative, inviting readers into a personal encounter with the divine.

John's Gospel throws us into a cosmic battle where the stakes couldn't be higher. This isn't just a nice story about a religious teacher, but about God breaking into a world that's been taken hostage by lies, oppression, and death. We're caught right in the middle of this struggle between light and darkness, truth and deception, life and death, and there's no sitting on the sidelines. The Gospel forces us to pick a side and shows us where we really stand when push comes to shove. For John's community, following Jesus wasn't about agreeing with certain ideas but about being pulled into God's mission to free the world from whatever forces keep it in chains. It's a call not just to think differently but to live differently, to stay connected to Christ the way he stays connected to God, and to become part of the solution in a world that desperately needs it.

At the same time, the Gospel speaks to the real challenges the early Christian community was facing, especially as they dealt with rejection and possible removal from the synagogue. It helps them understand who they are and how to stay strong in their faith. The Gospel does not just talk about who Jesus is in a spiritual or divine sense. It also shows how knowing Jesus can change a person's life and shape the way the whole community lives together.

John Chapter by Chapter

John 1 - John opens with the cosmic introduction of Jesus as the Word, present at creation, now dwelling among us. Unique to John is the divine Logos framing of Jesus' identity.

John 2 - At a wedding, Jesus performs His first miracle, turning water into wine. Unique to John is the wedding at Cana.

What Also Matters?

- **John 3** - In a quiet nighttime conversation, Jesus explains salvation. Unique to John is the story of Nicodemus.

- John 4 - Jesus crosses cultural boundaries to offer living water to a Samaritan woman at a well. Unique to John is the encounter with the Samaritan woman.

- John 5 - Jesus heals a man on the Sabbath and asserts His authority to judge and give life. John uniquely highlights Jesus' assertion of his equality with God.

- John 6 - Jesus feeds the five thousand, walks on water, and declares Himself the Bread of Life. Unique to John is the deep theological discourse following the feeding.

- John 7 - Amid growing opposition, Jesus promises rivers of living water to those who believe in Him, pointing to the coming Spirit. Unique to John is the unique imagery of living water tied to the Holy Spirit.

- John 8 - Jesus forgives an adulterous woman and declares, "I am the light of the world," confronting the Pharisees with His truth and authority.

- John 9 - Jesus restores sight to a man born blind, challenging the Pharisees and revealing Himself as the light that overcomes spiritual blindness. Unique to John is the detailed account of the blind man's healing.

- John 10 - Jesus calls Himself the Good Shepherd who lays down His life for His sheep. Unique to John is the Good Shepherd discourse.

- **John 11 - Jesus raises Lazarus from the dead, foreshadowing His own resurrection and proclaiming Himself the resurrection and the life. Unique to John is the Lazarus story.**

- John 12 - As Jesus enters Jerusalem, He predicts His death and speaks of being lifted up to draw all people to Himself.

John 13 - At the Last Supper, Jesus washes His disciples' feet, modeling servant leadership and giving a new commandment to love one another. Unique to John is the foot washing.

John 14 - Jesus comforts His disciples with the promise of the Father's house, the coming of the Spirit, and His role as the only way to the Father. Unique to John is the discourse.

John 15 - Jesus describes Himself as the true vine, calling His disciples to abide in Him and bear fruit through love and obedience. Unique to John is the vine metaphor.

John 16 - Jesus prepares His disciples for His departure, promising the Spirit of truth who will guide and empower them in His absence. Unique to John is the detailed teaching on the Holy Spirit as Comforter and Advocate.

John 17 - Jesus prays for Himself, His disciples, and all believers, asking for unity and that they may share in His glory. Unique to John is the High Priestly Prayer.

John 18 - Jesus is betrayed, arrested, and stands trial before Pilate, declaring that His kingdom is not of this world. Unique to John is the extended dialogue with Pilate.

John 19 - Jesus is crucified and declares, "It is finished," fulfilling His mission to bring salvation to the world. Unique to John is the emphasis on Jesus' control even in death.

John 20 - Jesus rises from the dead, appears to Mary Magdalene, and commissions His disciples. Unique to John is Jesus' post-resurrection encounter with Mary Magdalene.

John 21 - Jesus restores Peter and commissions him to "feed My sheep," reaffirming His mission to spread the gospel. Unique to John is this restorative dialogue with Peter.

ACTS

Though not a Gospel, Acts serves as the sequel to Luke's Gospel, detailing the dynamic origins of the early Church, propelled by the Holy Spirit. Beginning with the explosive events described in Acts 2, when the Spirit dramatically empowers the apostles in ways that transform everything, Acts narrates their courageous proclamation of the Gospel, their miraculous deeds, and the rapid expansion of a movement that withstood intense opposition. Central figures such as Peter, Stephen, and Paul rise as pivotal leaders, carrying the message of Jesus beyond the boundaries of Jerusalem and into the broader world.

Acts is fundamentally a story of community and belonging, underscoring the Holy Spirit's role in dismantling barriers of race, culture, and social status to forge a new humanity united in Christ. This narrative reflects the theological vision of a Church that is both diverse and unified, embodying the inclusive love of God. As readers journey through Acts, they encounter a grand narrative that is not only inspiring but also energizing, inviting them to participate in the ongoing mission of the Church. The book challenges believers to embrace the Spirit's empowerment, fostering communities of faith that transcend divisions and embody the reconciling work of Christ.

Must-Read Chapters

- [ ] Acts 1 - Jesus commissions His disciples and ascends to heaven, promising the Holy Spirit.
- [ ] **Acts 2 - The Holy Spirit empowers the apostles, and Peter's sermon leads to the birth of the Church.**

- [ ] Acts 3 - Peter heals a man who couldn't walk, leading to the proclamation of Jesus as the one who brings restoration.
- [ ] **Acts 7 - Stephen's speech recounts Israel's history, showing how God's plan always moves forward.**
- [ ] **Acts 9 - Saul's dramatic encounter with Jesus transforms him into Paul, the great apostle to the Gentiles.**
- [ ] Acts 10 - Peter's vision and Cornelius' conversion confirm that the gospel is for all people, Jew and Gentile alike.
- [ ] Acts 11 - Peter defends bringing the gospel to Gentiles, and the Church begins to see how big God's kingdom really is.
- [ ] Acts 15 - The early church decides that salvation comes by grace, not by adherence to the law.
- [ ] Acts 16 - Prison walls shake, chains fall, and a jailer finds salvation.
- [ ] Acts 28 - Paul's ministry in Malta and Rome and unhindered proclamation of the kingdom of God while under house arrest.

Paul's Letters
The Theology of Christ and His Church

No one has shaped Christian thinking more than Jesus himself, but Paul comes in a close second. His letters are loaded with big ideas and practical wisdom for real life. At the heart of everything Paul writes is his rock-solid conviction that Jesus's death and resurrection didn't just save some souls, but actually flipped the script on how the whole world works. Through Christ, Paul sees God putting everything back together again.

His letters tell that story while also dealing with the nitty-gritty problems facing these new Christian communities. He's constantly encouraging them, calling them out when they mess up, and giving them hope as they try to figure out how to live together. What makes Paul's writing so compelling is how he manages to be both deeply personal and universally relevant. He takes the most profound truths about God and connects them to everyday struggles, always bringing it back to grace, unity, and the kind of love that actually changes people's lives. Paul basically becomes the guy who helps us understand what Jesus's story means for how we're supposed to live and grow as God's people.

Reading Paul's letters can feel a bit like reading someone else's mail. You're stepping into an ongoing conversation, hearing only one side of it. Each chapter adds context, and jumping around can sometimes leave you more confused than inspired. These letters were meant to be heard, read aloud in gatherings, wrestled with, and lived out. They unpack Paul's vision of faith, grace, and community, one section at a time. Still, if you're short on time, there are chapters that cut straight to the heart of his message, places where theology and practical advice come together in ways that still move people today.

Not all of Paul's letters come without questions. While the New Testament includes thirteen letters that carry his name, scholars have long debated whether Paul actually wrote all of them. Some letters differ in style, vocabulary, or focus when compared to his more universally accepted writings like Romans, 1 and 2 Corinthians, Galatians, Philippians, 1 Thessalonians, and Philemon. Letters such as Ephesians and Colossians reflect Paul's theology but read differently enough to raise questions. 2 Thessalonians shifts in tone and topic from 1 Thessalonians. The Pastoral Epistles, which include 1 Timothy, 2 Timothy, and Titus, sound especially distinct, focusing heavily on church leadership and structure. Because of these differences, many scholars think some letters may have been written by followers of Paul, people shaped by his teaching and trying to carry his message forward in new contexts. Their goal was not to deceive, but to honor Paul's influence and continue guiding the growing Christian communities.

One last thought: Paul has been misunderstood more than just about any other biblical writer, often twisted to support ideas he never actually had or used to answer questions he wasn't even asking. Much of this confusion happens because people read him through the lens of modern debates rather than trying to understand what he was actually dealing with in his own time.

To read Paul well, remember that he was a first-century Jewish man writing letters to specific churches facing real, practical problems. He wasn't sitting in an office writing a theology textbook. Pay attention to what each community was actually struggling with, whether it was fights between different groups of Christians, questions about how to live as religious minorities in the Roman world, or everyday issues about how to get along with each other. Don't assume Paul is making blanket statements for all time when he might just be solving a particular problem for a particular group of people. Most importantly, let Paul speak for himself. He was passionate about God's love reaching everyone and spent his life arguing that the good news of Jesus brings people together rather than divides them.

ROMANS

Romans is a masterclass in theology, where Paul weaves the story of Israel into the sweeping narrative of God's faithfulness, culminating in the reconciling work of Christ. Through echoes of Israel's Scriptures, Paul unveils the Gospel as fulfilling God's covenant promises, a dramatic intervention in history that defeats sin, death, and the powers of the present age. The righteousness of God is not merely a concept but a transformative power, reshaping reality and forming a new community of Jews and Gentiles alike, united through faith and animated by the Spirit. Romans is not just a theological treatise; it is a call to embody this reconciled identity, living as a people whose lives testify to God's ongoing work of renewal in the world.

Many Christians have found Romans absolutely life-changing, but that doesn't mean it will immediately grab you the same way. The first few times I read Romans I just thought Paul had anger issues. In Romans, Paul is clearly working through his own stuff and you can feel his frustration. Don't get frustrated too. Paul's argument is complex and builds on itself in ways that can be confusing at first, and there's no shame in finding it difficult to follow. Dense and richly layered, Romans rewards slow, patient reading as you work to grasp its breathtaking vision of God's redemptive plan.

Must-Read Chapters

- [ ] Romans 1 - Paul introduces the power of the gospel, revealing humanity's need for God's righteousness.
- [ ] **Romans 3 - Paul explains how all have sinned, but are justified freely through Jesus Christ.**

Romans 5 - Through one man came death, but through another comes life, God's grace makes everything new.

Romans 6 - Believers are called to live free from sin's power, walking in newness of life.

Romans 8 - A triumphant chapter celebrating the freedom, hope, and love found in Christ.

Romans 10 - Faith comes by hearing, and the gospel is for everyone, because God's salvation refuses to be boxed in.

Romans 12 - A call to live transformed lives, marked by humility, love, and service, as worship to God.

Romans 14 - In God's kingdom, people come first, unity matters more than your preferences or disputes.

Romans 15 - Jews and Gentiles, together in Christ, singing one song, God's promises fulfilled in a harmony.

1 CORINTHIANS

First Corinthians addresses the real-world challenges faced by the early Christian church in Corinth. Paul tackles issues like divisions within the community, moral struggles, and confusion about spiritual matters. He emphasizes the importance of unity and love, reminding believers that their shared faith in Christ should bring them together despite differences. His advice: Stop making excuses and start being the body of Christ.

Paul highlights the significance of the resurrection, not just as a future event, but as a powerful force that can transform daily life. He stresses that love is more important than any spiritual gift, encouraging the Corinthians to focus on loving one another.

Additionally, Paul offers practical advice on living holy lives, covering topics such as marriage, worship, and moral behavior.

First Corinthians is both engaging and practical, challenging readers to apply the Gospel to their everyday lives. By reading the letter in sections, its insights can deeply impact personal growth and community life. It remains a valuable guide for Christians today, offering timeless wisdom for navigating faith and community challenges.

Must-Read Chapters

- [ ] 1 Corinthians 1 - Paul addresses divisions, calling believers to focus on the wisdom of the cross.
- [ ] 1 Corinthians 3 - God's the builder, we're the field, and all we do rests on the foundation of Christ.
- [ ] **1 Corinthians 12 - The Spirit gives gifts, and each one matters, because the body of Christ thrives when every part**
- [ ] **1 Corinthians 13 - Paul describes love as the ultimate marker of a life shaped by Christ.**
- [ ] **1 Corinthians 15 - Paul defends the resurrection of Jesus and its centrality to the Christian hope.**

2 CORINTHIANS

Second Corinthians gives us a deeply personal look at Paul's life and work. Like all letters of his time, it follows certain formal patterns, but Paul makes them meaningful. In this letter, he openly shares his struggles and victories, showing how he found strength in God during his weakest moments.

What sets this letter apart is how personal Paul gets. Instead of sticking to his usual formal tone, he opens with a genuine, heartfelt blessing. He shares his struggles in Ephesus not as bragging rights, but to show how God showed up when everything fell apart. Paul makes clear that real ministry doesn't start with strength. Instead, it starts with weakness, so there's no point in pretending you've got it all together.

Must-Read Chapters

- 2 Corinthians 3 - The old covenant fades, but the Spirit brings freedom and transforms us into the image of Christ.
- 2 Corinthians 4 - Treasure in jars of clay, God's power works through our weakness, so the glory is always His.
- **2 Corinthians 5 - In Christ, there's a new creation, a ministry of reconciliation, and a call to embody God's restoring love.**
- 2 Corinthians 8 - Generosity is grace in action, an overflow of God's abundance to meet the needs of others.
- 2 Corinthians 12 - God's grace is enough, His power shines brightest in our weakness.

GALATIANS

Galatians is a fiery and passionate declaration of freedom in Christ. Paul writes urgently to churches in Galatia (modern-day Turkey), addressing a crisis where other teachers insisted that non-Jewish converts must follow Jewish laws to be true Christians. Throughout the letter, Paul's anger and concern are evident as he warns against relying on human efforts or rules to earn salvation, emphasizing that it comes through faith in Christ alone.

While we only have Paul's perspective on the conflict, the letter offers a fascinating glimpse into early Christianity's growing pains as it separated from Judaism. This relatively short letter has had an enormous impact on Christian theology, particularly in its emphasis on grace over religious rules. Its themes of freedom, transformation through faith, and the power of God's unconditional grace continue to resonate.

Paul's theology, deeply shaped by his Jewish identity and hope for God's kingdom, is reinterpreted through the reality of Jesus' resurrection as the beginning of the new creation. Galatians is a quick, impactful read with a sharp focus on grace, providing insight into both the historical development of early Christianity and timeless questions about faith, identity, and freedom.

Read the Entire Letter

- [ ] Galatians 1 - The gospel isn't human, it's God's revelation, and it changes everything.
- [ ] Galatians 2 - Faith in Christ, not the law, is what makes us right with God.
- [ ] Galatians 3 - The law held us until faith came, now, in Christ, we are children of God.
- [ ] Galatians 4 - We're not slaves but heirs, adopted into God's family through Christ.
- [ ] **Galatians 5 - Freedom in Christ isn't for selfishness but for love and the Spirit's fruit.**

☐ Galatians 6 - Bear each other's burdens because we're called to sow what is good.

EPHESIANS

Ephesians is sort of like a battle hymn for God's grand plan to unite all things in Christ. Paul explores the Church's role as Christ's body, the beauty of grace, and the call to live holy and unified lives. He equips its readers for spiritual battles, urging them to put on the "armor of God." Ephesians unveils God's purpose, where the Church becomes the foretaste of new creation, embodying unity and reconciliation in a fractured world. The letter interestingly portrays the victory of Christ over the powers and principalities, calling believers to live as a sign of that victory through Spirit-empowered lives. Ephesians offers encouragement and a vision of living as God's people, compelling yet profound, challenging readers to embrace their identity as those already seated with Christ in the heavenly realms.

Read the Entire Letter

☐ Ephesians 1 - God's plan for everything, redemption, grace, and unity, is revealed in Christ

☐ **Ephesians 2 - We were dead, but grace made us alive and brought us into one family.**

☐ Ephesians 3 - Gentiles are fellow heirs, and the breadth of God's love surpasses all understanding.

☐ Ephesians 4 - United as one body, one Spirit, and one faith, we mature together into the complete expression of Christ.

- Ephesians 5 - Walk as children of light, reflecting Christ's love in all your interactions.
- Ephesians 6 - Clothe yourselves with the armor of God, standing resolute in His might.

PHILIPPIANS

Knowing that Paul wrote Philippians from a Roman prison might completely change how you read it. Here's a man in chains, in a dark Roman pit, facing an uncertain future, possibly even death, and yet this letter practically radiates with joy and hope. Despite his dire circumstances, Paul urges these Philippians to rejoice in the Lord, embrace humility, and keep moving forward in their spiritual journey.

You begin to learn that joy isn't a feeling, but rather a realization that Christ is enough. Centered on Christ's example of selfless love, Philippians becomes a masterclass in finding gratitude and resilience even when life gets brutal.

Beneath its surface, Philippians offers profound theological insights, challenging readers to embody Christ's mindset of humility, obedience, and sacrificial love. It underscores the transformative power of these virtues in everyday life, while acknowledging the tension between present challenges and future hope. This letter invites us to experience the dynamic reality of Christ's lordship, uniting our lives here and now with His eternal purpose.

Read the Entire Letter

- Philippians 1 - Even amidst trials, the gospel progresses, for Christ is supreme in all things.

- [ ] **Philippians 2 - Jesus willingly embraced the cross, exemplifying a life of service that we are called to emulate.**

- [ ] Philippians 3 - Nothing surpasses the value of knowing Christ and experiencing the power of His resurrection.

- [ ] Philippians 4 - Rejoice continually, place your trust in God's peace, and draw strength from Him to meet every challenge.

COLOSSIANS

Colossians often gets glossed over as just another letter about Christian living, but it's actually a bold confrontation with the powers that shape our world. In this short letter, Paul is delivering a prophetic challenge to the Roman Empire and its false promises of peace through domination and control.

This ancient confrontation speaks directly to our modern empire of consumerism, nationalism, and the illusion of security through economic and military dominance. Just as Rome offered "Pax Romana" built on violence and propaganda, our culture offers "peace" through consumption, brand loyalty, and political allegiance. Colossians cuts through these hollow promises, insisting that ultimate authority belongs to Christ and nothing else. In essence Paul is telling us that Christ is not part of your life; Christ is your life.

The letter addresses how our imaginations have been captured by cultural forces that tell us what to want, who to be, and what matters most. Paul calls readers to wake up and reimagine reality where Christ truly reigns, not just in personal faith but in how we think about power, community, economics, and politics.

Read the Entire Letter

☐ **Colossians 1** - Christ is the image of God, the center of creation, and the hope of glory.

☐ Colossians 2 - Live rooted in Christ, who overcomes all powers and brings wholeness and freedom.

☐ Colossians 3 - Put off the old self, put on the new, and let Christ shape everything.

☐ Colossians 4 - Pray, walk in wisdom, and live out Christ's love in every encounter.

1 THESSALONIANS

First Thessalonians is warm and encouraging, written to a young church navigating faith amid challenges. Paul's words are affirming, celebrating the Thessalonians' steadfast faith, abounding love, and unyielding hope. He underscores the profound impact of the Gospel on their lives, urging them to deepen their commitment to holiness as they eagerly anticipate the full realization of God's kingdom.

Paul emphasizes the imminent expectation of Christ's return, which was believed to be near. These church members thought Jesus was coming back really really soon. Paul had to clarify. This anticipation is not about predicting future events but about living in the present with a sense of urgency and hope. Paul encourages the Thessalonians to ground their lives in faith, love, and hope, actively preparing for the fulfillment of God's promises. His words serve as a reminder that the Christian life is about embodying the values of the kingdom of God here and now, rather than merely awaiting a future event.

Must-Read Chapters

1 Thessalonians 1 - Faith, love, and hope make the gospel visible in your life.

1 Thessalonians 4 - Live to please God, love each other, and live with hope for Christ's return

1 Thessalonians 5 - Be awake, be ready, and live in the light as you await the Lord.

2 THESSALONIANS

Second Thessalonians builds upon the foundational themes of the first letter, addressing and clarifying misunderstandings that had arisen within the church regarding the nature and timing of Christ's return. Paul's basically telling the church to stop staring at the clouds and get to work. Still, Paul's words are reassuring and pastoral, encouraging them to remain steadfast in their faith and to avoid the pitfalls of idleness or despair.

It becomes clear that Paul is writing to a church in crisis. They are hurting deeply, scared, and convinced they've been abandoned. They've endured suffering, and now a false teacher has added insult to injury by claiming that Jesus has already returned and left them behind. To paraphrase Paul is saying, "I know you're scared. I know it feels like God forgot you. But He hasn't. His timing isn't ours, and His plan is still unfolding."

The letter is concise yet powerfully focused, serving as a call to live with diligence, perseverance, and readiness. Paul underscores the necessity of continuing in faithful service and active discipleship, not merely as a response to future expectations, but as a testament to the transformative power of the Gospel in the present. It is a poignant reminder that the Christian life is one of hopeful anticipation, grounded in the assurance of Christ's ultimate victory and the establishment of God's kingdom.

Must-Read Chapters

- [ ] 2 Thessalonians 1 - God's justice is coming, He will bring relief and vindication to His people.
- [ ] 2 Thessalonians 2 - Don't be shaken; God's victory over evil is already assured.

1, 2 TIMOTHY, AND TITUS

Paul's letters to Timothy and Titus are basically the instruction manual for how early churches organized themselves, and they're still shaping how churches operate today. Ever wonder where terms like Presbyterian, Episcopal, Elder, and Deacon come from? They're all right here in these letters.

Paul talks about *presbyteroi* (literally "older ones"), the seasoned, wise leaders who guided the community, especially when it came to teaching and preaching. Presbyterian churches get their name from this Greek word because they're led by these elders. He also mentions *episkopoi* (meaning "overseers"), who kept watch over the spiritual health of the congregation. That's where we get Episcopal, referring to churches led by bishops. Then there are the *diakonoi* (meaning "servants"), who focused on the practical, hands-on work of caring for people's needs. Paul describes them as trustworthy people with servant hearts, and that's where our word deacon comes from.

What's fascinating is how Paul envisioned these roles working together to care for and guide God's people, creating a leadership structure that's lasted for centuries. These three letters pulse with urgency and passion, pushing church leaders to be courageous and stay committed to spreading the good news, no matter what obstacles they face.

Must-Read Chapters

- [ ] 1 Timothy 1 - God's mercy has transformed us; therefore, guard the gospel with faith and love.
- [ ] 1 Timothy 3 - Leadership in the Church is about character shaped by Christ.
- [ ] 1 Timothy 6 - Flee greed, pursue godliness, and trust in the riches of Christ.
- [ ] 2 Timothy 1 - Develop the gifts God has given you, for His Spirit empowers with strength, love, and self-control.
- [ ] 2 Timothy 2 - Be strong in grace, faithful in teaching, and endure for the sake of the gospel.
- [ ] 2 Timothy 3 - Scripture equips us for every good work, even in days of deception.
- [ ] 2 Timothy 4 - Preach the word, run the race, and trust God to complete the story.
- [ ] Titus 2 - Teach sound doctrine so that every generation lives out the gospel.
- [ ] Titus 3 - Saved by mercy, not works, now live out good deeds as a response to grace

PHILEMON

Philemon is written to a slaveholder, and we cannot escape its tension. Paul's words come from within a world where slavery is normal, but his appeal cracks the foundations of that world. He asks Philemon to receive Onesimus, not as property but as a brother. This act demands Philemon see Onesimus not through the distorted lens of ownership but through the transforming vision of Christ.

This letter does not explicitly condemn slavery, but I want to trust that it lays the groundwork for its eventual dismantling. Paul's plea forces a reimagination of relationships, where the Gospel disrupts the world's hierarchies, master and slave, powerful and powerless. To call Onesimus a brother in Christ is to challenge Philemon to unlearn his place in the imperial order and to learn Christ's order, where love replaces domination, and communion replaces exploitation.

In Philemon, the Gospel moves relationally, not abstractly. It speaks into the messy, unjust realities of a slaveholding world, not with condemnation alone, but with the hope of transformation. It asks us today to consider our own entanglements with systems of oppression and to live into the radical reconciliation that Christ makes possible.

Read the Entire Letter

- [ ] Philemon - Paul calls for a new kind of relationship, rooted in love and equality in Christ.

Pastoral Letters
Enduring Hope and a Final Vision

The remaining letters of the New Testament and Revelation address the challenges of faithfulness in a world often at odds with God's kingdom. They are intensely practical, offering wisdom for daily life, yet their theological depth points to the ultimate hope of God's redemptive plan. From encouraging perseverance in trials to envisioning a new creation where God reigns in glory, these writings call believers to endure with faith and anticipate the renewal of all things. These letters remind readers that faithfulness is not only a personal journey but also a communal witness, rooted in the transformative power of God's presence in both the present and the promised future.

HEBREWS

It's time to sit back and learn more about the Old Testament. Hebrews is intricate and awe-inspiring. Like a masterful sequel that honors the original story while revealing new depths, Hebrews bridges the Old Testament and the New Testament, revealing Jesus as the ultimate fulfillment of God's promises.

Jesus is portrayed as the perfect High Priest and sacrifice, surpassing the old system of laws and rituals, offering a once-for-all path to God. Hebrews emphasizes the necessity of unwavering faith, especially through trials, drawing inspiration from heroes who endured before them.

Rich with symbolism and theology, Hebrews invites readers into a deeper understanding of Christ, calling them to persevere, remain loyal, and have faith in a mission that transcends individual struggles and points to something far greater.

Additionally, Hebrews highlights the superiority of Christ over angels, Moses, and the old covenant, demonstrating His unique role in God's redemptive plan. The book also offers profound insights into the nature of faith, defining it as the assurance of things hoped for and the conviction of things not seen.

Like any great work that builds on what came before while opening new possibilities, Hebrews deepens our understanding of Christ's eternal significance and the transformative power of faith.

Must-Read Chapters

- [ ] Hebrews 1 - Jesus is revealed as God's ultimate Word, surpassing angels and fulfilling all of God's promises.
- [ ] Hebrews 2 - Jesus, fully human, shares in our suffering to defeat evil and bring salvation.
- [ ] Hebrews 4 - God invites us into a deep and abiding Sabbath rest, if only we trust enough to enter it.
- [ ] Hebrews 8 - Jesus is the mediator of a better covenant, written not on stone but on our hearts.
- [ ] Hebrews 10 - Jesus' once-for-all sacrifice replaces the old system, opening the way to God.
- [ ] **Hebrews 11 - A celebration of faith through the stories of those who trusted God throughout history.**
- [ ] Hebrews 12 - A cloud of witnesses surrounds us, calling us to endure, to run, to fix our eyes on Jesus.

JAMES

James is practical and direct, challenging believers to let their faith be visible in their actions. This letter, written by Jesus' brother, emphasizes justice, humility, and care for the vulnerable, calling out hypocrisy and encouraging authentic living. James reminds readers that faith without action is lifeless, and he offers wisdom for real-world challenges like controlling the tongue and dealing with conflict. Down-to-earth and highly applicable, it's a refreshing call to live out the Gospel with integrity.

James' epistle embodies a faith so intertwined with action that it resists any separation of belief from behavior, urging Christians to be doers of the word and not merely hearers, revealing that faith finds its fullest expression in love made concrete through deeds. Unlike Paul's complex theological arguments, James favors straightforward moral instruction, using vivid metaphors drawn from nature and everyday life to illustrate his points. His writing style reflects the Jewish wisdom tradition, with short, memorable teachings that address practical concerns while maintaining a deep spiritual foundation.

The letter particularly emphasizes the responsibility of wealthy believers toward the poor, making it a timeless voice for social justice within the Christian tradition. James bridges the gap between high religious ideals and daily Christian living, showing how faith should transform every aspect of life.

Must-Read Chapters

- James 1 - Caring for the poor and remaining unstained by the world, a reflection of the Torah's ethical demands.

What Also Matters?

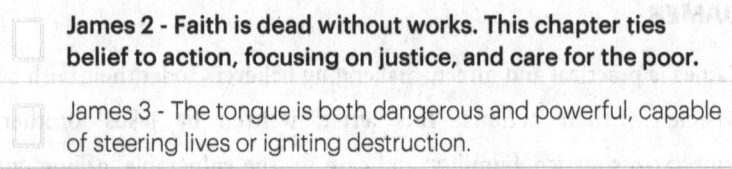

- [ ] James 2 - Faith is dead without works. This chapter ties belief to action, focusing on justice, and care for the poor.

- [ ] James 3 - The tongue is both dangerous and powerful, capable of steering lives or igniting destruction.

1 PETER

First Peter speaks to Christians navigating the tension between their allegiance to God's kingdom and life within a society that views them with suspicion. Addressed to believers scattered across Asia Minor, both Jewish and Gentile, who faced not just persecution but daily marginalization, the letter offers no easy fixes. Instead, it reframes their suffering through the story of Jesus: rejected by the world but vindicated by God.

Far from presenting suffering as meaningless, First Peter insists it's part of God's redemptive work. Just as Jesus's rejection led to resurrection and glory, so too will their faithfulness lead to vindication. The author draws deeply from Israel's identity, calling them a "chosen people," a "royal priesthood," a "holy nation," to remind these so-called outsiders that they are, in fact, insiders in God's renewed people.

Through rich Old Testament imagery and early Christian baptismal themes, the letter shows that what looks like failure in the world's eyes may actually be wisdom in God's. First Peter balances pastoral warmth with theological depth, encouraging believers to embrace their "resident alien" status not as a burden but as a calling to live with holiness, resilience, and hope grounded in Christ's victory.

Must-Read Chapters

1 Peter 1 - A new birth, a living hope, and an inheritance that never fades—this is the essence of the resurrection.

1 Peter 2 - Believers are a royal priesthood and a holy nation, chosen by God, with Christ as the cornerstone.

1 Peter 4 - Suffering unites you with Christ; therefore, arm yourselves with His mindset and love deeply.

2 PETER

Second Peter speaks directly to something we all face: how do we navigate a world full of conflicting voices claiming to speak for God? The letter confronts the reality of religious leaders who exploit faith for personal gain, twisting Jesus' message of liberation into something that serves their own interests. It's a sobering reminder that we need to stay grounded in the actual teachings of Jesus, his radical love, his concern for the marginalized, and his call to justice.

The letter tackles a question that still resonates today: if God is just and loving, why does suffering persist? Why haven't we seen the full realization of God's kingdom? Second Peter reframes this not as divine delay, but as divine patience. This perspective transforms waiting into hope. Instead of passively anticipating some distant future, we're invited to participate in bringing about the change we long to see.

Second Peter ultimately calls us to live as people of hope who refuse to accept the world as it is. It's about embodying God's character through our commitment to justice, our care for creation, our welcome of the stranger, and our pursuit of peace.

Read the Entire Letter

- [ ] 2 Peter 1 - God has given everything we need for life and godliness, be diligent in living it out.

- [ ] 2 Peter 2 - False teachers bring destruction, but God knows how to rescue the faithful.

- [ ] 2 Peter 3 - The Lord's return is not slow; it's patient, giving time for repentance and renewal.

1, 2, AND 3 JOHN

First John is a heartfelt exploration of love, God's love for us, our love for Him, and the love we're called to show one another. It encourages believers to live in the light, walk in truth, and let love shape every aspect of their lives. This letter reassures readers of God's faithfulness, reminding them that perfect love casts out fear and secures their salvation. Simple yet profound, First John invites deep reflection on living in God's love.

I've included Second and Third John here simply because they are each one chapter. Second John highlights love and obedience as inseparable hallmarks of a genuine faith while warning against deceivers who distort the Gospel. Third John celebrates the importance of hospitality and generosity in spreading the Gospel.

Must-Read Chapters

- [ ] 1 John 1 - Walk in the light, confess your sins, and find fellowship with God and each other.

> 1 John 4 - God is love, and love casts out fear, because love comes from Him.

> 1 John 5 - Faith in Christ triumphs over the world, granting us life and assurance through Him.

> 2 John - Walk in truth and love, but avoid endorsing anything that contradicts Christ.

> 3 John - Walk in truth, warmly receive fellow laborers, and reject anything that causes division in the Church.

JUDE

Jude is a bold and urgent call to defend the faith against the infiltration of false teachers and ungodly influences. Through vivid and striking imagery, Jude warns of impending judgment for those who distort the truth and lead others astray. At the same time, the letter offers reassurance to believers of God's unfailing power to protect and preserve them in the face of such threats. The letter concludes with a majestic doxology, a resplendent celebration of God's glory, majesty, and sovereignty, which stands as one of the most beautiful and theologically rich passages in all of Scripture. Despite its brevity, Jude's message is potent and inspiring, instilling confidence in God's ability to keep His people safe, steadfast, and faithful amidst the challenges and deceptions of the world.

Read the Entire Letter

> Jude - Contend for the faith, for grace is not a license to sin, and God preserves those who are His.

REVELATION

Revelation has become one of the most misunderstood books in the Bible because people approach it with the wrong assumptions. The popular idea that it's a secret code for predicting future events is a recent invention that contradicts how Christians read this book for nearly 1,800 years.

This confusion stems from dispensationalism, a theological system created by John Nelson Darby in 19th-century Britain. Darby had no formal theological training. He was a lawyer who developed his theories while bedridden after a riding accident, likely under the influence of the opium-based painkillers common in that era. His approach treated Revelation like a detailed timeline of future events, despite contradicting centuries of Christian interpretation. Though his ideas gained popularity, especially through the Scofield Reference Bible, they've led to wild modern speculations about barcodes being the "mark of the beast" or politicians being the Antichrist.

The original Christian audience understood Revelation completely differently. They lived under Roman rule and faced real persecution. When John wrote about the beast or Babylon, readers immediately recognized coded descriptions of the Roman Empire. The beast's number 666 likely pointed to Emperor Nero, whose persecution of Christians was still fresh in memory. This wasn't about the distant future but about their present reality.

Revelation belongs to apocalyptic literature, a genre that used symbolic imagery to communicate safely under hostile governments. Just as political cartoons today use symbols their audience recognizes, John used imagery that spoke directly to his readers' situation.

Reading it without this context is like trying to understand a Depression-era cartoon without knowing the history.

The book's real purpose was strengthening believers facing immediate challenges. It called Christians to resist imperial pressure, maintain their identity, and trust God's justice when earthly justice failed. The visions of God's throne and the Lamb's victory weren't chronological predictions but reminders that despite Rome's apparent power, God remained in control.

Revelation functions as resistance literature, encouraging believers to see through empire's lies and maintain hope despite suffering. Rather than creating anxiety about future catastrophes, it calls believers to courage, hope, and faithful commitment to Christ's way of love and justice.

Must-Read Chapters

- Revelation 1 - Jesus stands among the lampstands, the faithful witness calling His people to endure under Rome's shadow.

- Revelation 4 - A throne in heaven, a vision of true power, contrasting the empire's fleeting dominion.

- Revelation 5 - The slaughtered Lamb is the only one worthy, His sacrifice unmasks Rome's violence.

- Revelation 13 - The beast rises, the empire exposed as a counterfeit power demanding allegiance.

- Revelation 18 - Babylon's fall is Rome's collapse, her wealth and violence judged by God.

- **Revelation 21 - A new Jerusalem, where justice and peace reign, eclipsing Rome's failed vision of power.**

chapter 8

Who Is God?

Who is God? That's the ultimate question, isn't it? It's the one that hums beneath the surface of every sacred text, every whispered prayer, every moment when life feels too big, too raw, or too impossible to hold. The question doesn't require an answer as much as it dares us to look deeper, wonder harder, and stand in awe of something we can never fully explain.

The creation story in Genesis begins where all good stories do: in the dark. Hebrew scholar Robert Alter translates it as "welter and waste," an impactful, yet haunting phrase. It speaks of everything unresolved, the void we fear most, a place of chaos and formlessness. It's not just a blank slate; it's worse. And yet, this is precisely where God begins. God doesn't flinch in the face of it.

The ancient Israelites wanted us to understand this about God: He is the One who spins galaxies into being, not out of nothing, but out of welter. Welter means overwhelming turbulence. Waste is what has been discarded, unwanted, or deemed beyond use. And what does God do? He speaks life into the waste. The creation account is not a scientific manual or philosophical theory. It's a revelation. It shows us a God who creates and re-creates, who brings beauty out of brokenness, order out of chaos, light out of the deep.

When Moses stumbled across that burning bush in the middle of nowhere, he had the nerve to ask God for a name. God's answer was pretty wild: "I Am Who I Am." Not exactly what you'd put on a business card, right? But that's the point. This wasn't just God dodging the question or being mysterious for the sake of it.

"I Am" is less about labeling and more about existing in the most fundamental way possible. It's like God was saying, "I'm not a thing you can pin down or categorize. I'm the very fact that anything exists at all." Some people think the name Yahweh actually sounds like breathing, like the most basic thing we do to stay alive. Every breath becomes a kind of prayer, whether we realize it or not.

This changes everything about how we think about the divine. Instead of some distant ruler keeping score, we're talking about the source of life itself, the reason there's something rather than nothing. It's an invitation to stop trying to figure God out like a math problem and start paying attention to the mystery of simply being alive.

Approachable Attributes of God

Psalm 145 tells us that God is great and deserves all our praise, but his greatness is so vast we can't even wrap our minds around it. God breaks every box we try to put him in. But here's what's amazing: this God who's beyond our understanding actually wants to be known.

That's where Jesus comes in. In Christ, the mystery becomes a real person. The infinite God enters our world, walking around Palestine, eating with people society had written off, crying at funerals, and opening his arms to a world desperately hungry for love.

God isn't just a bunch of separate qualities thrown together. His holiness doesn't cancel out his compassion. His love doesn't ignore justice. Instead, everything about God works together perfectly. The cross shows us this most clearly, where justice and grace meet head-on, and death gets defeated completely.

This overview looks at different aspects of God's character as shown throughout the Bible. Each passage highlights something distinct about who God is, helping us build a fuller, more personal picture of his nature from both the Old and New Testaments.

- Genesis 1:1-31 - God is the Creator
- Genesis 21:33 - God is eternal
- Exodus 3:1-6 - God is holy
- Exodus 20:1 - The LORD is our God
- Exodus 20:1-20 - God is the commandment giver
- Exodus 34:6-7 - God is slow to anger
- Numbers 23:19 - God is truthful and reliable
- Deuteronomy 7:9 - God is faithful and covenant-keeping
- Deuteronomy 32:3-4 - God is flawless

Who Is God?

- [ ] 1 Samuel 1:9-20 - God is the hearer of our prayers
- [ ] 1 Kings 3:1-15 - God is the source of wisdom
- [ ] 1 Kings 17:1-24 - God is our sustainer
- [ ] 1 Chronicles 16:8-36 - God is good
- [ ] Psalm 18:1-6 - God is our refuge
- [ ] Psalm 23:1-6 - God is our shepherd
- [ ] Psalm 30:2-3 - God is a healer
- [ ] Psalm 86:15 - God is compassionate and gracious
- [ ] Psalm 116:5 - God is righteous and merciful
- [ ] Isaiah 40:28 - God is everlasting and untiring
- [ ] Isaiah 44:3-5 - God is the source of our blessings
- [ ] Jeremiah 18:1-6 - God is the potter
- [ ] Ezekiel 11:16 - God is sanctuary
- [ ] Matthew 1:18-25 - God is with us
- [ ] Matthew 25:31-46 - God is just
- [ ] Luke 7:36-50 - God is forgiving
- [ ] John 1:1-5 - God is the Word
- [ ] John 3:16-17 - God is our savior

- John 4:24 - God is Spirit
- Acts 17:25 - God is self-sufficient
- Romans 11:33-36 - God is wise
- Galatians 4:6 - God is personal
- Ephesians 2:14 - God is peace
- Ephesians 6:10-20 - God is our protector
- Philippians 4:19 - God is a provider
- James 2:23 - God is a friend
- 1 John 1:5 - God is light
- 1 John 4:7-21 - God is love

Theological Attributes of God

As Christianity spread and grew, theologians found they needed better language to talk about God. What started as simple faith statements gradually developed into more complex theological vocabulary. This might seem like making things unnecessarily complicated, but it's actually a good thing. God is incredibly complex, so our ways of understanding and discussing the divine need to be sophisticated enough to handle that complexity.

These theological terms work like tools in a toolbox. They help us put words to experiences and beliefs that would otherwise be impossible to express clearly. Sure, they can never fully capture who

God is. In fact, you'll notice that many of these concepts seem to contradict each other. God is both knowable and unknowable, both near and far, both unchanging and responsive. That's not sloppy thinking. That's what happens when finite minds try to grasp infinite reality.

Think of it like trying to describe the ocean to someone who's never seen it. You might talk about its vastness, its power, its beauty, its danger. Each description captures something true, but none of them alone gives you the full picture. Theological language works the same way. It gives us a framework for exploring and discussing the nature of God, even when we know our words are just pointing toward a mystery that's always bigger than our ability to explain it.

- [ ] Psalm 90:1-2 - God is ascetic (beyond creation)
- [ ] Psalm 107:1 - God is omnibenevolent (Perfectly good)
- [ ] Psalm 139:7-10 - God is omnipresent (everywhere)
- [ ] Psalm 147:4-5 - God is omniscient (all-knowing)
- [ ] Malachi 3:6 - God is immutable (unchanging)
- [ ] Matthew 28:16-20 - God is trinity (Father, Son, Holy Spirit)
- [ ] Luke 1:37 - God is omnipotent (unlimited)
- [ ] Acts 17:24-28 - God is imminent (knowable)
- [ ] Romans 11:33-36 - God is transcendent (unknowable)
- [ ] Philippians 2:5-11 - God is incarnate (human and divine)

- [ ] Colossians 1:15-20 - God is preeminent (supreme)
- [ ] 2 Timothy 1:9-10 - God is atemporal (eternal / outside of time)
- [ ] James 1:17 - God is impassible (unchanging)

chapter 9

Who Is Jesus Christ?

Jesus of Nazareth remains one of history's most compelling figures. Even skeptical historians agree he existed as a real person, a Jewish teacher who lived in first-century Palestine during the Roman Empire. He was born to a woman named Mary when Augustus Caesar ruled Rome, and grew up in Nazareth, a small town most people had never heard of.

Before becoming a traveling teacher, Jesus worked with his hands. The original Greek word suggests he was some kind of craftsman or builder, maybe working with wood, stone, or both. It was honest work, the kind that calluses your hands and teaches you patience. Nothing about his background suggested he would become someone history would remember.

But around age thirty, something shifted. Jesus began teaching publicly, drawing crowds throughout the Galilee region. He spoke in synagogues and out in the open, gathering a diverse group of followers who found something magnetic about his message. He talked about God's kingdom in ways that made it feel both urgent and hopeful, describing a reality where divine love could break into everyday life.

What made Jesus different wasn't just his teaching, though. People claimed he healed the sick and performed other extraordinary acts. Whether you believe those accounts literally or see them as powerful symbols, they clearly meant something profound to the people who witnessed them. His message and actions created both devoted followers and serious opposition, especially from religious leaders who saw him as a threat to their authority.

The historical consensus is clear about how his story ended: Jesus was crucified by Roman authorities around 30-33 CE. The Roman historian Tacitus and the Jewish historian Josephus, neither of whom were Christians, both confirm this basic fact. Jewish temple authorities had him arrested, and the Roman governor Pontius Pilate ordered his execution.

For Christians, Jesus isn't just a figure from the past. We believe something unprecedented happened after his death, that he came back to life, proving he was more than just a remarkable teacher. This conviction that Jesus was God in human form, living among us, shapes how Christians understand literally everything else.

From this perspective, Jesus represents God's direct involvement in human history. His life becomes a window into what divine love actually looks like when it takes on flesh and blood. His death becomes meaningful not just as a tragedy, but as God's way of addressing the deep brokenness in our world. And his resurrection becomes the ultimate sign that death doesn't have the final word.

This isn't simply ancient history for people who follow Jesus today. Many experience him as an ongoing presence, someone who continues to transform lives, build communities, and inspire people to work for justice and healing in our world. The movement he started has certainly had its failures and caused real harm at times, but it has also motivated countless acts of compassion, social reform, and personal transformation across two millennia.

The invitation to follow Jesus is more than accepting certain beliefs or even truths. It's about entering into a way of life oriented around love, forgiveness, and hope for transformation, both personal and social. It's messy, challenging, and deeply human work, but for millions of people, it's also been the most meaningful thing they've ever discovered.

The Person of Jesus

I've created this list to walk you through Jesus' life step by step, with checkboxes so you can track your progress. But I need to be upfront about something: putting Jesus' life in perfect chronological order is genuinely difficult, and any attempt involves educated guesswork.

The Gospels weren't written as chronological biographies. The Gospel writers were more interested in theological themes than precise timelines. They arranged stories to make specific points about who Jesus was and what his life meant, not necessarily to create a day-by-day historical record.

In fact, each Gospel has a different organizing principle. Matthew groups Jesus' teachings into major speeches. Luke arranges material to show Jesus' journey toward Jerusalem. John selects specific events to demonstrate Jesus' divine nature. Mark, while probably the earliest, still arranges events thematically rather than strictly chronologically.

Also, the Gospels sometimes place the same event at different points. For example, Jesus' cleansing of the temple appears early in John's Gospel but near the end in the other three. Scholars debate which timing is historically accurate, if either.

More so, many events have no clear time markers. The Gospels often use vague transitions like "after this" or "then," making it impossible to know exactly when things happened in relation to each other.

Then there's John. John includes many events and conversations not found in the other Gospels, and it's often unclear where these fit chronologically with the shared material.

For this list, I've used Mark's Gospel as the primary framework because most scholars consider it the earliest and possibly closest to a chronological sequence. When I reference the Gospels, I follow their traditional biblical order (Matthew, Mark, Luke, John), but the overall timeline follows Mark's structure.

For events that appear only in one Gospel, especially John's unique material, I've made my best estimate about where they fit chronologically. These placements should be understood as reasonable guesses rather than historical certainties.

This uncertainty doesn't diminish the value of studying Jesus' life chronologically. Even an approximate timeline helps us understand the flow of his ministry, the development of opposition against him, and how his message unfolded. Just remember that the precise order of events remains, in many cases, an educated guess based on the best available evidence.

- An Angel Tells Mary About Jesus - Luke 1:26-38
- Jesus Is Born - Matthew 1:18-25; Luke 2:1-7
- Young Jesus at the Temple - Luke 2:22-52
- Jesus Is Baptized - Matthew 3:13-17; Mark 1:9-11; Luke 3:21-22; John 1:32-34
- Jesus Is Tempted in the Wilderness - Matthew 4:1-11; Mark 1:12-13; Luke 4:1-13
- Jesus Calls His First Disciples - Matthew 4:13-22; Mark 1:16-20; Luke 5:1-11; John 1:35-51
- Water Turned to Wine - John 2:1-11
- Passover when Jesus Cleanses the Temple - John 2:12-25
- Nicodemus Visits Jesus at Night - John 3:1-21
- Jesus Talks with a Woman at the Well - John 4:3-42
- Jesus Reads Scripture in His Hometown - Luke 4:16-30
- Jesus Heals an Official's Son - John 4:46-54
- Jesus Heals in the Synagogue - Mark 1:21-28; Luke 4:31-37
- Jesus Heals Simon's Mother-in-law - Matthew 8:14-17; Mark 1:29-34; Luke 4:38-41
- Jesus Heals a Man with Leprosy - Matthew 8:1-4; Mark 1:40-45; Luke 5:12-16
- Jesus Heals a Paralyzed Man - Matthew 9:1-8; Mark 2:1-12; Luke 5:17-26

Who Is Jesus Christ?

- [ ] Jesus Calls Matthew the Tax Collector - Matthew 9:9-13; Mark 2:13-17; Luke 5:27-32
- [ ] Jesus Heals on the Sabbath - Matthew 12:9-21; Mark 3:1-12; Luke 6:6-11
- [ ] Jesus Calms the Storm - Matthew 8:18-27; Mark 4:35-41; Luke 8:22-25
- [ ] Jesus Frees a Man from Demons - Matthew 8:28-34; Mark 5:1-20; Luke 8:26-39
- [ ] Jesus Heals a Woman and Raises a Girl - Matthew 9:18-26; Mark 5:21-43; Luke 8:40-56
- [ ] Jesus Is Rejected in Nazareth - Matthew 13:54-58; Mark 6:1-6; Luke 4:16-30
- [ ] Jesus Feeds 5,000 People - Matthew 14:13-21; Mark 6:30-44; Luke 9:10-17; John 6:1-15
- [ ] Jesus Walks on Water - Matthew 14:22-33; Mark 6:45-52; John 6:16-21
- [ ] Jesus Heals Many at Gennesaret - Matthew 14:34-36; Mark 6:53-56
- [ ] Jesus Heals a Woman's Daughter - Matthew 15:21-28; Mark 7:24-30
- [ ] Jesus Restores Hearing and Speech - Mark 7:31-37
- [ ] Jesus Feeds 4,000 People - Matthew 15:32-39; Mark 8:1-10
- [ ] Jesus Heals a Blind Man - Mark 8:22-26
- [ ] The Transfiguration - Matthew 17:1-13; Mark 9:1-13; Luke 9:28-36
- [ ] Jesus Heals a Boy with an Unclean Spirit - Matthew 17:14-20; Mark 9:14-29; Luke 9:37-43

Who Is Jesus Christ?

- Jesus Heals the Blind and the Possessed - Matthew 9:27-34
- Jesus Heals a Man at the Pool - John 5:1-15
- Jesus Confronts Religious Leaders - John 5:16-47
- Jesus Gives the Sermon on the Mount - Matthew 5:1-7:29; Luke 6:17-49
- Jesus Heals a Soldier's Servant - Matthew 8:5-13; Luke 7:1-10
- Jesus Raises a Widow's Son - Luke 7:11-17
- Jesus Offers Rest for the Weary - Matthew 11:25-30
- A Woman Anoints Jesus' Feet - Luke 7:36-50
- Jesus Teaches at the Festival - John 7:11-53
- A Woman Caught in Adultery - John 8:1-11
- Jesus Debates the Pharisees - John 8:12-59
- Jesus Heals a Man Born Blind - John 9:1-41
- Jesus Calls Himself the Good Shepherd - John 10:1-21
- Jesus Teaches During Hanukkah - John 10:22-30
- Jesus Sends Out 70 Followers - Luke 10:1-16
- The Good Samaritan - Luke 10:25-37
- Mary and Martha Welcome Jesus - Luke 10:38-42
- Jesus Teaches the Lord's Prayer - Matthew 6:9-13; Luke 11:1-4

- [ ] Jesus Teaches About Returning Spirits - Matthew 12:43-45; Luke 11:24-28
- [ ] The Sign of Jonah - Matthew 12:38-42; Luke 11:29-32
- [ ] Jesus Teaches on Light - Matthew 5:15; 6:22-23; Luke 11:33-36
- [ ] Jesus Confronts the Pharisees - Matthew 23:1-39; Luke 11:37-54
- [ ] Jesus Heals on the Sabbath - Luke 13:10-17; 14:1-6
- [ ] Jesus Heals a Man with Swelling - Luke 14:1-6
- [ ] Jesus Heals Ten Men - Luke 17:11-19
- [ ] Jesus Blesses Children - Matthew 19:13-15; Mark 10:13-16; Luke 18:15-17
- [ ] Jesus Talks to a Rich Man - Matthew 19:16-26; Mark 10:17-27; Luke 18:18-27
- [ ] Jesus Heals the Blind Near Jericho - Matthew 20:29-34; Mark 10:46-52; Luke 18:35-43
- [ ] Jesus Visits Zacchaeus - Luke 19:1-10
- [ ] Jesus Raises Lazarus - John 11:1-44
- [ ] Jewish Leaders Plot Against Jesus - John 11:45-53
- [ ] Jesus Enters Jerusalem - Matthew 21:1-11; Mark 11:1-10; Luke 19:29-44; John 12:12-19
- [ ] Jesus Curses a Fig Tree - Matthew 21:17-22; Mark 11:11-14, 19-23
- [ ] Jesus Clears the Temple - Matthew 21:12-16; Mark 11:15-18; Luke 19:45-48

- [ ] Jesus Is Challenged by Leaders - Matthew 21:23-27; Mark 11:27-33; Luke 20:1-8

- [ ] Jesus Gives the Greatest Commandment - Matthew 22:34-40; Mark 12:28-34

- [ ] Religious Leaders Plan His Death - Matthew 26:1-5; Mark 14:1-2; Luke 22:1-2

- [ ] A Woman Anoints Jesus - Matthew 26:6-13; Mark 14:3-9; Luke 7:36-50; John 12:1

- [ ] Greeks Seek Jesus and a Voice Speaks - John 12:20-36

- [ ] Judas' Betrayal - Matthew 26:14-16; Mark 14:10-11; Luke 22:3-6

- [ ] Jesus Shares the Last Supper - Matthew 26:17-30; Mark 14:12-26; Luke 22

- [ ] Jesus' Final Words to His Disciples - John 14-17

- [ ] Jesus Prays in Gethsemane - Matthew 26:36-46; Mark 14:32-42; Luke 22:40-46; John 18:1

- [ ] Jesus Heals a Man's Ear - Luke 22:50-51; John 18:10

- [ ] Jesus Is Arrested - Matthew 26:47-56; Mark 14:43-52; Luke 22:47-53; John 18:2-11

- [ ] Jesus Before the Priests - Matthew 26:57-58; Mark 14:53-54; Luke 22:54-65; John 18:12-27

- [ ] Jesus Before the Sanhedrin - Matthew 26:59-68; Mark 14:55-65; Luke 22:66-71

- [ ] Peter Denies Jesus - Matthew 26:69-75; Mark 14:66-72; Luke 22:54-62; John 18:15-27

- [ ] Jesus and Pilate - Matthew 27:1-14; Mark 15:1-5; Luke 23:1-6; John 18:33-40

Who Is Jesus Christ?

- [ ] Jesus Before Herod - Luke 23:7-12
- [ ] Jesus Is Sentenced - Matthew 27:15-26; Mark 15:6-15; Luke 23:13-25; John 18:29; 19:16
- [ ] Soldiers Mock Jesus - Matthew 27:27-31; Mark 15:16-20; Luke 23:36-37; John 19:1-3
- [ ] Jesus Is Crucified - Matthew 27:32-44; Mark 15:21-32; Luke 23:26-39; John 19:17-24
- [ ] Jesus' Mother at the Cross - John 19:25-27

The Parables

People expect religious teachers to give clear, straightforward answers. However, Jesus sure didn't. Instead he told stories that left his listeners scratching their heads. A scholar once observed that these stories work like time bombs, seeming harmless at first but exploding with meaning later when you least expect it.

Consider the parable of the workers in the vineyard. Some people work all day in the scorching heat, others show up at the last hour, but everyone gets paid the same wage. That's not fair by any normal standard, and Jesus knew it. The story is supposed to make you uncomfortable with your assumptions about fairness and reward.

Jesus' parables work like a door that's both open and closed. If you're really listening and willing to have your world turned upside down, the story opens up and shows you something profound about how God works. But if you're just looking for confirmation of what you already believe, the story stays locked. This isn't accidental. Jesus faced the reality that some of his deepest truths could only be grasped by those willing to release their assumptions.

At the center of almost every parable is this idea: God's kingdom is breaking into our world, but not in the way anyone expected. It doesn't come with armies or political power. It shows up in unexpected places, through unlikely people, in ways that often seem backwards.

The kingdom appears through a despised Samaritan who shows mercy, through a father who welcomes back a rebellious son, through a master who pays workers generously regardless of hours worked. These stories suggest that God's way of doing things often contradicts human expectations.

Unfortunately, his Parables don't let you stay neutral. They force you to take a position. When Jesus tells the story of the Good Samaritan, he's not just teaching about kindness in general. He's confronting his listeners with a question: "Will you act with mercy toward people you've been taught to despise?"

The parables create what scholars call "productive tension." You have to choose: Will you cling to your old way of seeing things, or will you let the story change how you understand God, yourself, and the world around you?

So, when you encounter a parable, resist the urge to quickly figure out "the moral of the story." Instead, let yourself sit with the discomfort, the questions, the ways the story challenges your assumptions. Ask yourself: What is this story asking me to reconsider?

The goal isn't to solve the parable like a puzzle, but to let it work on you over time. The best parables keep surprising you, revealing new layers of meaning as you encounter them at different stages of your life.

- [ ] Let Your Light Shine - Mark 4:21-25; Matthew 5:14-16; Luke 8:16-18; 11:33-36
- [ ] A Farmer Scatters Seeds - Mark 4:3-20; Matthew 13:3-23; Luke 8:5-15
- [ ] Seeds That Grow on Their Own - Mark 4:26-29
- [ ] The Tiny Mustard Seed - Mark 4:30-32; Matthew 13:31-32; Luke 13:18-19
- [ ] Wheat and Weeds Grow Together - Matthew 13:24-30, 36-43
- [ ] A Little Yeast Makes a Big Difference - Matthew 13:33; Luke 13:20-21
- [ ] Treasure Hidden in a Field - Matthew 13:44
- [ ] The Pearl Worth Everything - Matthew 13:45-46
- [ ] A Net Full of Fish - Matthew 13:47-50
- [ ] Two People Owe a Debt - Luke 7:41-43
- [ ] The Good Samaritan - Luke 10:30-37
- [ ] The Rich Man Who Built Bigger Barns - Luke 12:16-21
- [ ] Be Ready - Mark 13:35-37; Luke 12:35-48
- [ ] Building on a Solid Foundation - Matthew 7:24-27; Luke 6:47-49
- [ ] A Tree That Doesn't Bear Fruit - Luke 13:6-9
- [ ] The Wedding Party Is Ready - Matthew 22:1-14
- [ ] Ten Bridesmaids Waiting - Matthew 25:1-13

- Investing What You've Been Given - Matthew 25:14-30; Luke 19:11-27
- Ten Servants and the Master's Money - Luke 19:11-27
- Workers Hired at Different Times - Matthew 20:1-16
- A Father and Two Sons - Matthew 21:28-32
- Tenants Who Refused the Owner - Mark 12:1-12; Matthew 21:33-46; Luke 20:9-19
- Learn from the Fig Tree - Mark 13:28-31; Matthew 24:32-35; Luke 21:29-33
- Sheep and Goats at the Final Judgment - Matthew 25:31-46
- The Lost Sheep - Matthew 18:10-14; Luke 15:3-7
- The Lost Coin - Luke 15:8-10
- The Lost Son Comes Home - Luke 15:11-32
- The Shrewd Manager - Luke 16:1-13
- The Rich Man and Lazarus - Luke 16:19-31
- The Persistent Widow - Luke 18:1-8
- Two Prayers: One Prideful, One Humble - Luke 18:9-14
- Don't Patch Old Clothes with New Fabric - Mark 2:21-22; Matthew 9:16-17; Luke 5:36-38
- New Wine Needs New Wineskins - Mark 2:22; Matthew 9:17; Luke 5:37-38
- The Servant Who Wouldn't Forgive - Matthew 18:21-35

Self Reflective Attributes of Jesus

When Moses asked God for his name at the burning bush, God responded with the mysterious phrase "I Am Who I Am" (Exodus 3:14). This wasn't just a name but a declaration of God's eternal, self-existing nature. For first-century Jews, this phrase carried enormous weight as the most sacred way God had revealed himself.

When Jesus began making his own "I am" statements, his Jewish listeners would have immediately recognized the connection. He wasn't just describing himself using metaphors; he was claiming to possess the same eternal, divine nature that God revealed to Moses.

- [ ] Exodus 20:1 - I am the LORD your God
- [ ] John 6:35 - I am the bread of life
- [ ] John 8:12 - I am the light of the world
- [ ] John 10:7 - I am the gate of the sheep
- [ ] John 10:11 - I am the good shepherd
- [ ] John 11:25 - I am the resurrection and the life
- [ ] John 14:6 - I am the way, the truth, and the life
- [ ] John 15:1 - I am the true vine
- [ ] John 8:23 - I am from above; I am not from this world
- [ ] John 8:58 - Before Abraham was, I am
- [ ] John 18:5-6 - I am he

From Jesus to Christ

The four Gospels all introduce Jesus with weighty titles, but in different ways. Mark opens boldly: "The beginning of the good news about Jesus Christ, God's Son." Matthew immediately calls him "the Christ" in his genealogy. Luke has angels announcing: "Your savior is born today in David's city. He is Christ the Lord." John shows Andrew telling Peter: "We have found the Messiah," with the writer adding helpfully, "which is translated Christ."

Both the Greek *Christos* and Hebrew *Messiah* mean "the anointed one." In ancient Israel, prophets, priests, and kings were anointed with oil as a sign of God's choosing them. Over time, especially during foreign occupation, "Messiah" came to represent the ultimate anointed leader who would restore Israel's independence and establish God's reign.

Jesus completely upended messianic expectations. Most first-century Jews anticipated a Messiah who would be a military and political leader, someone who would drive out the Romans and restore Israel to glory. They expected strength, victory, and national triumph.

Instead, they got a carpenter's son from Nazareth who spoke about loving enemies and taking up crosses. Rather than conquering Rome, Jesus was executed by Roman authorities. The idea of a crucified Messiah seemed like a contradiction in terms.

Paul's letters, written before the Gospels, become crucial here. Writing with theological hindsight, Paul saw something that wasn't immediately obvious to Jesus' first followers. For Paul, the resurrection changed everything. The cross, which seemed like the ultimate failure of messianic hopes, became the very means through which God accomplished salvation.

In Paul's hands, "Christ" evolves from a title describing Jesus' role to something deeper, a way of talking about God's entire plan for healing a broken world. While Paul writes with theological clarity about who Christ is, the Gospels show us the slower process of people gradually recognizing Jesus' true identity. They capture the confusion, questions, and moments of breakthrough that characterized encounters with Jesus.

Understanding this movement from "Jesus" to "Christ" helps us grasp how divine truth reveals itself in human history. Jesus of Nazareth was a specific person, but "Christ" represents the universal significance of that life for all people and times.

The title "Christ" represents the Christian conviction that in Jesus, God entered human history definitively to bring healing, hope, and transformation. It's a confession that this particular Jewish teacher somehow embodies God's ultimate response to human need and divine love for the world.

- [ ] John 20:30 - Jesus is the Christ, God's Son
- [ ] Acts 4:11 - Jesus is the stone that was rejected
- [ ] Romans 10:4 - Christ is the end (culmination/goal) of the law
- [ ] Romans 10:12 - Jesus is Lord of all
- [ ] 1 Corinthians 1:13 - Christ is not divided
- [ ] 1 Corinthians 1:24 - Christ is God's power and God's wisdom
- [ ] Colossians 1:27 - Christ is in you

- 1 Corinthians 3:11 - Jesus Christ is the foundation
- 1 Corinthians 15:20 - Christ is risen from the dead
- Ephesians 2:14 - Christ Jesus is our peace
- Ephesians 3:20 - Christ Jesus is the cornerstone
- Ephesians 5:23 - Christ is the head of the Church
- Colossians 1:15 - Christ is the image of the invisible God
- Colossians 3:1 - Christ is seated at the right hand of God.
- Colossians 3:11 - Christ is all and in all
- Hebrews 9:15 - Christ is the mediator of a new covenant

ISAIAH 1:17

Learn to do right
Seek justice
Defend the oppressed
Take up the cause
of the fatherless
Plead the case
of the widow

part 3

Walk Its Path
Transform Your Journey

chapter 10

What Is Faith in Action?

When I first started exploring faith, reading the Bible, going to church, trying to understand who God is, justice wasn't even on my mind. Looking back, that's pretty ironic since I was studying criminal justice in college. I wasn't planning to become a cop or anything, but I was fascinated by the contradictions in our legal system.

One of my professors, a former federal prosecutor, told us something that stuck with me. He said he couldn't bring himself to attend sentencing hearings for the murderers he'd helped convict. Even though he believed in the process, he couldn't watch someone receive the death penalty. That tension between believing in justice and struggling with its execution planted something in me: a nagging sense that things weren't as simple as they seemed.

Fast forward a few years to my first job as a pastor. I quietly moved the American flag out of the sanctuary. I wasn't trying to start trouble or make some grand political statement. I just felt like the church's first loyalty should be to God's kingdom, not any earthly nation. Boy, was I naive about how that would go over.

Despite coming from a military family myself, I suddenly became the most unpopular person in town. I had no idea how deeply people connect their faith with their love of country, or how threatening it feels when someone suggests those might be two different things.

But here's what surprised me about that church, even the people who were furious with me still treated me with kindness. A retired couple taught me about environmental stewardship and how our daily choices affect the planet. Tobacco farmers shared how they'd switched to growing grass for lawns because they couldn't keep supporting an industry they felt was hurting people. A lawyer quietly took on cases for people who couldn't afford representation. A doctor and his wife showed me what real community care looked like. Another couple grew their own vegetables and opened my eyes to issues around hunger and access to healthy food. I was learning, even if I didn't have words for what I was learning yet.

Then came a moment that really woke me up. Someone asked me point-blank: "What's your position on homosexuality?" I wasn't ready for that question. I'd cared for LGBTQ+ people in my churches and in my own family, but no one had ever forced me to think through what I actually believed theologically.

I said the most honest thing I could: "My approach is the same for everyone. We're all made in God's image, and I try to welcome people the way Jesus did." It wasn't a bad answer, but the question haunted me. I realized I'd been coasting on good intentions without doing the hard work of really understanding what my faith demanded.

That's when it hit me. I had missed something huge. The church has caused real harm to real people, and I hadn't fully grasped that reality. I had been treating liberation theology like an optional course when it was actually the main curriculum. The Bible's central story is about God freeing people from oppression.

Here's what I've come to understand: every system we live within (legal, political, economic, even religious) has flaws built right into it. These aren't just occasional mistakes; they're patterns that consistently benefit some people while harming others. If our faith doesn't acknowledge this reality, then we're missing something essential about what the Bible actually teaches.

Real justice, the kind Jesus demonstrated and the Old Testament prophets demanded, isn't the same as charity. It's not about "helping people less fortunate than us." It's not about pretending we don't see race or class differences. It's not about being polite or keeping the peace.

True biblical justice is disruptive. It's about restoring dignity to people who've been stripped of it. It means listening to stories that make us uncomfortable. It means recognizing that sin isn't just about individual bad choices, it's also about participating in systems that harm others, even when we benefit from those systems. Instead of just asking "Who did something wrong?" it asks "Who's been hurt, and how do we help heal that harm?"

So when people say that social justice is just a trendy distortion of real Christian values, I have to respectfully disagree. Social justice is biblical. It's what love looks like when it gets involved in the messy realities of public life. It's what happens when faith stops being just a private feeling and starts walking around in the world where people are actually suffering.

The gospel isn't simply asking us to believe certain things about God. It's calling us to participate in God's work of making things right, not as a hobby or side project, but as the main point. I had to learn this the hard way. I'm still learning. But now I understand: every system around us needs healing. And honestly, so do we.

The beautiful thing is that this work of justice isn't something we have to figure out alone. It's what God has been doing all along, and we get to be part of it. That's not a burden, it's an invitation to something bigger and more meaningful than we could create on our own.

Advocating for Social Justice

Oscar Romero, the Salvadoran archbishop who was assassinated for speaking out against injustice, once said something that cuts right to the heart of what faith should be: "A church that doesn't provoke any crises, a gospel that doesn't unsettle, a word of God that doesn't get under anyone's skin, a word of God that doesn't touch the real sin of the society in which it is being proclaimed—what gospel is that?"

His words challenge us to ask a hard question: if our faith never makes us uncomfortable, never pushes us to confront the world's pain and injustice, then what exactly are we following?

Social justice isn't something we add to our faith like an optional accessory. It's what happens when love gets involved in public life. When we look at the Bible's story from beginning to end, justice isn't just one theme among many; it's woven throughout the entire narrative. From the very beginning, we see that God cares deeply about how people treat each other and whether society works for everyone or just the privileged few.

The Old Testament prophets understood this. Isaiah, Jeremiah, Amos, Micah, and others weren't just offering religious advice or feel-good spiritual guidance. They were calling out corrupt systems, economic exploitation, and leaders who abused their power. They held up a mirror to their society and demanded that God's people actually live out the righteousness and compassion they claimed to believe in.

When Amos declared, "Let justice roll down like waters, and righteousness like an ever-flowing stream," he wasn't being poetic for poetry's sake. He was crying out for real, systemic change. These prophets condemned the exploitation of poor people, the neglect of vulnerable families, and nations that failed to reflect God's character in how they operated. For them, justice wasn't an abstract concept; it was practical, urgent, and deeply connected to what it means to know God.

Jesus picked up where the prophets left off. When he talked about the Kingdom of God, he wasn't just describing some distant future hope. He was painting a picture of how things could be different right now. Jesus challenged the Roman Empire's power structures, lifted up people who had been pushed to the margins, brought healing to those society had written off, and confronted religious leaders who had lost touch with what really mattered.

The Sermon on the Mount reads like a blueprint for building a just and compassionate society. Jesus' parables about the Good Samaritan, the unforgiving servant, the rich man and Lazarus, and separating sheep from goats all carry powerful social implications about how we're supposed to treat each other, especially those who are struggling.

What Is Faith in Action?

Jesus didn't die just to secure individual tickets to heaven. He came to usher in a completely new way of living: one marked by justice, mercy, humility, and love. And he calls everyone who follows him to start embodying that new reality right here, right now.

This means we need to think about both personal transformation and systemic change. The biblical understanding that all of humanity is broken reminds us that sin isn't just about individual bad choices; it's also embedded in the systems and structures that shape our world. Personal change is absolutely essential, but it's incomplete if it doesn't transform how we live in community, love our neighbors, and confront injustice when we see it.

When we talk about human brokenness, we're not saying that people are as terrible as they could possibly be. We're recognizing that sin touches every part of our lives: our hearts, our institutions, our communities, even our best intentions. Injustice isn't just "out there" somewhere. It lives in how we benefit from broken systems, how we look the other way when it's convenient, and how we choose safety and comfort over standing with people who are suffering.

But here's the hope: grace is bigger than all of that. God's grace doesn't just forgive us; it transforms us. We're not just saved from something; we're saved for something meaningful. We're called to lives of compassion, genuine community, justice-seeking, and the work of building a world that looks more like what Jesus envisioned.

That work touches every area of life. Justice means asking hard questions about how we treat workers, how wages are set, how resources get distributed, and whether our economic systems serve everyone or just those who are already comfortable. It means honestly facing the ongoing reality of racism and the ways it continues to distort our institutions, policies, and relationships. It means doing the difficult work of dismantling what divides us and rebuilding what brings us together.

It means caring for our environment not because it's politically trendy, but because creation itself is suffering and God cares deeply for the most vulnerable people, who are usually the first and worst affected by environmental damage. It means standing alongside people who have been marginalized and recognizing the inherent dignity in every person, regardless of where they come from, who they are, or who they love.

Justice isn't something we pursue in isolation. It's inherently communal; it's what discipleship looks like when lived out in relationship with others. The early Christian communities understood this. They shared meals, resources, and responsibility for each other. They believed that how they lived together actually mattered. They saw the church as meant to be a glimpse of what the world could look like when it's working the way it's supposed to.

Jesus never promised that following him would be easy. In fact, he was pretty clear that it would be challenging. But he also promised that God's kingdom is already breaking into our world. He showed us that power can be laid down rather than grasped, that enemies can be loved rather than destroyed, and that injustice can be resisted not through violence but through courage, truth-telling, and sacrificial love.

- Genesis 1:27 - Reflect God's image in yourself and others
- Genesis 38:1-30 - Speak up against abuse
- Exodus 1:1-14 - Protect the dignity and humanity of all people

What Is Faith in Action?

- [ ] Exodus 22:21 - Treat immigrants and foreigners with respect
- [ ] Exodus 23:6 - Stand up for the poor
- [ ] Leviticus 19:9-10 - Share food and resources with those in need
- [ ] Leviticus 19:13 - Pay fair wages and honor workers' rights
- [ ] Leviticus 19:15 - Judge fairly
- [ ] Leviticus 19:18 - Show love and kindness to others
- [ ] Leviticus 25:8-13 - Create time for rest and restoration for all
- [ ] Leviticus 25:35-36 - Support those struggling financially
- [ ] Numbers 35:9-28 - Build safe spaces for people fleeing danger
- [ ] Deuteronomy 10:18 - Care for outsiders
- [ ] Deuteronomy 14:29 - Provide for widows and orphans
- [ ] Deuteronomy 15:7 - Be generous with your resources
- [ ] Deuteronomy 20:19-20 - Care for the environment
- [ ] Deuteronomy 23:12-14 - Prioritize public health and cleanliness
- [ ] 1 Samuel 13:19-21 - Equip people with resources to thrive
- [ ] Psalm 9:9 - Know that God is a defender of the oppressed
- [ ] Psalm 12:5 - Trust that God hears the cries of the poor
- [ ] Psalm 34:6 - Stand with the desperate, because God does

- [ ] Psalm 72:1-7 - Prioritize justice and fairness for all
- [ ] Psalm 82:3-4 - Defend the rights of the weak and poor
- [ ] Psalm 120:6-7 - Strive for peace, even in a conflicted world
- [ ] Psalm 140:12 - Trust that God will secure justice for the needy
- [ ] Proverbs 14:31 - Show kindness to the poor
- [ ] Proverbs 17:23-26 - Reject bribes and corruption
- [ ] Proverbs 19:17 - Worship God by caring for the poor
- [ ] Proverbs 23:10-11 - Respect the rights and property of others
- [ ] Proverbs 23:29-35 - Avoid excess and addictions
- [ ] Proverbs 31:8-9 - Speak out for the voiceless
- [ ] Isaiah 2:2-4 - Work toward peace
- [ ] Isaiah 41:17-20 - Restore hope by standing with those in need
- [ ] Isaiah 58:6-7 - Worship God by welcoming the outcast
- [ ] Isaiah 58:6-12 - Rebuild broken communities
- [ ] Isaiah 61:1 - Know God's preference for the oppressed
- [ ] Jeremiah 22:1-5 - Treat immigrants and refugees with fairness
- [ ] Jeremiah 22:3 - Fight against oppression
- [ ] Ezekiel 18:7 - Help the hungry and homeless

What Is Faith in Action?

- [ ] Micah 6:8 - Seek justice, love mercy, and walk humbly
- [ ] Amos 5:24 - Let justice roll down like waters
- [ ] Zechariah 7:10 - Protect and care for the most vulnerable
- [ ] Matthew 2:16-18 - Grieve for those who suffer
- [ ] Matthew 6:14-15 - Forgive others
- [ ] Matthew 7:12 - Treat others how you want to be treated
- [ ] Matthew 10:5-15 - Care for the sick and vulnerable
- [ ] Matthew 19:13-15 - Value and protect children
- [ ] Matthew 25:35-36 - See Jesus in all people
- [ ] Mark 1:40-45 - Be like Jesus, bringing healing to all
- [ ] Mark 10:21 - Let go of material wealth to help the poor
- [ ] Luke 3:11 - Share your surplus with those who lack basic needs
- [ ] Luke 4:18 - Heal the brokenhearted
- [ ] Luke 10:25-28 - Love God and your neighbor as yourself
- [ ] Luke 14:13-14 - Invite and care for those excluded by society
- [ ] Luke 21:10-19 - Stay strong in faith, even in persecution
- [ ] John 4:3-26 - Honor the dignity of women
- [ ] Acts 4:32-35 - Share resources so no one is in need

- Acts 20:35 - Find joy in giving rather than receiving
- Romans 12:13 - Practice radical hospitality and inclusion
- Romans 12:18 - Be peacemakers in a divided world
- 1 Corinthians 12:19-26 - Celebrate the value of everyone's work
- Galatians 3:23-29 - Embrace unity and equality in Christ
- Ephesians 4:32 - Forgive others as God forgives you
- Hebrews 13:1-3 - Care for prisoners
- James 1:26-27 - Care for the vulnerable in society
- James 2:14-17 - Put your faith to work
- 1 John 3:17-18 - Show love through action, not just words

Living Ethically

Discipleship is not about mastering moral techniques or self-improvement through heroic effort. It is about being formed by God's story, allowing the Spirit to reshape our desires so that we become people who naturally embody God's character. This formation doesn't modify behavior; it reconstitutes our identity as citizens of God's peaceable kingdom.

The virtues Paul describes are not achievements we accomplish through moral exertion but gifts that emerge from our participation in God's life. We do not manufacture love or patience; these virtues are formed in us as the community of faith schools us in kingdom practices.

Love flows from recognizing we exist because we are first loved by God. Patience develops as we learn to inhabit God's time rather than our anxious schedules. Kindness takes root as we practice the generosity shown toward us. These are communal practices requiring the church to be the kind of community that makes such virtues intelligible.

Living faithfully also demands reading Scripture with recognition that it bears the marks of particular cultures, including social arrangements that, when baptized uncritically, have legitimized oppression. Scripture's authority lies not in timeless principles but in narrating God's redemption in ways that train us to see our lives as part of that ongoing drama.

This is not gentle invitation to personal improvement but radical call to be formed as citizens of an alternative polis, the church, which embodies God's peace in a world organized by violence. Our discipleship will be marked by failure, but God's mercy sustains the community that dares to live as if resurrection has begun transforming all creation.

- [ ] Exodus 20:1-17 - The Ten Commandments
- [ ] Deuteronomy 10:12-13 - The Call to Covenant Faithfulness
- [ ] Proverbs 6:16-19 - The Importance of Integrity
- [ ] Matthew 5:1-12 - The Beatitudes

What Is Faith in Action?

- [ ] Matthew 22:37-40 - The Greatest Commandment
- [ ] Matthew 28:18-20 - The Great Commission
- [ ] John 15:5 - The Vine and the Branches
- [ ] Acts 2:42-47 - The Fellowship of Believers
- [ ] Romans 12:9-21 - The Marks of True Christian Love
- [ ] 1 Corinthians 13 - The Way of Love
- [ ] 2 Corinthians 5:17-21 - The Ministry of Reconciliation
- [ ] Galatians 5:22-23 - The Fruit of the Spirit
- [ ] Ephesians 4:1-3 - The Unity of the Spirit
- [ ] Ephesians 6:10-18 - The Armor of God
- [ ] Philippians 2:5-11 - The Christ Hymn
- [ ] Philippians 4:8 - Meditating on What Is Good
- [ ] Colossians 3:12-17 - Clothed in Christlike Virtues
- [ ] 1 Thessalonians 5:14-18 - Living in the Spirit's Community
- [ ] 1 Timothy 6:11-16 - The Good Fight of Faith
- [ ] Hebrews 11 - The Hall of Faith
- [ ] Hebrews 13:1-3 - The Call to Hospitality and Compassion
- [ ] 2 Peter 1:5-8 - The Ladder of Virtues

chapter 11

Where Can I Find Hope?

Sometimes, students approach me, asking where they can turn in the Bible to find peace and comfort. With AI and Google just a click away, they're searching for something deeper, more profound than a list of verses. They're longing for connection, wisdom, and a sense of hope. I am deeply grateful to walk with them in those moments. A strong Christian community exists for this reason. To comfort those in distress and stand together in times of need is a sacred calling. So, if you or someone you love is facing illness, grief, or any kind of crisis, please know that you don't have to face it alone.

Grief is Normal

Grief is one of life's universal experiences, yet it remains deeply personal. While many of us may move through typical stages of grief, no two journeys are the same. The path is shaped by the circumstances of the loss, the depth of your relationship with the person, and your unique personal and spiritual history.

Whether you're mourning the loss of a loved one or anticipating their passing, grief brings a whirlwind of emotions, intense, painful, and yet often transformative. Sudden or traumatic losses can amplify these feelings, overwhelming you with their abruptness. Anticipated losses, on the other hand, may create a complex blend of sorrow and reflection. Yet, in all its forms, grief invites us to wrestle with life's fragility, deepen our gratitude for those we love, and strengthen our connections with those who remain.

Navigating Emotional Pain

Grief isn't the only source of deep pain. Life's challenges, broken relationships, job loss, betrayal, or setbacks can wound us profoundly. Recognizing this pain isn't weakness; it's a courageous step toward healing.

Healing begins with honest acceptance of what you're feeling. It's okay to hurt. Suppressing pain only prolongs its grip. When you acknowledge emotions without judgment, you take the first step toward release.

Self-care becomes essential: prayer, meditation, walking, creative expression like journaling or music. These provide outlets for processing emotions and restoring balance.

Equally important is seeking support. Emotional pain isn't meant to be carried alone. Connect with trusted friends, family, or faith community. For many, reaching out to a counselor is pivotal. Asking for help isn't failure; it's strength.

Turn to Scripture for comfort. The Bible offers timeless truths and unshakable promises for times of loss, pain, or anxiety. Here are some of the Bible's most comforting passages when life feels overwhelming.

God Is Always With Us

- [ ] Genesis 28:15 - God promises to always be with you
- [ ] Exodus 33:14 - The Lord's presence brings rest and peace
- [ ] Deuteronomy 31:6 - Be strong; God will never leave you
- [ ] Deuteronomy 33:27 - The eternal God is our refuge
- [ ] Joshua 1:9 - Be courageous; God is by your side
- [ ] Psalm 34:18 - The LORD is close to the brokenhearted
- [ ] Isaiah 41:10 - Do not fear; God will strengthen you
- [ ] Isaiah 43:1-2 - God stays with you through trials
- [ ] Hebrews 13:5-6 - God will never leave or forsake you

God Gives Us Strength

- [ ] Exodus 15:2 - God is your strength and salvation
- [ ] Psalm 23:4 - God protects you even in dark times
- [ ] Isaiah 40:31 - Those who hope in God will be renewed

- [ ] Psalm 46:1-3 - God is our refuge and strength
- [ ] Habakkuk 3:19 - God makes you strong to overcome
- [ ] Colossians 1:11 - Be strengthened with God's power

God Brings Us Peace

- [ ] Psalm 62:1-2 - Rest in God, your rock and salvation
- [ ] Proverbs 3:5-6 - Trust God; He will make your paths straight
- [ ] Isaiah 26:3 - Trusting God brings perfect peace
- [ ] John 14:27 - Jesus gives peace, not as the world does
- [ ] Philippians 4:6-7 - Do not be anxious about anything

God Gives Us Hope

- [ ] Psalm 62:5-6 - Our hope comes from God
- [ ] Psalm 71:5 - God is our hope
- [ ] Isaiah 40:31 - We will soar like eagles
- [ ] Jeremiah 29:11 - God knows your plans
- [ ] Lamentations 3:22-23 - God's love is steadfast
- [ ] Micah 7:8 - When you're in darkness, God is your light

- [ ] Romans 5:3-5 - Trials produce perseverance and hope
- [ ] Romans 8:24-25 - Hope requires patience and trust
- [ ] 1 Peter 1:3 - Through Christ, we have a living hope

God Watches Over Us

- [ ] Psalm 27:1 - The Lord is your light and salvation
- [ ] Psalm 55:22 - Cast your cares on the LORD
- [ ] Psalm 56:3 - When you're afraid, trust in God
- [ ] Psalm 121:1-2 - Your help comes from the Lord
- [ ] Isaiah 49:16 - God has engraved you on His hands
- [ ] 1 Peter 5:7 - Give your worries to God

God Gives Us Courage

- [ ] Deuteronomy 31:6 - Be strong and courageous in God
- [ ] Psalm 118:6 - God emboldens us to face adversity
- [ ] Isaiah 35:4 - Be strong and fearless; God will save you
- [ ] Jeremiah 32:27 - Nothing is too hard for the Lord
- [ ] Luke 1:37 - Nothing is impossible with God

Where Can I Find Hope?

- [ ] Acts 18:9-10 - Don't be afraid; God is with you

God Comforts Us

- [ ] Psalm 73:26 - God is your strength when your heart fails
- [ ] Psalm 94:19 - God's comfort gives joy in anxiety
- [ ] Matthew 5:4 - Blessed are those who mourn
- [ ] John 16:22 - Your sorrow will turn to joy
- [ ] 2 Corinthians 1:3-4 - God comforts you to comfort others
- [ ] 2 Corinthians 4:16-18 - Do not lose heart
- [ ] 2 Corinthians 12:9-10 - God is strong in your weakness
- [ ] 1 Peter 5:10 - God will restore and strengthen you

God Restores Us

- [ ] Zephaniah 3:17 - God rejoices over you with singing
- [ ] Matthew 11:28 - Jesus gives rest to the weary
- [ ] Mark 4:39-40 - Jesus calms the storms in your life
- [ ] Romans 8:38-39 - Nothing can separate you from God's love
- [ ] Revelation 21:4 - God will wipe away all tears and end pain

God Guides and Encourages Us

- [ ] 1 Chronicles 16:11 - Seek the Lord's strength always
- [ ] Romans 12:12 - Be joyful, patient, and prayerful
- [ ] Philippians 4:13 - You can do all things through Christ
- [ ] 1 Thessalonians 5:16-18 - Rejoice, pray, and give thanks
- [ ] Hebrews 10:24-25 - Encourage one another to do good

chapter 12

How Do I Grow?

Faith is a living, breathing relationship with God that shapes every aspect of our lives. Yet many churches, while inviting people to worship and share their beliefs, often stop short of teaching practical ways to grow in faith. This gap leaves many feeling that their faith is weak or stagnant, yearning for something more but unsure how to achieve it.

Truth is, faith grows through intentional cultivation. It requires active participation and thrives when we nurture it and carve out space to take hold in our everyday moments. The challenge is that faith too often becomes confined to a few select areas of life—worship, quick prayers before meals, or moments when we need comfort in hard times. But faith was always meant to flourish at the center of our lives. It is designed to transform the whole, spilling over into how we work, how we rest, how we love, and how we serve.

Many people experience a watered-down faith. This faith feels distant and hollow, where God seems more like a backdrop to life than the One animating it. This isn't just a personal struggle; it reflects a culture that undervalues or misunderstands the depth of a real, vibrant relationship with Christ. Rediscovering that depth requires returning to the basics, not just as ideas but as practices. It means renewing our sense of purpose, realigning our habits with God's will, and making faith something we live, not just think about.

You can't give what you don't have, right? If you long to inspire others or pass on a living, growing faith, it begins with investing in your journey. Practices like prayer, reading scripture, worshiping with intention, and serving others are not chores or checklists. They are lifelines that anchor you to God's presence and reshape your heart to reflect His truth. These rhythms of faith do more than connect you to God; they prepare you to live out His love in a world desperate for it.

Living this way is not easy. Life pulls us in a thousand directions; sometimes, even finding a quiet moment feels impossible. But the beauty of faith is that it is built in small, ordinary acts. It grows when you whisper a prayer in the middle of a busy day (I pray a lot when I drive), choose gratitude in moments of frustration, or offer kindness even when it costs you something. These simple moments create ripples. They deepen your connection to God and touch the lives of those around you. Faith is contagious. When people see authentic faith, faith that moves, breathes, and loves, they are drawn to it.

The journey of faith isn't about perfection; it's about being present with God and allowing His presence to transform us. Through spiritual disciplines, we create space for this divine encounter, not as a burden but as a gift that allows our faith to breathe, grow, and overflow into every corner of our lives. These practices become the fertile soil where deep roots grow, anchoring us in truth and nurturing a faith that doesn't just survive but thrives, bearing fruit that nourishes both our souls and the world around us.

Read the Bible

- [ ] Joshua 1:8 - Meditate on God's word day and night
- [ ] Psalm 119:105 - God's word is a lamp and light
- [ ] Proverbs 4:20-21 - Be attentive to God's word
- [ ] Isaiah 40:8 - The Word of God stands forever
- [ ] Luke 11:28 - Blessed are those who hear the word of God
- [ ] Romans 15:4 - Scripture is written to give us hope
- [ ] Colossians 3:16 - Let the word dwell richly as you teach

Bear Each Other's Burdens

- [ ] Exodus 23:5 - Help even your enemy with their burden
- [ ] Proverbs 17:17 - A true friend loves and supports in adversity
- [ ] Isaiah 58:6-7 - Share with the hungry and shelter the oppressed
- [ ] John 13:34 - Love one another as Christ loved us

How Do I Grow?

- [ ] Romans 15:1 - The strong bear with the weak to build them up
- [ ] 1 Corinthians 12:26 - If one member suffers, all share the burden
- [ ] Galatians 6:2 - Carry each other's burdens to fulfill Christ's law
- [ ] Ephesians 4:2 - Bear with one another in love
- [ ] Philippians 2:4 - Look to the interests of others, not your own
- [ ] Hebrews 10:24-25 - Encourage one another toward love

Celebrate and Show Joy

- [ ] Psalm 30:11 - Turn mourning into dancing and joy
- [ ] Psalm 118:24 - Rejoice in each day God has made
- [ ] Psalm 150:6 - Praise God in celebration with every breath
- [ ] Ecclesiastes 3:4 - A time to weep, a time to dance
- [ ] Acts 2:46 - Celebrate daily with glad and sincere hearts
- [ ] 1 Corinthians 5:8 - Celebrate with sincerity and truth

Build Community

- [ ] Acts 2:44-47 - Believers shared with joy and unity
- [ ] 1 John 1:7 - Walking in light fosters unity

- [ ] Acts 2:42 - Devote yourself to teaching, fellowship, and prayer
- [ ] Hebrews 3:13 - Encourage one another daily

Practice Confession

- [ ] Leviticus 5:5 - When guilt is realized, confess the sin committed
- [ ] Numbers 5:7 - Confess sins and make restitution for wrongs
- [ ] Psalm 32:5 - Confess to the Lord for forgiveness
- [ ] Proverbs 28:13 - Confessing sin leads to mercy

Honor Confidentiality

- [ ] Proverbs 11:13 - Trustworthy people keep confidences
- [ ] Proverbs 25:9-10 - Handle private matters with respect
- [ ] Matthew 18:15 - Keep arguments and disagreements private
- [ ] James 3:5-6 - The tongue's words can destroy

Fast with Purpose

- [ ] Exodus 34:28 - Moses fasted to meet God
- [ ] Ezra 8:23 - Fasting brings God's guidance

How Do I Grow?

- [ ] Nehemiah 1:4 - Fast with prayer in seeking God
- [ ] Psalm 69:10 - Fasting humbles the soul
- [ ] Isaiah 58:6-12 - True fasting brings justice and freedom
- [ ] Daniel 10:3 - Fast for spiritual focus
- [ ] Matthew 6:16-18 - Fast in secret to honor God
- [ ] Acts 13:2 - Fasting leads to hearing God's call

Forgive Freely and Pursue Reconciliation

- [ ] Matthew 6:14-15 - Forgiving others brings God's forgiveness
- [ ] Matthew 18:15-16 - Resolve conflicts peacefully and directly
- [ ] Luke 6:37 - Forgive, and you will be forgiven
- [ ] 2 Corinthians 5:18-20 - Be ministers of reconciliation
- [ ] Ephesians 4:32 - Be kind, compassionate, and forgiving
- [ ] Colossians 3:13 - Forgive others as the Lord forgave you

Show Generosity and Practice Sharing

- [ ] Matthew 6:19-21 - Invest in eternal treasures
- [ ] Luke 3:11 - Share with those in need

- [ ] 2 Corinthians 9:6-7 - Give cheerfully and generously
- [ ] Hebrews 13:16 - Do good and share with others

Cultivate Gratitude

- [ ] 1 Chronicles 16:34 - Give thanks for God's enduring love
- [ ] Psalm 100:4 - Enter God's presence with thanksgiving
- [ ] Ephesians 5:20 - Always give thanks to God
- [ ] 1 Thessalonians 5:18 - Give thanks in every situation

Show Hospitality

- [ ] Leviticus 19:34 - Treat strangers like family
- [ ] Romans 12:13 - Share with those in need
- [ ] Titus 1:8 - A good person loves to host others
- [ ] 1 Peter 4:9 - Show hospitality happily, without complaining

Meditate and Pray

- [ ] Joshua 1:8 - Meditate for guidance and success
- [ ] Psalm 1:2 - Meditate on God's law day and night

- [ ] Matthew 6:6 - Seek God in private, personal prayer
- [ ] Philippians 4:6 - Present your requests with thanksgiving

Practice Patience

- [ ] Psalm 37:7 - Be still and trust God to act
- [ ] Psalm 40:1 - God hears those who wait patiently
- [ ] Proverbs 14:29 - Patience brings wisdom, not anger
- [ ] Ecclesiastes 7:8 - Patience leads to better endings than pride
- [ ] Romans 12:12 - Be patient in trouble and stay prayerful
- [ ] Galatians 6:9 - Don't grow weary in doing good
- [ ] James 1:4 - Persevere to grow in maturity

Seek Counsel

- [ ] Proverbs 15:22 - Seek advisors for sound plans
- [ ] Proverbs 20:5 - Wise counsel helps uncover deep truths
- [ ] Romans 12:2 - Professional help supports renewing our minds
- [ ] Philippians 4:6-7 - Prayer complements professional help
- [ ] James 5:16 - Sharing struggles with others fosters healing

- [ ] Psalm 102:18 - Record God's works for future generations
- [ ] Habakkuk 2:2 - Write down the vision for others to see

Live Simply and Consume Less

- [ ] Ecclesiastes 4:6 - Contentment is better than constant striving
- [ ] Luke 12:15 - Life isn't about having lots of stuff
- [ ] Philippians 4:11-13 - Learn to be content no matter what
- [ ] 1 Timothy 6:6-8 - Be content with what you have
- [ ] Titus 2:11-12 - Embrace simplicity

Embrace Silence, Rest, and Take Retreats

- [ ] Exodus 20:8-11 - Rest on the Sabbath, keeping it holy
- [ ] Psalm 46:10 - Be still and know God is Lord
- [ ] Mark 1:35 - Jesus prayed alone in solitude
- [ ] Mark 2:27 - The Sabbath is made for our benefit
- [ ] Mark 6:31 - Come away and rest
- [ ] Luke 5:16 - Jesus withdrew to pray

chapter 13

What Is God's Plan?

Students often ask me, "what is God's plan for my life?" They don't always say it outright. Sometimes, it sounds more like, "Hey, Steve, you should preach on God's purpose." That's not just a casual suggestion, is it? It's the cry beneath a thousand sleepless nights, the quiet ache for clarity, meaning, and direction. It's that pull toward something deeper, something eternal.

And here's the thing, you're not alone in asking. This isn't just a question for the restless and uncertain; it's a question that's echoed across the centuries. Theologians, thinkers, and dreamers like Aquinas, who was known for connecting faith with reason, and Luther, who redefined faith as something lived out in daily work. Wesley, who was relentless in his call to personal holiness and transformation, also wrestled with it. Because it's THE question. The one we can't shake. The one that keeps pulling us toward God.

What Is God's Plan?

Aquinas would probably tell us that God's plan isn't locked away in some distant heaven. It's here, in the rhythm of creation itself. Look around: the order, the beauty, the logic of everything. God's fingerprints are everywhere, including on you. Your ability to think, reason, and create is part of His plan. So don't ignore it. Use it. Study deeply. Think critically. Make decisions that honor Him. And your gifts are no accident. You're stepping into His plan when you use your gifts to love, serve, and contribute. Whether helping a friend or taking a leap toward a career that excites and terrifies you, God's plan unfolds over time and with every faithful step you take.

Luther is more straight to the point. Martin Luther, who taught that all work, not just church work, is holy, would probably look us in the eye and say, "Don't overthink it." God's plan isn't reserved for the spiritual elite. It's in your everyday work. Even that part-time job you're tired of. That class project. That shift at the coffee shop. It's all holy ground when you approach it with faith. Every spreadsheet you fill out, every meal you prepare, and every line of code you write can be sacred when done with love or meaning. Your desk, kitchen, and study room are not just spaces but can be altars. Your work isn't just a task. It can be worship.

Calvin is a little more formal but less passionate. John Calvin, who saw God's sovereignty in every detail of life, reminds us to zoom out and see the big picture. God's sovereignty is vast, he might say. It's cosmic. Your life, choices, and relationships are pieces of a much bigger puzzle than you. Calvin would want us to see this as freeing, that we're not the story's center, but our life matters because it's connected to God's bigger plan. Even the tiny things, like the meeting you're dreading or the chore you've been putting off, are moments where you're invited to reflect God's order, creativity, and love in the world.

John Wesley added that it's not just about what you do. It's about who you're becoming. Every challenge, every act of love, and every hard choice are all shaping you. God is using your work, studies, and relationships to grow you in patience, humility, and courage. Wesley would tell us be transformed by it! Because when your heart aligns with God, your calling becomes more than a task. It becomes your path to holiness.

Dorothy Day lived a fierce life demanding much of herself and others. She found purpose as an activist who lived the Gospel among the poor. She looked at the poor, the hungry, the hurting, and the forgotten and realized God's plan isn't just about your career or happiness, but it's about love. Radical love. She would encourage us to take risks. Volunteer. Share. Give what you have. Sit with someone who feels invisible. That's where you'll meet Christ. That's where your life starts to echo the Gospel. That's where you'll start to see God's plan.

- Genesis 1:27-28 - Reflect God's image
- Genesis 2:15 - See work as part of God's design for you
- Psalm 32:8 - Trust God's instruction and guidance
- Psalm 37:23-24 - Be confident in God
- Psalm 46:10 - Remember God's in control, not you
- Psalm 139:13-16 - Embrace your intentional creation by God

What Is God's Plan?

- [ ] Proverbs 3:5-6 - Trust God to guide your steps
- [ ] Proverbs 16:9 - Submit your plans to God's direction
- [ ] Ecclesiastes 3:1 - Recognize God's timing
- [ ] Ecclesiastes 4:9-12 - Find strength in community
- [ ] Isaiah 30:21 - Listen for God's voice, directing your way
- [ ] Isaiah 41:10 - Draw strength from God's presence
- [ ] Isaiah 43:1-7 - Know you are called and loved
- [ ] Isaiah 58:11 - Rely on God's provision
- [ ] Jeremiah 1:5 - Understand you were known
- [ ] Jeremiah 29:11 - Rest in God's plans for your future and hope
- [ ] Micah 6:8 - Act with justice, mercy, and humility
- [ ] Matthew 5:13-16 - Shine as salt and light in the world
- [ ] Matthew 6:33 - Seek God's kingdom above all things
- [ ] Matthew 25:34-40 - Serve others
- [ ] John 15:16 - Bear fruit that lasts through God
- [ ] Romans 8:28 - Trust God works all things for your good
- [ ] Romans 12:1-8 - Use your gifts to serve in community
- [ ] 1 Corinthians 10:31 - Live for His glory in all you do

What Is God's Plan?

- [ ] 1 Corinthians 12:4-11 - Embrace your spiritual gifts
- [ ] 2 Corinthians 5:17 - Walk as a new creation in Christ
- [ ] 2 Corinthians 5:18-20 - Share in the ministry of reconciliation
- [ ] Ephesians 4:1 - Live a life worthy of God's calling
- [ ] Philippians 1:6 - Be confident in God's work in your life
- [ ] Philippians 1:9-11 - Seek discernment and wisdom in prayer
- [ ] Philippians 2:13 - Let God work in and through you
- [ ] Philippians 4:6-7 - Receive peace through prayer
- [ ] Philippians 4:13 - Rely on Christ's strength
- [ ] Colossians 3:17 - Honor God in all you do
- [ ] 1 Thessalonians 5:11 - Build up and encourage others
- [ ] 1 Thessalonians 5:16-18 - Rejoice, pray, and give thanks
- [ ] 2 Timothy 1:9 - Walk in holiness through His calling
- [ ] Hebrews 10:24-25 - Encourage and inspire each other
- [ ] Hebrews 12:1-2 - Run with perseverance
- [ ] James 1:5 - Ask for His wisdom when you lack it

chapter 14

What Verses We Love?

In the darkest valleys of human experience, certain verses break through like lightning, illuminating the path forward when all other lights have failed. The verses we hold close often speak to the deepest parts of who we are, meeting us in moments of joy, sorrow, or longing. For someone who has faced rejection or hardship, a verse about God's unfailing love can feel like a lifeline. It affirms their worth and anchors them in a love that never falters. These words resonate deeply because they connect us to God's greater story, a story that reminds us who we are and invites us into something far greater than ourselves.

But these verses are more than just lifelines. They are living reminders of God's promises, carrying hope and assurance through seasons of doubt or uncertainty. Faith, at its core, is more than belief. It is a relationship, an ongoing dialogue, an encounter with a God who meets us right where we are. The verses we treasure turn profound truths into deeply personal experiences, touching our hearts and shaping the way we live.

As we reflect on these verses over time, they begin to take root within us, bringing peace and renewal. They remind us who God is and who we are called to be. In the quiet moments of fear or struggle, they still our hearts, grounding us in truth and giving us strength to extend love and grace to others. Over time, these verses deepen our understanding of God's character. His compassion, His justice, and His unrelenting desire for restoration become clearer to us. With that understanding comes a renewed sense of purpose, a courage to live with conviction and hope.

Faith doesn't stop with us. It calls us outward, inviting us to participate in God's work of healing and renewal in the world. The verses that resonate most often carry a quiet invitation, urging us to live out Christ's love in practical, tangible ways. They become markers of identity and transformation, connecting us to the larger story God is telling. It is a story of redemption and reconciliation. Through these words, we are reminded that we are not just recipients of His grace but active participants in His ongoing work.

Below, I've shared some of the verses that have been especially meaningful to me and to countless others.

- [ ] Genesis 1:1 - In the beginning, God created
- [ ] Genesis 1:27 - God created humankind in his image
- [ ] Genesis 12:2 - I will make of you a great nation

What Verses We Love?

- [ ] Leviticus 19:18 - Love your neighbor as yourself
- [ ] Numbers 6:24-26 - The Lord bless you and keep you
- [ ] Deuteronomy 6:4-9 - Hear, O Israel; Love the Lord your God
- [ ] Deuteronomy 31:6 - He will never leave you or forsake you
- [ ] Joshua 1:9 - Be strong and courageous
- [ ] Joshua 24:15 - But as for me and my household
- [ ] Ruth 1:16 - Where you go, I will go
- [ ] 1 Samuel 16:7 - The Lord looks at the heart
- [ ] Nehemiah 8:10 - The joy of the Lord is your strength
- [ ] Job 19:25 - I know that my redeemer lives
- [ ] Psalm 23 - The Lord is my shepherd
- [ ] Psalm 27:1 - The Lord is my light and my salvation
- [ ] Psalm 32:8 - I will instruct you and teach you
- [ ] Psalm 34:8 - Taste and see that the Lord is good
- [ ] Psalm 37:4 - Take delight in the Lord
- [ ] Psalm 46:1 - God is our refuge and strength
- [ ] Psalm 46:10 - Be still and know that I am God
- [ ] Psalm 51:10 - Create in me a pure heart

What Verses We Love?

- [ ] Psalm 96: 1-3 - Sing to the Lord a new song
- [ ] Psalm 100 - Make a joyful noise
- [ ] Psalm 103:1-5 - Praise the LORD, my soul
- [ ] Psalm 107:1 - Give thanks to the Lord
- [ ] Psalm 119:105 - Your word is a lamp for my feet
- [ ] Psalm 121:1-2 - I lift up my eyes to the hills
- [ ] Psalm 139:13-16 - You knit me together in my mother's womb
- [ ] Psalm 150 - Praise God with instruments and dance
- [ ] Proverbs 3:5-6 - Trust in the Lord with all your heart
- [ ] Proverbs 9:10 - The fear of the Lord is the beginning
- [ ] Ecclesiastes 3:1-8 - To everything there is a season
- [ ] Ecclesiastes 4:9 - Two are better than one
- [ ] Isaiah 6:8 - Here am I, send me
- [ ] Isaiah 9:6 - For to us a child is born
- [ ] Isaiah 40:28-31 - Those who hope in the Lord
- [ ] Isaiah 41:10 - Fear not, for I am with you
- [ ] Isaiah 43:19 - See, I am doing a new thing!
- [ ] Isaiah 53:5 - He was pierced for our transgressions

What Verses We Love?

- [ ] Isaiah 55:8 - My thoughts are not your thoughts
- [ ] Isaiah 58:11 - The Lord will guide you
- [ ] Isaiah 66:13 - As a mother comforts her child
- [ ] Jeremiah 1:5 - Before I formed you in the womb
- [ ] Jeremiah 29:11 - For I know the plans I have for you
- [ ] Jeremiah 33:3 - Call to me and I will answer you
- [ ] Lamentations 3:22-23 - His mercies are new every morning
- [ ] Hosea 6:6 - God desires mercy, not sacrifice
- [ ] Amos 5:24 - Let justice roll on like a river
- [ ] Micah 6:8 - What does the Lord require of you
- [ ] Zephaniah 3:17 - The LORD your God is with you
- [ ] Matthew 4:4 - We can not live on bread alone
- [ ] Matthew 5:3-12 - Blessed are the poor in spirit
- [ ] Matthew 5:14-16 - You are the light of the world
- [ ] Matthew 6:9-13 - Our Father in heaven
- [ ] Matthew 6:33 - Seek first the kingdom of God
- [ ] Matthew 7:12 - Do to others
- [ ] Matthew 11:28 - Come to Me, all you who are weary

What Verses We Love?

- [ ] Matthew 17:20 - Faith as small as a mustard seed
- [ ] Matthew 18:20 - Where two or three are gathered
- [ ] Matthew 22:37-40 - Love the Lord your God
- [ ] Matthew 25:40 - Whatever you did for the least of these
- [ ] Matthew 28:19-20 - Go and make disciples
- [ ] Mark 10:27 - All things are possible with God
- [ ] Luke 2:11 - A Savior has been born
- [ ] Luke 6:38 - Give, and it will be given to you
- [ ] John 1:1 - In the beginning was the Word
- [ ] John 3:16 - For God so loved the world
- [ ] John 8:12 - I am the light of the world
- [ ] John 10:10 - I came that they may have life
- [ ] John 11:25-26 - I am the resurrection and the life
- [ ] John 14:1-3 - Do not let your hearts be troubled
- [ ] John 14:6 - I am the way, the truth, and the life
- [ ] John 14:27 - Peace I leave with you
- [ ] John 15:5 - I am the vine; you are the branches
- [ ] John 15:12-13 - Love each other as I have loved you

What Verses We Love?

- [ ] Acts 4:12 - No other name under heaven
- [ ] Romans 1:16 - For I am not ashamed of the gospel
- [ ] Romans 5:3-5 - Hope does not disappoint
- [ ] Romans 6:23 - Wages of sin is death
- [ ] Romans 8:28 - All things work together for good
- [ ] Romans 8:31 - If God is for us, who can be against us
- [ ] Romans 8:38-39 - Nothing can separate us from God's love
- [ ] Romans 10:9 - If you declare with your mouth, "Jesus is Lord..."
- [ ] Romans 10:17 - Faith comes from hearing
- [ ] Romans 12:2 - Do not conform to this world
- [ ] Romans 15:13 - May the God of hope fill you
- [ ] 1 Corinthians 13:4-13 - Love is patient, love is kind
- [ ] 2 Corinthians 5:7 - Walk by faith, not by sight
- [ ] 2 Corinthians 5:17 - If anyone is in Christ
- [ ] 2 Corinthians 12:9 - My grace is sufficient for you
- [ ] Galatians 2:20 - I have been crucified with Christ
- [ ] Galatians 5:22-23 - The fruit of the Spirit is
- [ ] Galatians 6:2 - Carry each other's burdens

What Verses We Love?

- [ ] Ephesians 2:8-9 - By grace you have been saved
- [ ] Ephesians 3:20 - Glory to God, who is able to do far beyond
- [ ] Ephesians 4:32 - Be kind and compassionate
- [ ] Ephesians 6:10-12 - Be strong in the Lord
- [ ] Philippians 1:6 - He who began a good work in you
- [ ] Philippians 2:5-11 - Let the same mind be in you
- [ ] Philippians 4:4 - Rejoice in the Lord always
- [ ] Philippians 4:6-7 - Do not be anxious about anything
- [ ] Philippians 4:13 - I can do all things through Christ
- [ ] Colossians 3:15 - Let the peace of Christ rule in your hearts
- [ ] 1 Thessalonians 5:16-18 - Rejoice always
- [ ] 2 Timothy 3:16-17 - All scripture is inspired
- [ ] 2 Timothy 4:7 - I have fought the good fight
- [ ] Hebrews 4:12 - For the word of God is alive and active
- [ ] Hebrews 11:1 - Faith is the assurance of things hoped for
- [ ] Hebrews 12:1-2 - Run with perseverance
- [ ] Hebrews 13:8 - Jesus is the same yesterday and today
- [ ] James 1:2-4 - Consider it pure joy

What Verses We Love?

- [ ] James 1:5 - If any of you lacks wisdom
- [ ] James 1:19 - Be quick to listen, slow to speak
- [ ] 1 Peter 2:9 - You are a chosen people, a royal priesthood
- [ ] 1 Peter 5:7 - Cast all your anxiety on him
- [ ] 1 John 1:9 - If we confess our sins,
- [ ] 1 John 4:4 - Greater is He that is in you
- [ ] 1 John 4:7-8 - God is love
- [ ] 1 John 4:19 - We love because he first loved us

chapter 15

What Is Discipleship?

Discipleship is not a hashtag, not a bumper sticker, and not something you "speak into existence" with enough pseudo-spiritual confidence to land a book deal. No, discipleship is the inconvenient, often painful, always transformative process of following Jesus Christ, not your feelings, not your pastor's TikTok, and certainly not your own assumptions about what God owes you.

True discipleship isn't about self-improvement, personal success, or divine endorsement of your plans. It's about Jesus. Following Him. Listening when you'd rather speak. Losing when you'd rather win. Carrying crosses, not clout. And it is certainly not the sentimental slog of bad theology dressed in Christian clichés.

The bumper sticker theology of "The Bible says it, I believe it, that settles it" misses the point entirely. Discipleship means wrestling with Scripture, not wielding it like a blunt instrument. Jesus didn't stand on the Mount and shout, "Just do what the Torah says!" Instead, He reimagines the Law in Matthew 5 through 7, intensifying its demands and exposing shallow interpretations. "You have heard it said," He begins, then He turns everything upside down. Literalism without transformation is lazy theology, and lazy theology makes for lazy disciples.

This wrestling extends to understanding the full scope of God's story. You don't get to throw out half the Bible because you don't understand Leviticus. Jesus says clearly in Matthew 5 that He did not come to abolish the Law, but to fulfill it. The story of God didn't start in Bethlehem. If you want to follow Jesus, start in Genesis. Our faith is rooted in a long, complicated covenantal history, and discipleship means honoring the God who works through the whole of it.

Too many have turned faith into superstition with a Christian label. "If you have enough faith, everything will work out" isn't faith, it's fantasy. Romans 12 doesn't promise an easy life; it demands a renewed mind. Faith doesn't fix everything; it forms you in the middle of everything. And if your faith only works when life works, it isn't faith at all.

This misunderstanding leads to the prosperity gospel's most toxic lie: that we can manipulate God through our spiritual transactions. "Sow a seed to reap a blessing!" "Name it and claim it!" Enough. Jesus did not humble Himself in Philippians 2 so you could treat God like a vending machine. True discipleship doesn't ask, "What can I get from God?" but "How can I give my life to follow Christ?" Micah 6 makes it clear that God desires justice and humility, not seed money and spiritual pyramid schemes.

Perhaps nowhere is bad theology more dangerous than when it comes to suffering and mental health. "God won't give you more than you can handle" sounds comforting until you remember Psalm 22, where Jesus Himself cries out, "Why have You forsaken me?" That doesn't sound like someone managing fine. Discipleship means not having all the answers, it means trusting a God who doesn't always explain, but who always shows up. Sometimes suffering is just suffering, and faith is trusting God anyway.

The church's response to mental health reveals how deeply we've misunderstood discipleship. "Pray it away." "You just need to believe harder." Tell that to Elijah under the broom tree, begging to die in 1 Kings 19. Or to Jesus sweating blood in Gethsemane. The idea that faith cures mental illness is not just theologically bankrupt, it's dangerous. Psalm 23 promises that God walks with us through the valley, not that we get to skip it entirely.

Modern Christianity has fallen for the same temptation Satan offered Jesus in Matthew 4, political power and cultural dominance. "Take back America for Christ!" "The Church must reclaim the government!" But Jesus refused political power. Why are we so obsessed with it? Philippians 2 shows the real path: humility, service, and suffering love. Discipleship is not domination.

This obsession with power extends to our obsession with purity culture. "Avoid certain people, they're ungodly." "Date a Christian or date the Devil." Yet Jesus seemed pretty comfortable around prostitutes, tax collectors, and Roman soldiers. Luke 10's Good Samaritan tears down the very walls we love to put up. Discipleship doesn't mean finding the cleanest, safest spiritual echo chamber. It means embodying Christ in the mess of real life and real people. Christianity isn't a country club.

The "victorious living 24/7" crowd needs to meet the apostle Paul, who begged God to take away his thorn in 2 Corinthians 12. God didn't. Instead, God gave him grace, which is more than most church slogans promise. Following Jesus means walking with a limp. Real discipleship embraces weakness, because that's where Christ shows up strongest. Real Christians struggle, and that struggle is not a bug in the system, it's a feature.

This struggle reveals discipleship's ultimate truth: it isn't about you. "Everything happens for a reason." "God's got a plan for your tragedy." Maybe, but Job would like a word. So would Jesus at Lazarus's tomb, weeping. God is not the author of your heartbreak, and discipleship isn't about rationalizing your pain. It's about trusting a suffering Savior who joins us in it.

So what is discipleship, stripped of its cultural baggage and spiritual clichés? Discipleship is the daily death of ego. It's letting go of certainty, prosperity theology, and cultural Christianity. It's washing feet, not winning arguments. It's opening Scripture with trembling hands, not throwing verses like grenades. It's following a Messiah who was homeless, crucified, and came back not with revenge, but resurrection.

Discipleship isn't trendy. It won't sell out a conference. It won't fit on a t-shirt or translate well to social media. But it will transform your life, because transformation, not comfort, not success, not even happiness, is the point.

Jesus didn't say, "Repeat this prayer after me and live your best life." He said, "Take up your cross and follow me." And He meant it. The path is narrow, the gate is small, and the journey is hard. But it leads to life, real life, not the counterfeit version peddled by those who have forgotten that following Jesus was never supposed to be easy. It was only supposed to be worth it.

Discipleship is Knowing Whose You Are

You are not here by accident. Your life has meaning and purpose. The Psalmist reminds us that God knit us together in our mother's womb, declaring that we are "fearfully and wonderfully made." Similarly, Jeremiah speaks of how God knew us before we were born and set us apart for His purposes. These truths point to God's initiative in our lives, not our own efforts.

More than this, all humanity was created in God's image, which reflects the intrinsic value and dignity of every person. To be made in God's image means we were created for relationship with Him, with one another, and with creation.

> Psalm 139:13
> You are the one who created my innermost parts;
> you knit me together while I was still in my mother's womb.
> CEB

> Jeremiah 1:5
> Before I formed you in the womb I knew you,
> and before you were born I consecrated you;
> NRSVue

> Genesis 1:26
> Then God said, "Let us make humanity
> in our image to resemble us
> so that they may take charge of the fish of the sea,
> the birds in the sky, the livestock, all the earth,
> and all the crawling things on earth.
> CEB

Discipleship is Receiving God's Invitation

Discipleship begins with God's grace, revealed through Jesus Christ. It is an act of divine hospitality, where God welcomes us into communion with Himself and others. Through baptism, we are drawn into the life of God by the Spirit and our identity is reshaped as beloved children of God. In fact, to be called a Christian (literally taking on the name of Christ) was often a family decision in the early church. When babies were baptized, priests would ask the parents what name they were giving the child. This act symbolized the child's taking on Christ, dying into the depths of the water, and rising into life as a Christian.

> Romans 6:3-4
> Or don't you know that all who were baptized into Christ Jesus were baptized into his death? Therefore, we were buried together with him through baptism into his death, so that just as Christ was raised from the dead through the glory of the Father, we too can walk in newness of life.
> CEB

Discipleship is Trusting God

Many church traditions place heavy emphasis on belief, focusing on the need to mentally assent to certain doctrines or say the right words to secure one's salvation. But belief, as understood in Scripture, is far more than intellectual agreement. The Greek word for belief *pisteuo* connotes trust, faithfulness, and reliance. When Jesus said, "Believe in God; believe also in me," He invited His followers into a trusting relationship, not merely a mental acknowledgment of His divinity. The earliest Christians placed their trust in Jesus with their whole hearts. Today, however, many Christians approach belief as an intellectual exercise, disconnected from the relational trust that the apostles and early church exemplified. Discipleship invites us to reclaim this trust, a wholehearted reliance on God that transforms our lives.

> Romans 10:9
> Because if you confess with your mouth "Jesus is Lord" and in your heart you have faith that God raised him from the dead, you will be saved.
> CEB

Discipleship is Seeking Justice

God's agenda is justice, mercy, and compassion, not self-preservation or power plays. Or consider those who prioritize "sharing Jesus" but turn a blind eye to the physical needs of the very people they're trying to evangelize. The gospel isn't just something to believe; it's a way of being.

We probably all know Christians who align themselves more with the ideologies of their political party than with the Sermon on the Mount. They'll fight to keep prayer in schools but remain indifferent when their neighbor can't afford medical care. They cry, "love the sinner, hate the sin," while refusing to truly love the sinner with the kind of costly love Christ demands.

To follow Jesus is to live under His Lordship, which means embodying a radical hospitality, prioritizing the vulnerable, and living in ways that challenge the powers of this world. Discipleship isn't just about personal salvation; it's about forming a people whose lives proclaim that Jesus is Lord, and everything else isn't.

This is good news. It's uncomfortable news, but it's good news. And it's news that we've been invited to accept, embrace, live, and carry forward.

> Isaiah 1:17
> Learn to do good;
> seek justice;
> rescue the oppressed;
> defend the orphan;
> plead for the widow.
> NRSVue

> Matthew 22:21
> Give to Caesar what belongs to Caesar and to God what belongs to God.
> CEB

Discipleship is Formational

For centuries, Christian institutions have weaponized the Great Commission in Matthew 28, turning it into a mandate for cultural conquest and spiritual colonialism. We've seen missionaries destroy indigenous cultures, evangelists prey on the vulnerable, and churches obsess over conversion numbers while ignoring systemic injustice. But what if we've completely misunderstood what Jesus was actually asking of us?

Jesus wasn't calling his followers to become spiritual salespeople or religious recruiters. The heart of his final instructions had nothing to do with building an empire or expanding an institution. The original Greek word *mathēteusate*, which gets translated as "make disciples," doesn't mean "convert people to your religion." It means something far more subversive: "apprentice them into a radically different way of being human."

Imagine this: in first-century Palestine, under Roman occupation, when someone chose to follow a rabbi, they weren't joining a religious club. They were entering a countercultural movement. They lived with their teacher, sharing meals with tax collectors and sex workers, challenging religious authorities, and learning to see the world through the eyes of the marginalized. This wasn't academic theology but embodied resistance to systems of oppression.

A disciple wasn't someone who agreed with a doctrinal statement. They were apprentices learning a dangerous craft: how to live as if the kingdom of God was already here. They absorbed their rabbi's radical vision, his subversive practices, his willingness to prioritize love over law, people over institutions, justice over tradition.

This changes everything about how we understand Christian mission. Baptism becomes less about a membership ritual and more about stepping into a completely new identity. Teaching becomes less about lecturing and more about mentoring and walking alongside someone as they learn to navigate life in a new way. And conversion? That's not a one-time event but an ongoing process of becoming more fully human, more fully alive.

This kind of transformation requires more than good intentions. Real change (the kind that dismantles white supremacy, redistributes wealth, and centers the voices of those society silences) doesn't happen through prayer meetings alone. It requires sustained commitment to justice work, community organizing, and the slow, often frustrating work of changing systems from within.

The early Christian communities got this. They weren't building megachurches but creating mutual aid networks. They weren't focused on evangelistic campaigns but on economic redistribution. They shared resources, cared for the sick, and challenged the empire's death-dealing policies through radical acts of love and resistance.

For those of us trying to follow Jesus today, this perspective shifts our focus from persuasion to participation. Instead of trying to win arguments, we're learning to embody a different way of being in the world. Instead of measuring success by decisions made, we're looking for transformation that happens slowly, authentically, and in community.

This is discipleship as Jesus intended it: not a moment of agreement but a lifetime of learning, not individual belief but communal transformation, not conquest but cultivation of human flourishing.

> Matthew 28:19-20
> Go therefore and make disciples of all nations,
> baptizing them in the name of the Father
> and of the Son and of the Holy Spirit
> and teaching them to obey everything
> that I have commanded you.
> And remember, I am with you always, to the end of the age.
> NRSVue

Discipleship is Living as Agents of Reconciliation

To follow Jesus is to take up the work of reconciliation. As those who have been forgiven, we are called to extend that same forgiveness, not as a sentimental gesture but as an act of obedience and participation in God's redemptive mission. Forgiveness is not the erasure of wrongdoing, nor does it ignore justice, but it opens the door for healing between individuals, within communities, and across societies. More so, discipleship is inseparable from peacemaking. Jesus did not come to maintain polite civility but to dismantle hostility at its roots. As Paul writes, Jesus is our peace, breaking down the dividing wall and creating one new humanity in place of the old divisions. Reconciliation, then, is not peripheral to the gospel; it is its very essence. This vision is neither easy nor idealistic. To follow Jesus is to stand in that tension—to seek justice without vengeance, to tell the truth without hatred, and to work for peace even when the wounds of division run deep.

> Colossians 3:13
> Be tolerant with each other and,
> if someone has a complaint against anyone,
> forgive each other. As the Lord forgave you,
> so also forgive each other.
> CEB

> Ephesians 2:14
> For he is our peace;
> in his flesh he has made both into one
> and has broken down the dividing wall,
> that is, the hostility between us
> NRSVue

Discipleship is Belonging to a Community of Love

The church is not merely a gathering of individuals but a foretaste of God's kingdom, a community where all are welcome and valued. Following Jesus means joining the body of Christ, where we learn to love and be loved, to forgive and be forgiven, through the messiness and beauty of shared life. In this community, we discover that our diversity is a strength, enriching our collective journey of faith. The sacraments, especially communion, nourish our journey with Christ and one another.

> Acts 2:42
> They devoted themselves
> to the apostles' teaching and to fellowship,
> to the breaking of bread and to prayer.
> NIV

Discipleship is Building God's Kingdom

Discipleship is not a retreat into private spirituality; it is a call to action. Faith, if it is not lived out, is lifeless. To follow Jesus is to embody His mission, caring for the poor, standing for justice, and reflecting His mercy and love in a world desperate for redemption. We are not merely called to believe; we are called to build His Kingdom. Not only to profess faith but to practice it. Not just to pray but to participate. A faith that remains passive is a faith that remains powerless. But a faith that moves, serving, sacrificing, and speaking up, becomes a force that reshapes the world.

> James 2:14
> In the same way, faith is dead
> when it doesn't result in faithful activity.
> CEB

Discipleship is Surrendering

The way of Jesus is the way of the cross, an inescapable path marked by hardship, suffering, and, at times, opposition. It is not a road we choose because we are particularly strong or faithful. More often, it is the road that finds us, ready or not. Nonetheless, it is an invitation to walk through it, upheld by a love that does not waver, even when our bodies, dreams, and plans do. Yet, paradoxically, it is in these very struggles that we encounter the sufficiency of God's grace. Sometimes we think we lack faith if the grace doesn't erase pain. But that's not what grace does. Instead, grace meets us in the hospital waiting room, in the sleepless nights, in the quiet griefs we carry alone. Paul reminds us, God's power is made perfect in weakness. Discipleship is not about being "blessed" in the way the world counts blessings, such as health, wealth, or certainty. Rather, it is a daily surrender to God's transforming work, where our imperfection becomes the very instrument of His strength.

> 2 Corinthians 12:9-10
> My grace is sufficient for you,
> for power is made perfect in weakness.
> So I will boast all the more gladly of my weaknesses,
> so that the power of Christ may dwell in me.
> NRSVue

Discipleship is a Living Thankfully

Every work we do, every act of service, every gift we offer, every step of growth we pursue, and every neighbor we love flows from gratitude. This isn't just positive thinking or good manners but an orientation of the heart and mind that transforms us at the deepest level, both spiritually and neurologically.

Modern neuroscience shows us that gratitude literally rewires the brain, strengthening neural pathways for empathy, resilience, and joy. What researchers are discovering now, however, ancient wisdom has always known. Long before we could map brain scans, the scriptures understood this fundamental truth: our capacity to love grows out of our experience of being loved first.

Gratitude becomes the soil in which discipleship grows, nourished by the continuous discovery of how deeply we are known and cherished. It's this wonder that sustains us through the difficult work of following Jesus, turning service from burden into joy.

> 1 John 4:19
> We love because God first loved us.
> CEB

About the Author

Rev. Stephen Cheyney serves as the University Minister for Niner United, the ecumenical campus ministry endorsed by the Episcopal, Lutheran (ELCA), Presbyterian Church (USA), and United Methodist denominations at the University of North Carolina at Charlotte. He also serves on the faculty of UNC Charlotte's Department of American Studies. With a doctorate from Emory University and a graduate degree from Duke University, his focus of study is the intersection of religion, ethics, and politics, which offers fresh insights into the Bible's enduring relevance in both historical and contemporary contexts.

stephen.cheyney@charlotte.edu
pages.charlotte.edu/scheyney

www.ingramcontent.com/pod-product-compliance
Lightning Source LLC
Chambersburg PA
CBHW011614290426
44110CB00021BA/2589